AGENTS OF
PARADOX

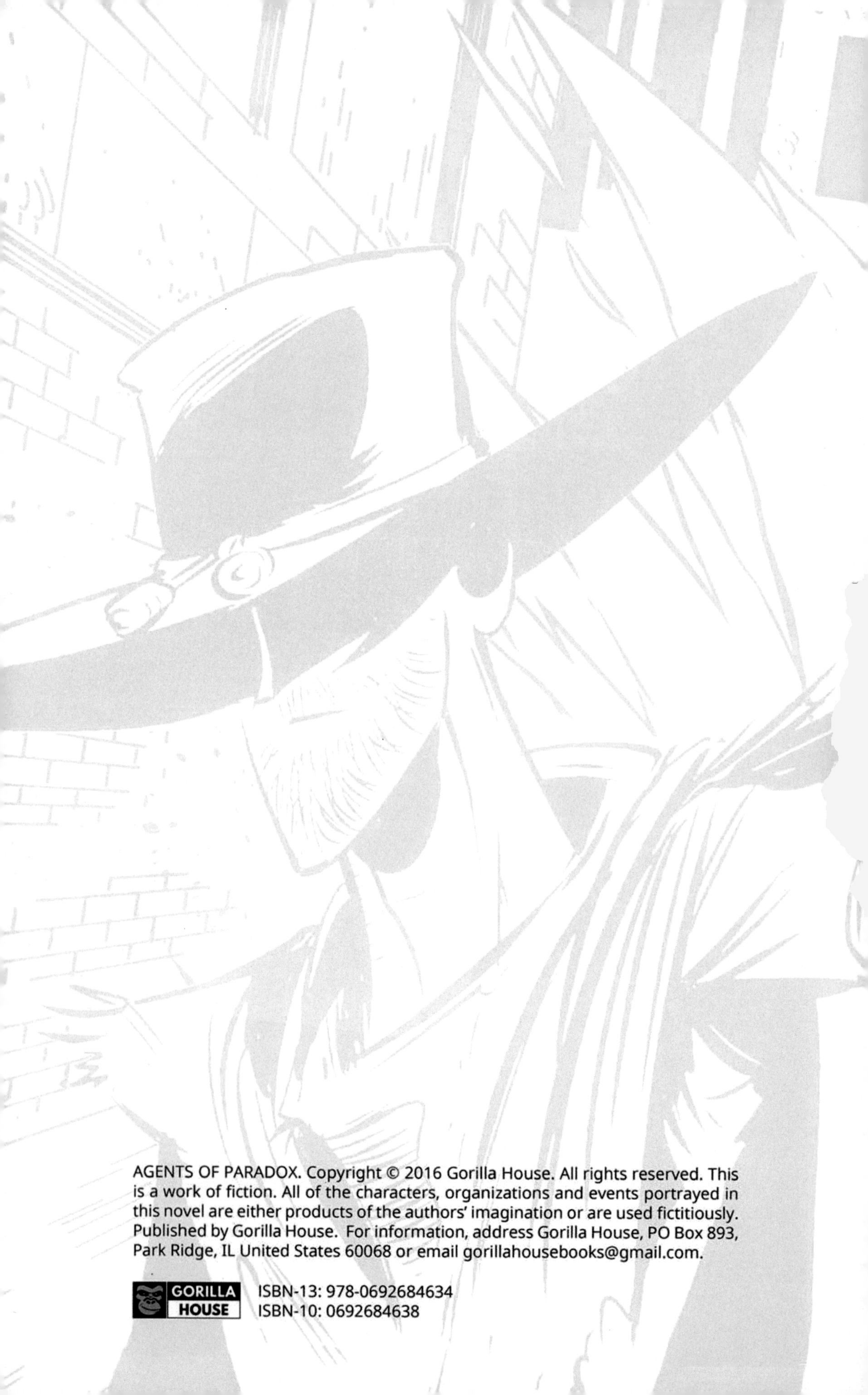

Published by Gorilla House. For information, address Gorilla House, PO Box 893, Park Ridge, IL United States 60068 or email gorillahousebooks@gmail.com.

GORILLA HOUSE

ISBN-13: 978-0692684634
ISBN-10: 0692684638

AGENTS OF PARADOX

WRITER
JACK McGUIGAN

ARTIST
JOHN FORTUNE

COLORIST
VANESSA KIRBY

"Agents of Paradox" is a crowdfunded book, made possible in part by the following individuals:

A. R. Bing, Adam Winnett, Adam Wollet, Al Sparrow, Alex Hoffmeyer, Alexander Gudenau, Alison Lavery, Amber Lanagan, Andrew Estrada, Andrew Funk, Andy Barbieri, Angela Garneata, Anthony Cecchini, ARKVINDICTA, Barron Snyder, Ben Thomas, Bob Bretall, Brandon Eaker, Brian Wessel, Caleb Michael Smith, Charles Sarratt, Chris Ferrell, Christian Berger, Christina Peck, Christo van Wyk, Chuck & Jeannie, Colten Lewis, Conor O'Donnell, Cristiane Weber, D. Victoria, Dan Goodchild, Daniel Kirrene, David Ocepek, Diana McGillivray, Don Meyer, Duell Mitchell, Dustin Andrews, Emmis Touron, Eric Grau, Erick Blandin, Fred Chamberlain, Gary Trimarchi, Gavin & Greta Zimmerman, Geoff Skinner, Gerald-Philippe Seguin, Henrik Lindhe, J. C. Lee, Jackie Pokryfke, Jane-Elizabeth (meow) ^w^, Jason Crase, Jason Fliegel, Jeremie Lariviere, Joachim Verhagen, Joe Clark, Joey Groah, Jon Olsen, Jonas Schiött, Jonathan Maxwell, Joseph Hawkins, Josh Frisch, Joshua Beale, Jussi Myllyluoma, Justin Phillips, Justin Rising, Kai Nikulainen, Karen H., Kat L., Kay McGuigan Nolan, Keith Robinson, Lachlan Matthew-Dickinson, Larry Edwarrds, Les Ironside, Leslie M., Liam *compelledorphan* Simmons, Luca T Romano, Macaire Grambauer, MAD, Margaret St. John, Mark E. Brown, Mark Wilhelm, Markus Zwinger, Martin Rudat, Matt Carr, Matt Christoff, Matt Kliemann, Matthias Frank, Michael J. Pokryfke, Michael Vaz, Mitchell Berry, Mr. Dancer, the Murphy family, Nath Kai, Olga Wegehaupt, Olivier Vigneresse, Pascal Tremblay, Patrick Miller, Patrick Trahey, Pete Asick, Peter McQuillan, Peter, Karen, Grace, Rose and Henry Harper, Robert Collier, Robert Early, Robert James Dunn, Robert L. Vaughn, Ron Bandish JR, Rory Fowlie, Ryan Linich, Sam Ludriks, Sarah M. Adams, Sebastian Nawrocki, Seto Konowa, Shervyn, Steve Lord, Stew Sizer, Stuart Lofthouse, Susan Knutson, the Schiller Family, Thomas Krech, Tom James Allen Jr, Tom Sullivan, Veronika Knurenko, Vijay Varman, Will Haley, and the Woodruff family.

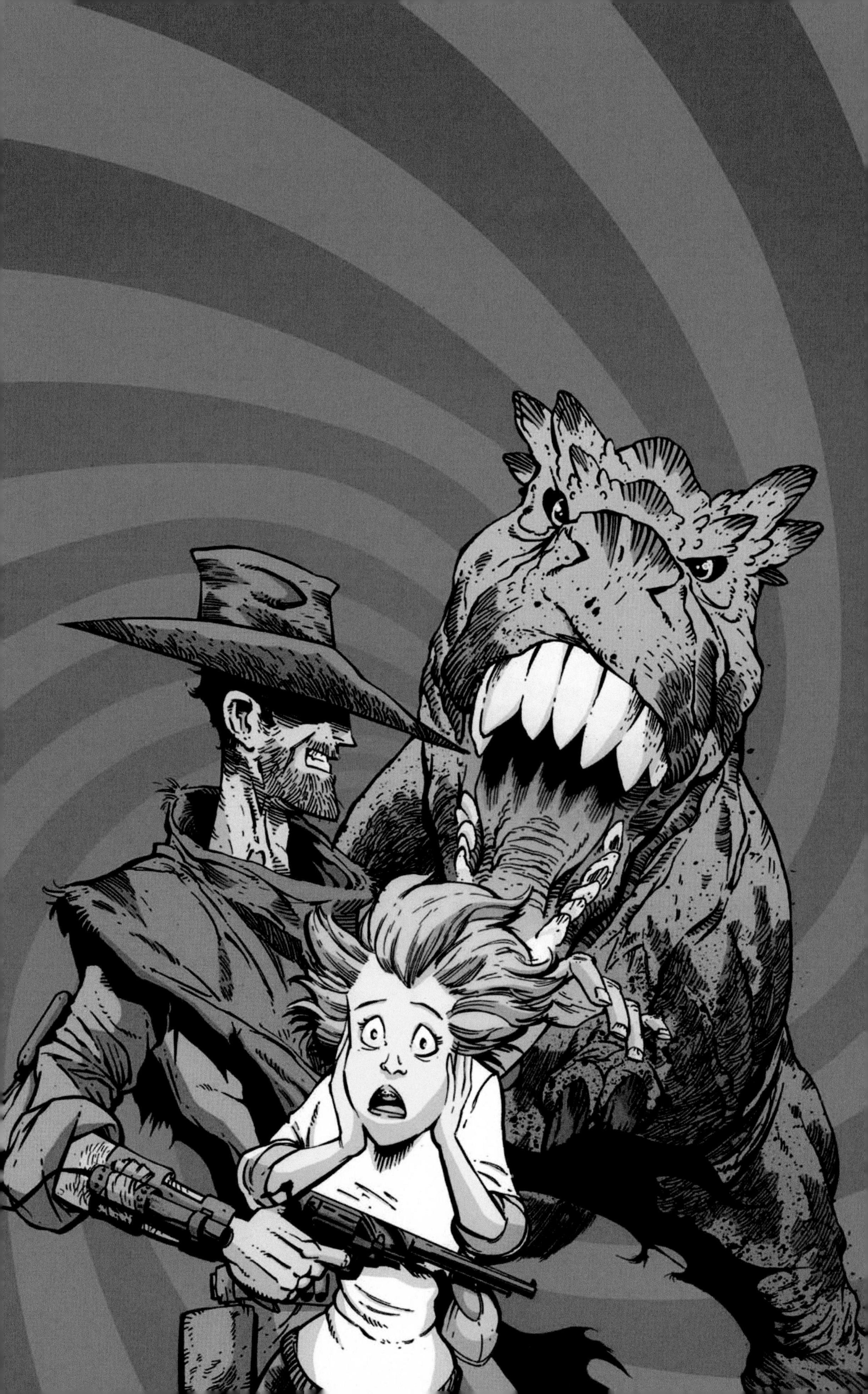

ISSUE ONE

"TIME BREAKS"

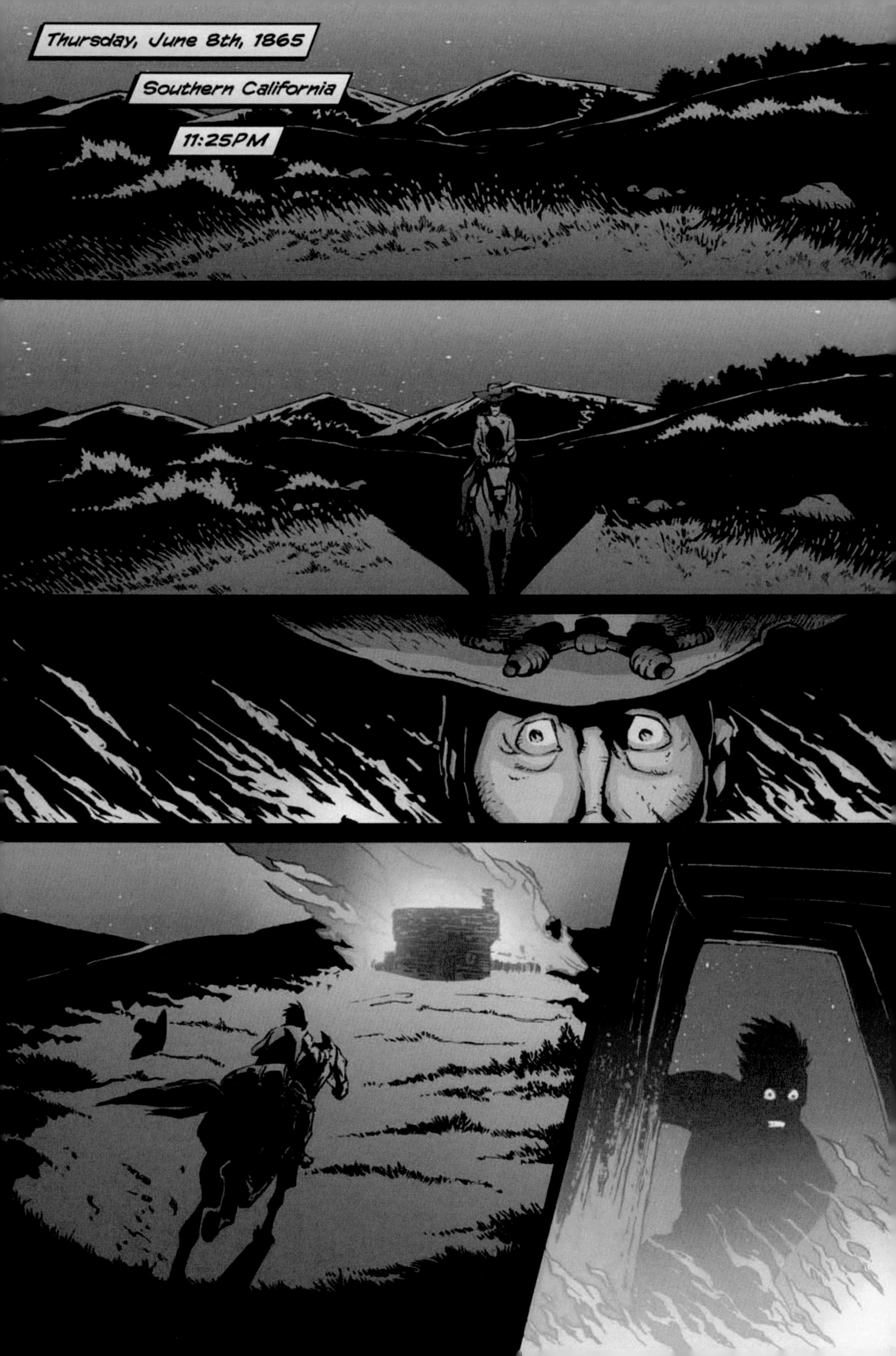
Thursday, June 8th, 1865
Southern California
11:25PM

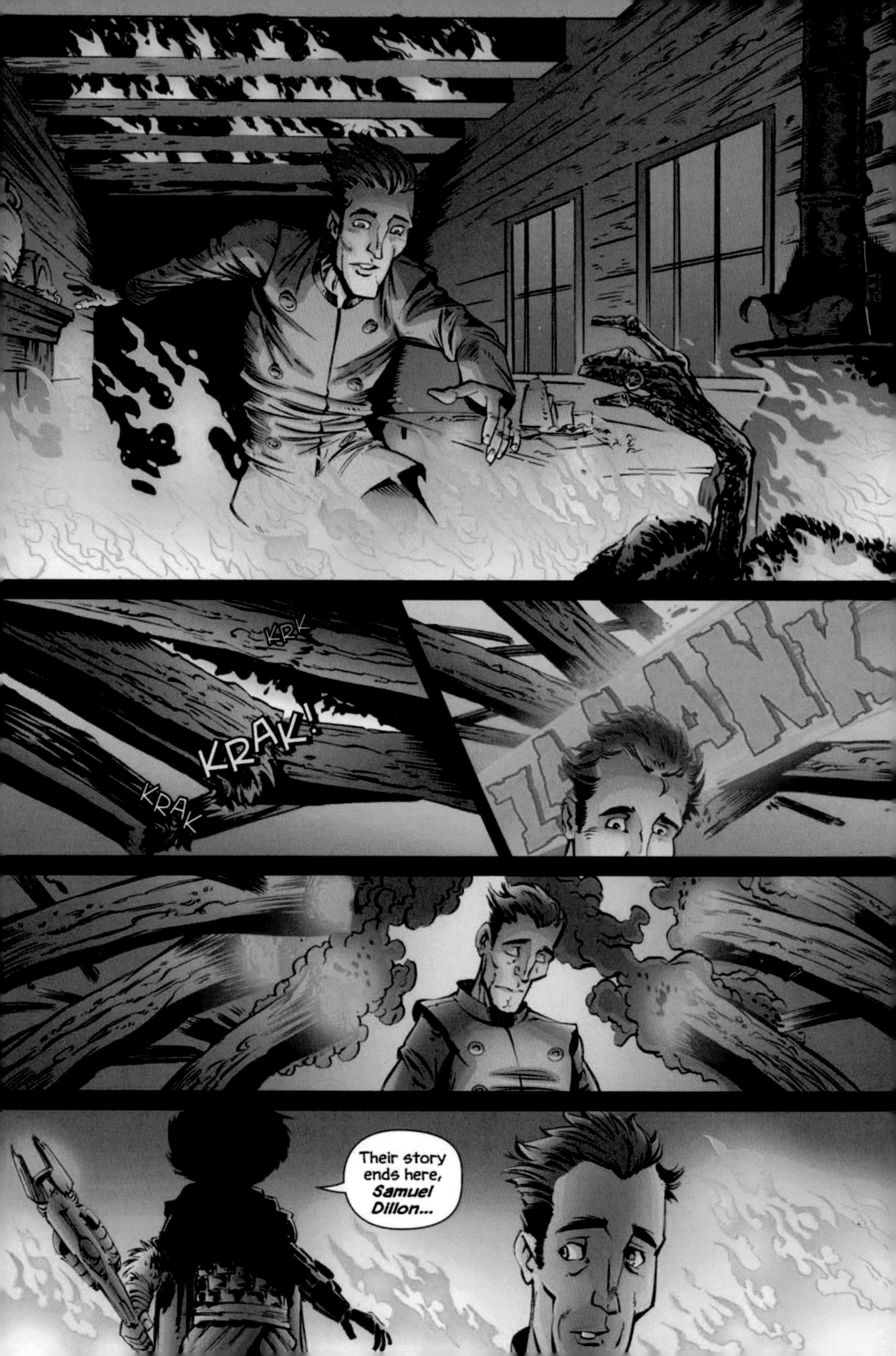
KRK
KRAK!
KRAK
ZAKANK
Their story ends here, *Samuel Dillon...*

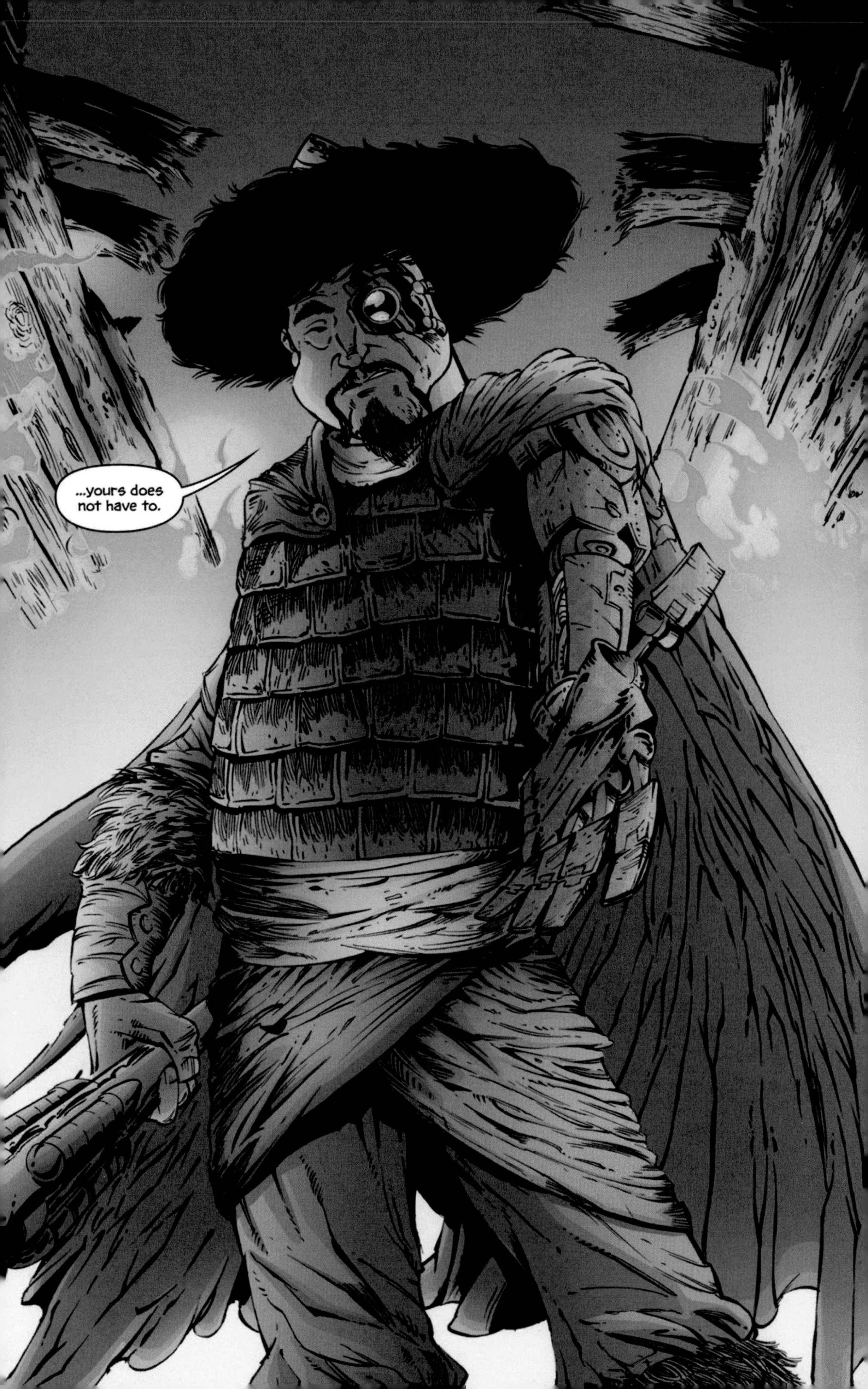
...yours does
not have to.

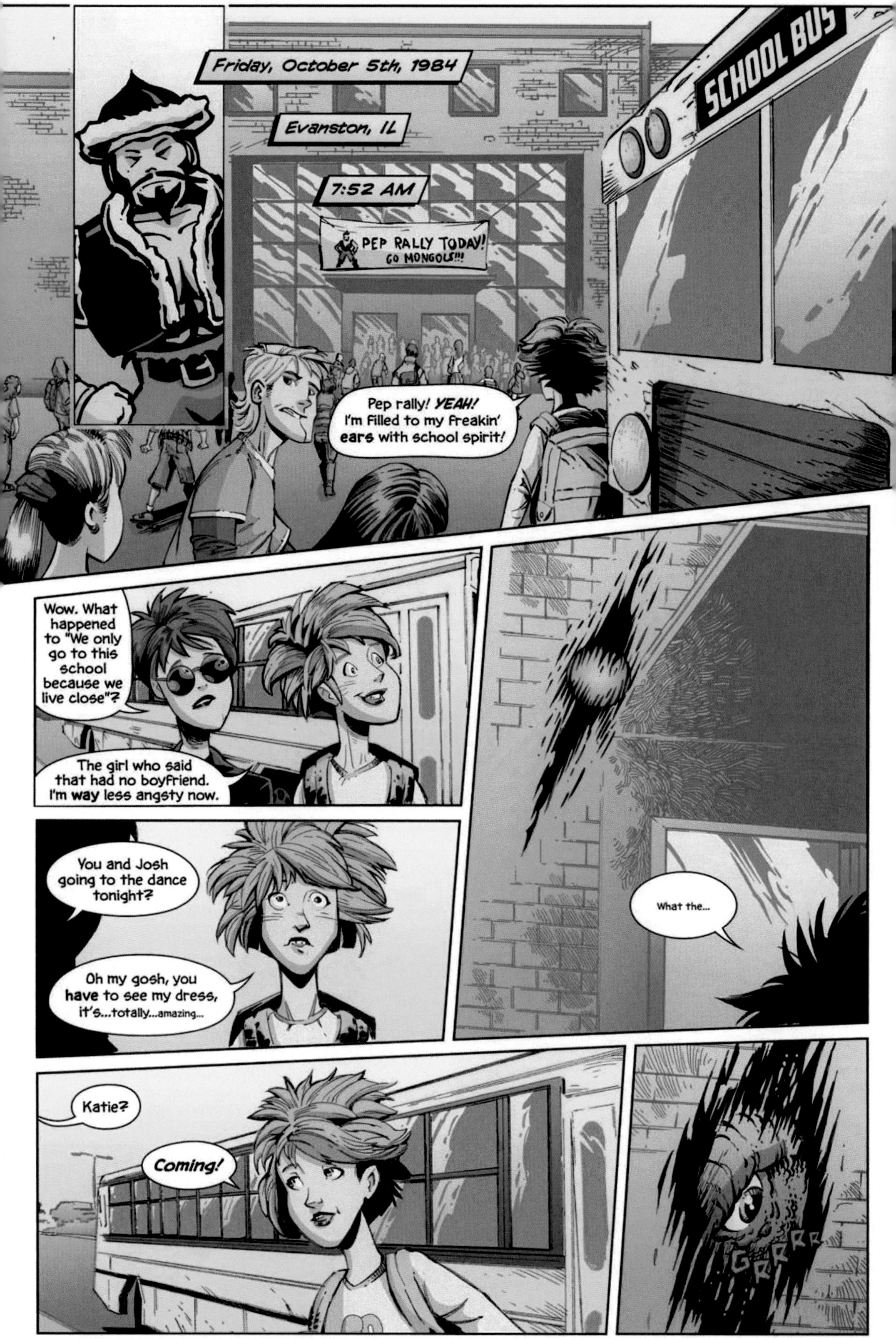
Friday, October 5th, 1984
Evanston, IL
7:52 AM
PEP RALLY TODAY! GO MONGOLS!!!
SCHOOL BUS
Pep rally! YEAH! I'm filled to my freakin' ears with school spirit!
Wow. What happened to "We only go to this school because we live close"?
The girl who said that had no boyfriend. I'm way less angsty now.
You and Josh going to the dance tonight?
Oh my gosh, you have to see my dress, it's...totally...amazing...
What the...
Katie?
Coming!
GRRRR

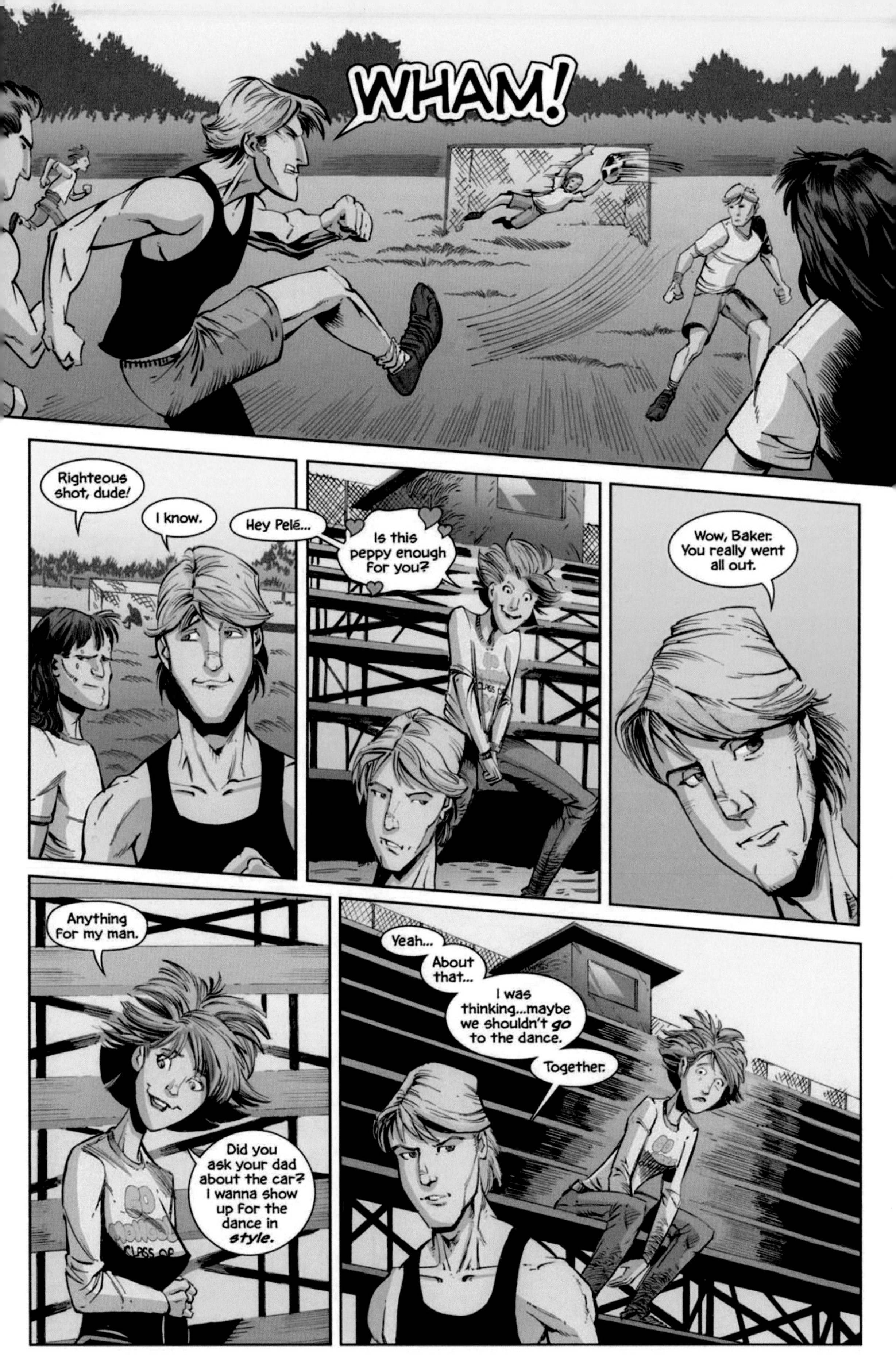
WHAM!
Righteous shot, dude!
I know.
Hey Pelé...
Is this peppy enough for you?
Wow, Baker. You really went all out.
Anything for my man.
Did you ask your dad about the car? I wanna show up for the dance in *style.*
Yeah...
About that...
I was thinking...maybe we shouldn't *go* to the dance.
Together.

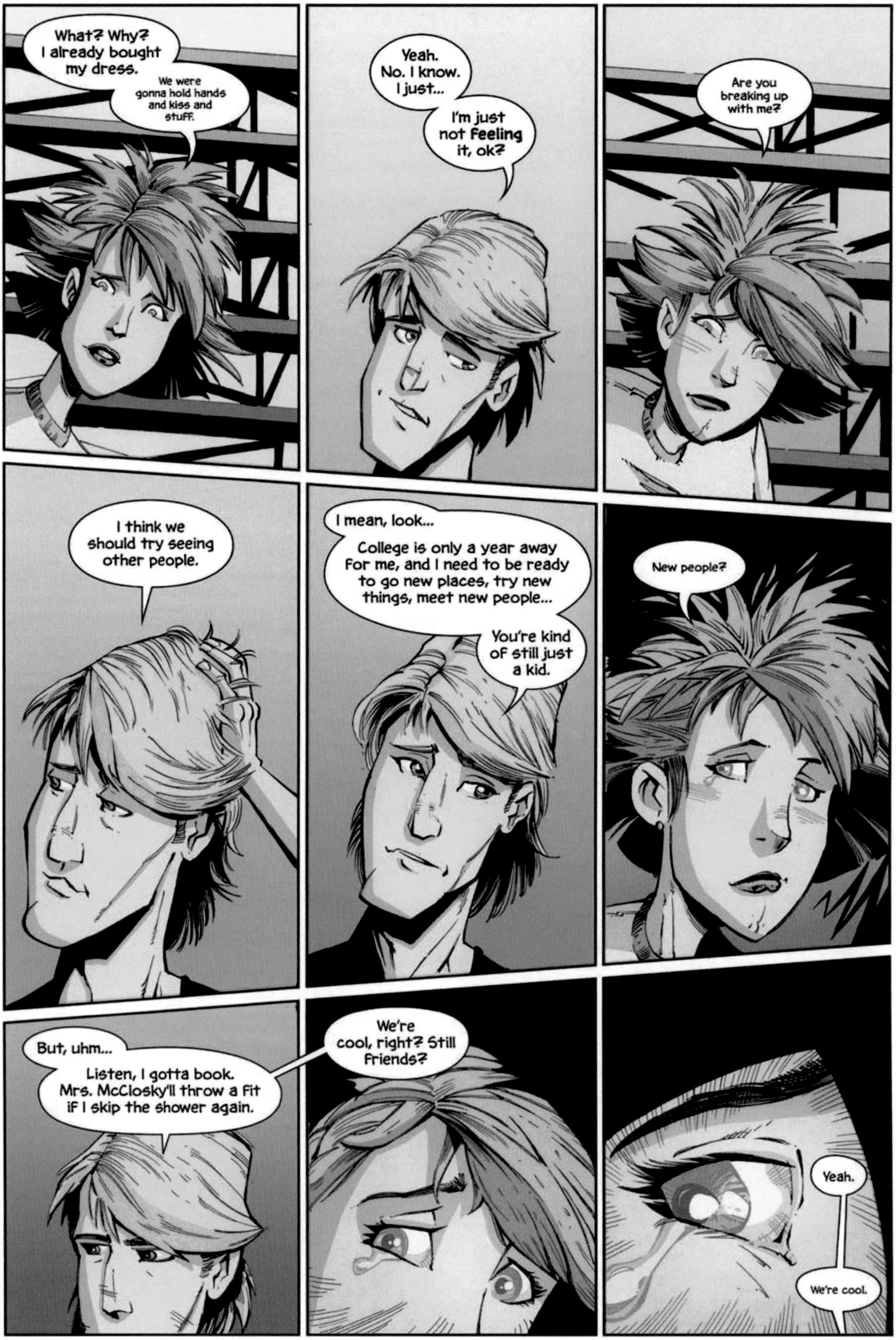
What? Why? I already bought my dress.
We were gonna hold hands and kiss and stuff.
Yeah. No. I know. I just...
I'm just not feeling it, ok?
Are you breaking up with me?
I think we should try seeing other people.
I mean, look...
College is only a year away for me, and I need to be ready to go new places, try new things, meet new people...
You're kind of still just a kid.
New people?
But, uhm...
Listen, I gotta book. Mrs. McClosky'll throw a fit if I skip the shower again.
We're cool, right? Still friends?
Yeah.
We're cool.

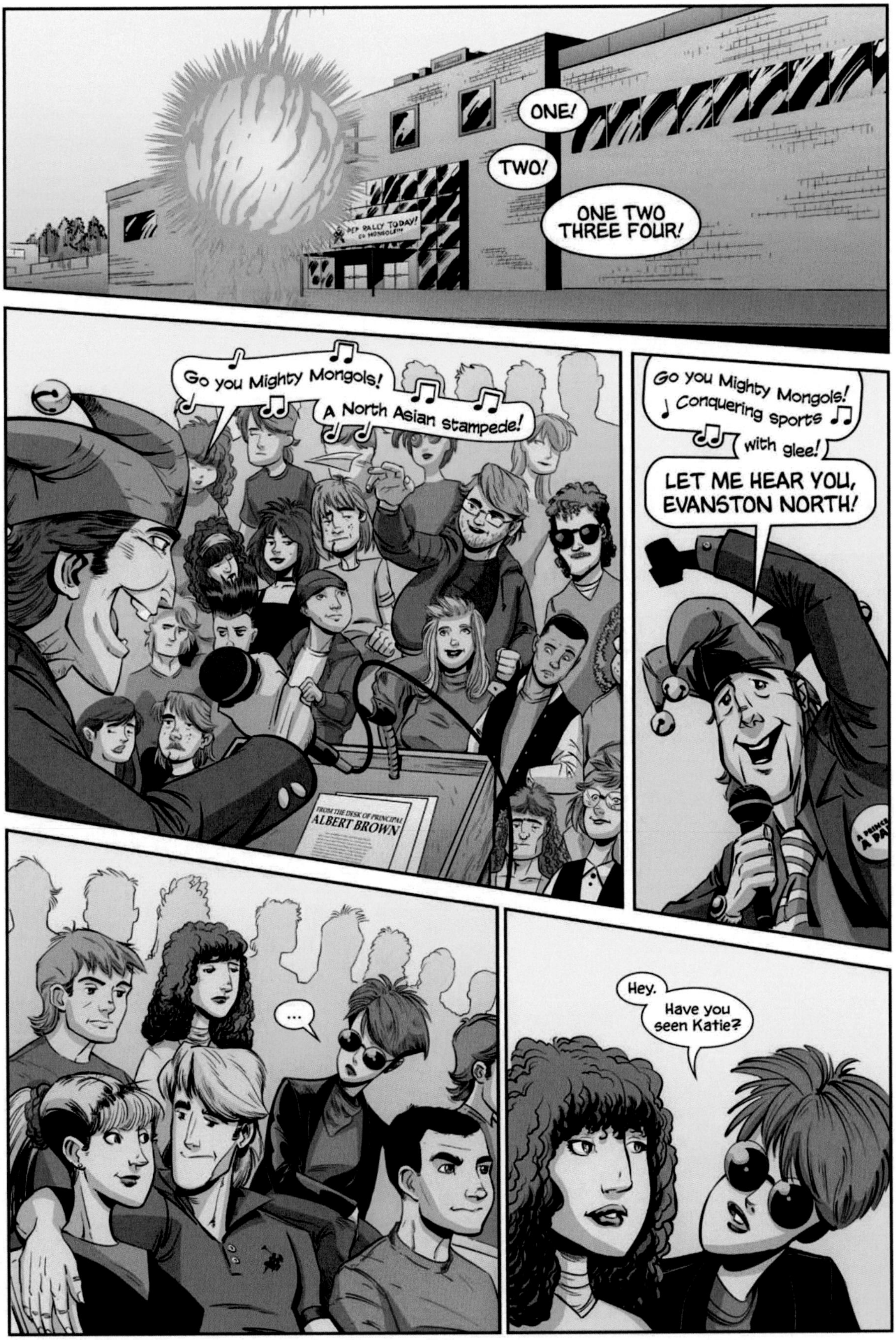
ONE!
TWO!
ONE TWO THREE FOUR!
Go you Mighty Mongols!
A North Asian stampede!
FROM THE DESK OF PRINCIPAL ALBERT BROWN
Go you Mighty Mongols! Conquering sports
with glee!
LET ME HEAR YOU, EVANSTON NORTH!
...
Hey.
Have you seen Katie?

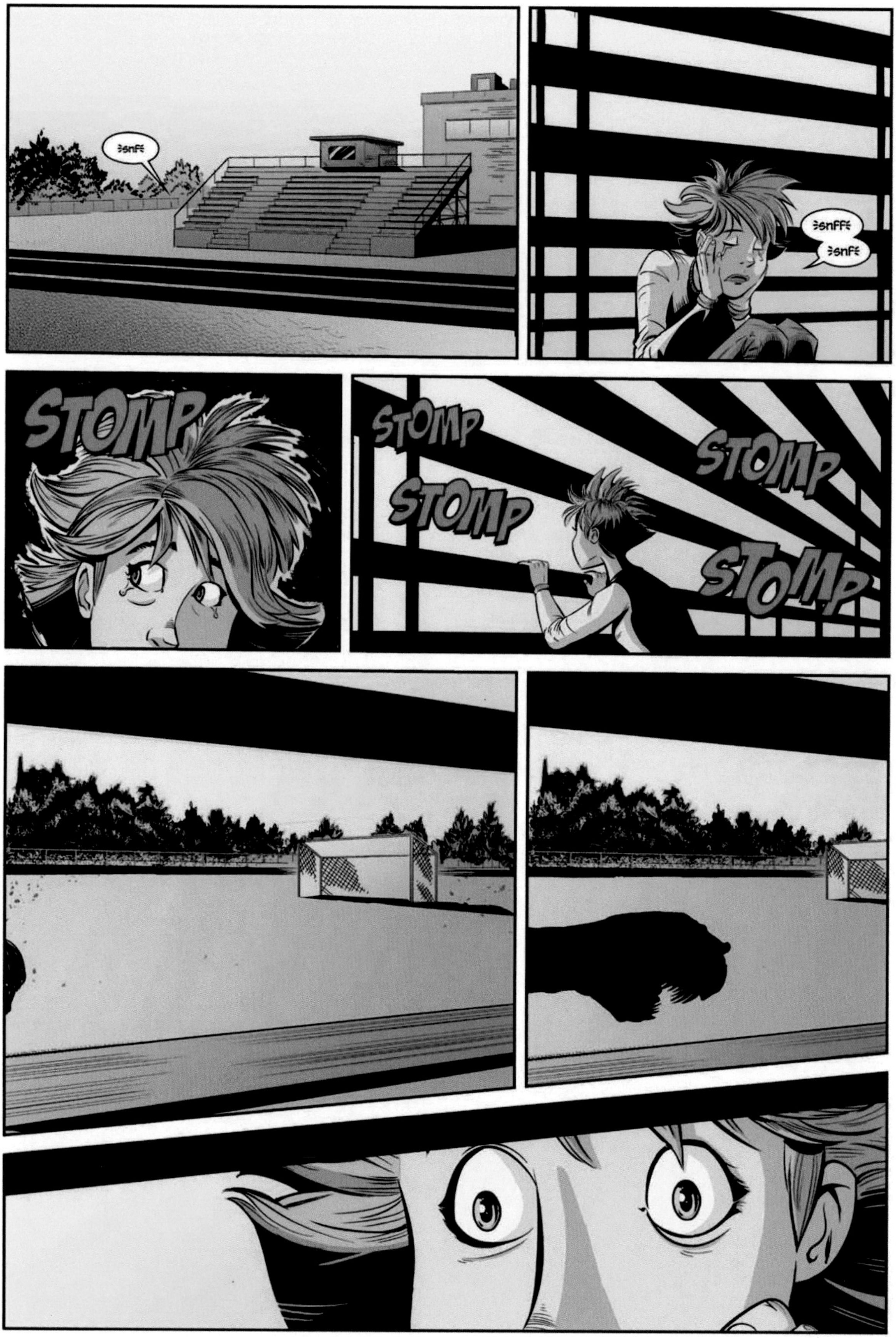
snf
snff
snf
STOMP
STOMP
STOMP
STOMP
STOMP

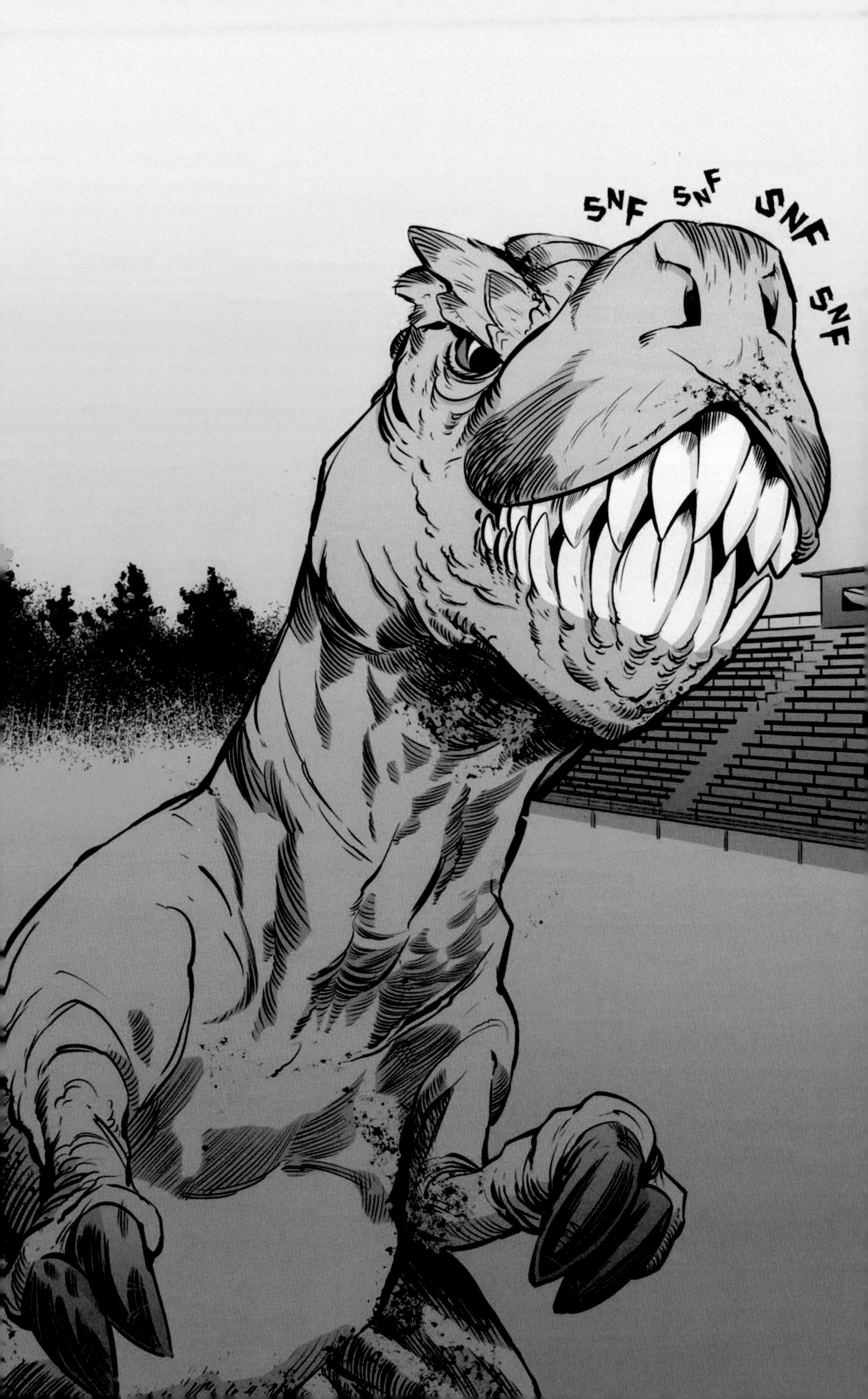
SNF SNF SNF
SNF SNF

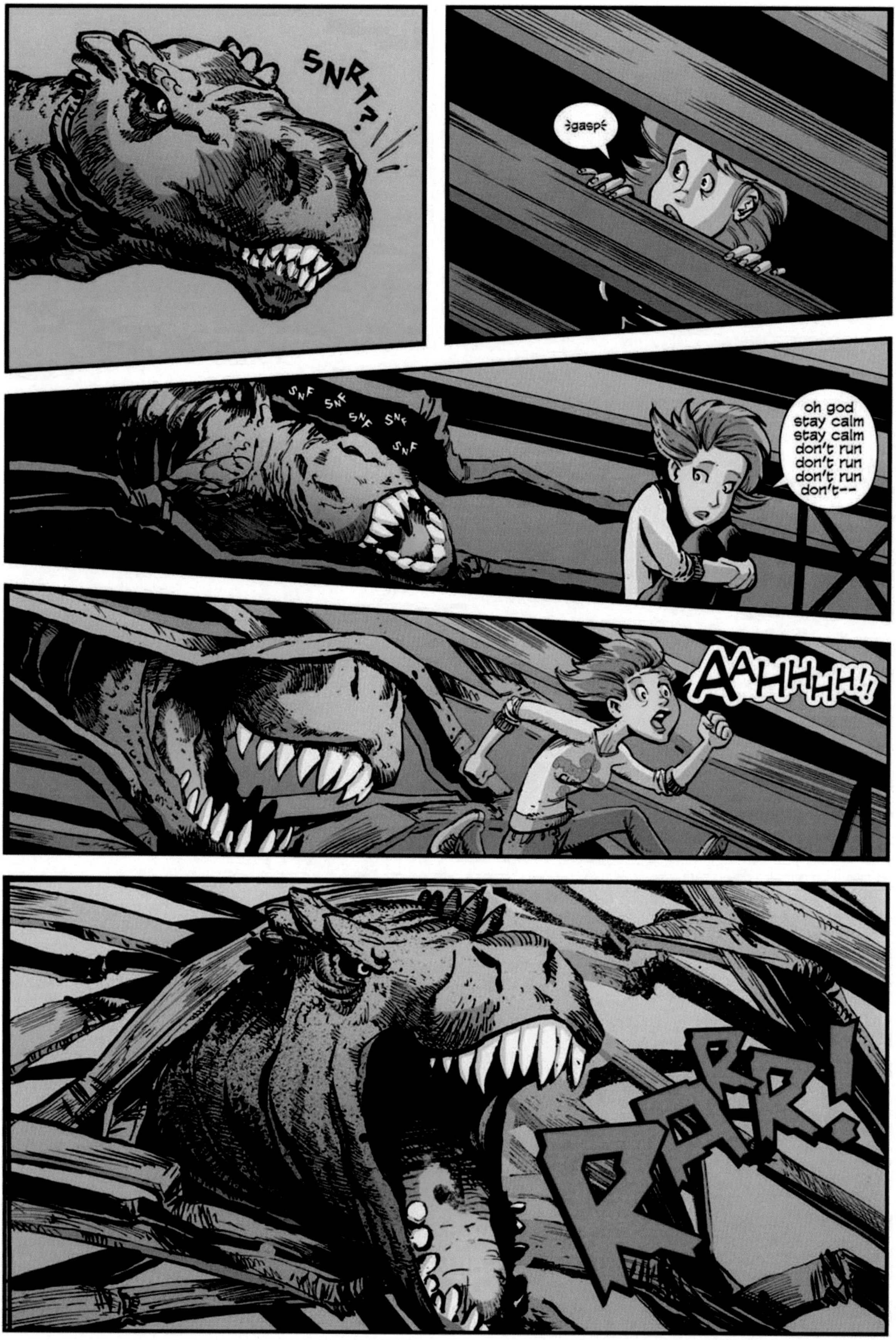
SNRT?
gasp
SNF SNF SNF SNF SNF
oh god stay calm stay calm don't run don't run don't run don't--
AAHHHHH!!
RRRR!

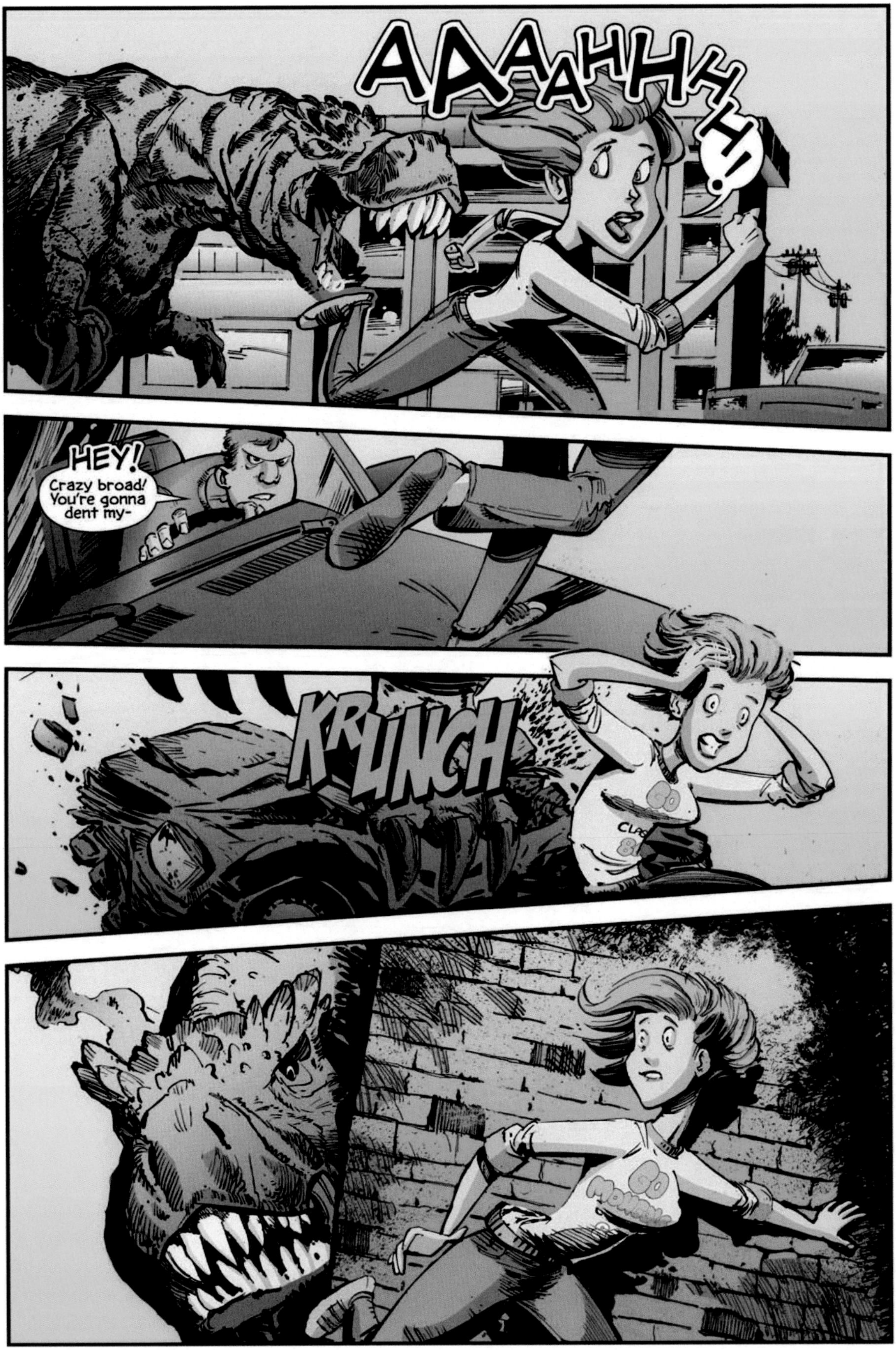
AAAAHHHH!
HEY! Crazy broad! You're gonna dent my-
KRUNCH

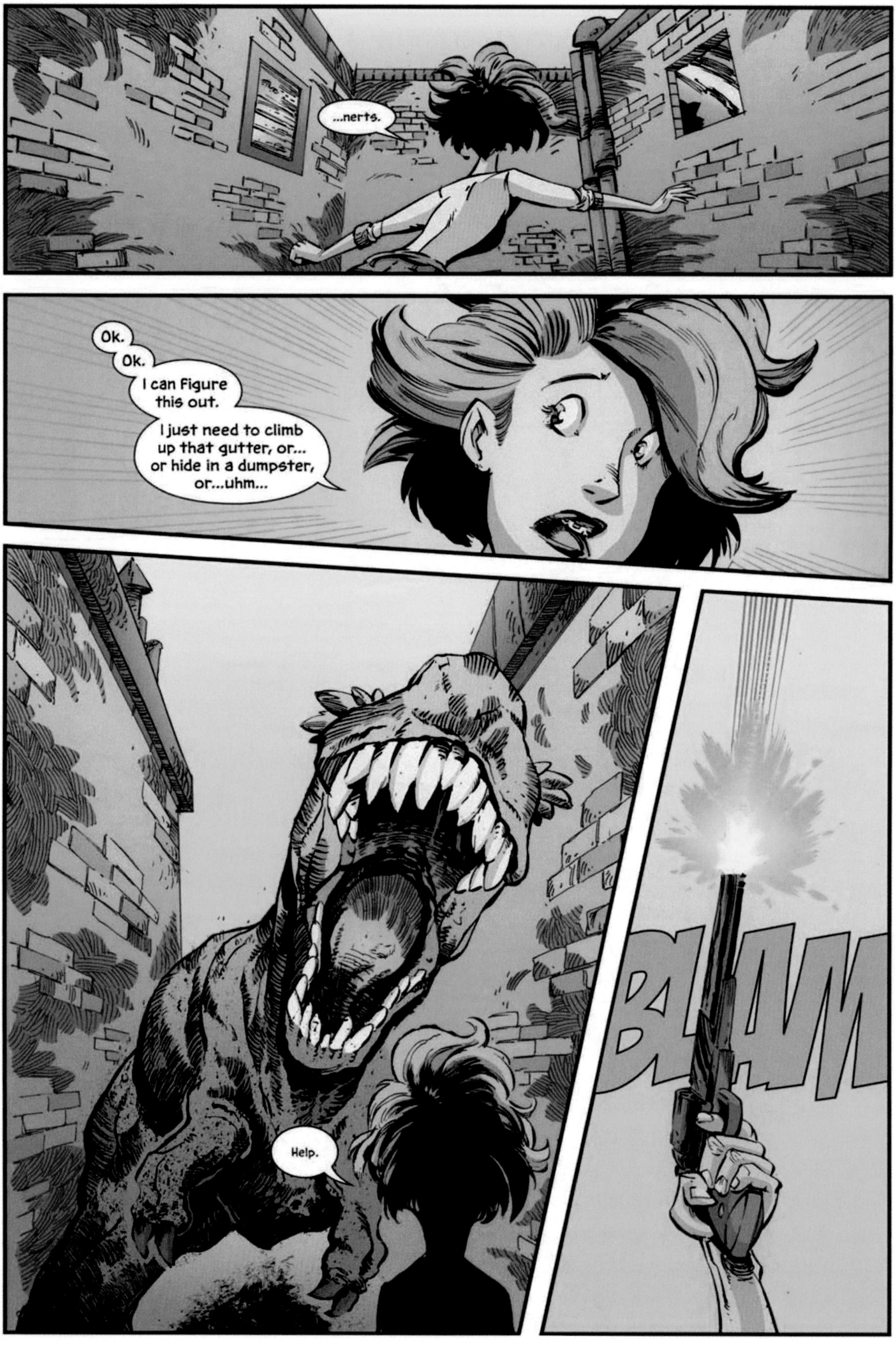
...nerts.
Ok.
Ok.
I can figure this out.
I just need to climb up that gutter, or... or hide in a dumpster, or...uhm...
Help.
BLAM

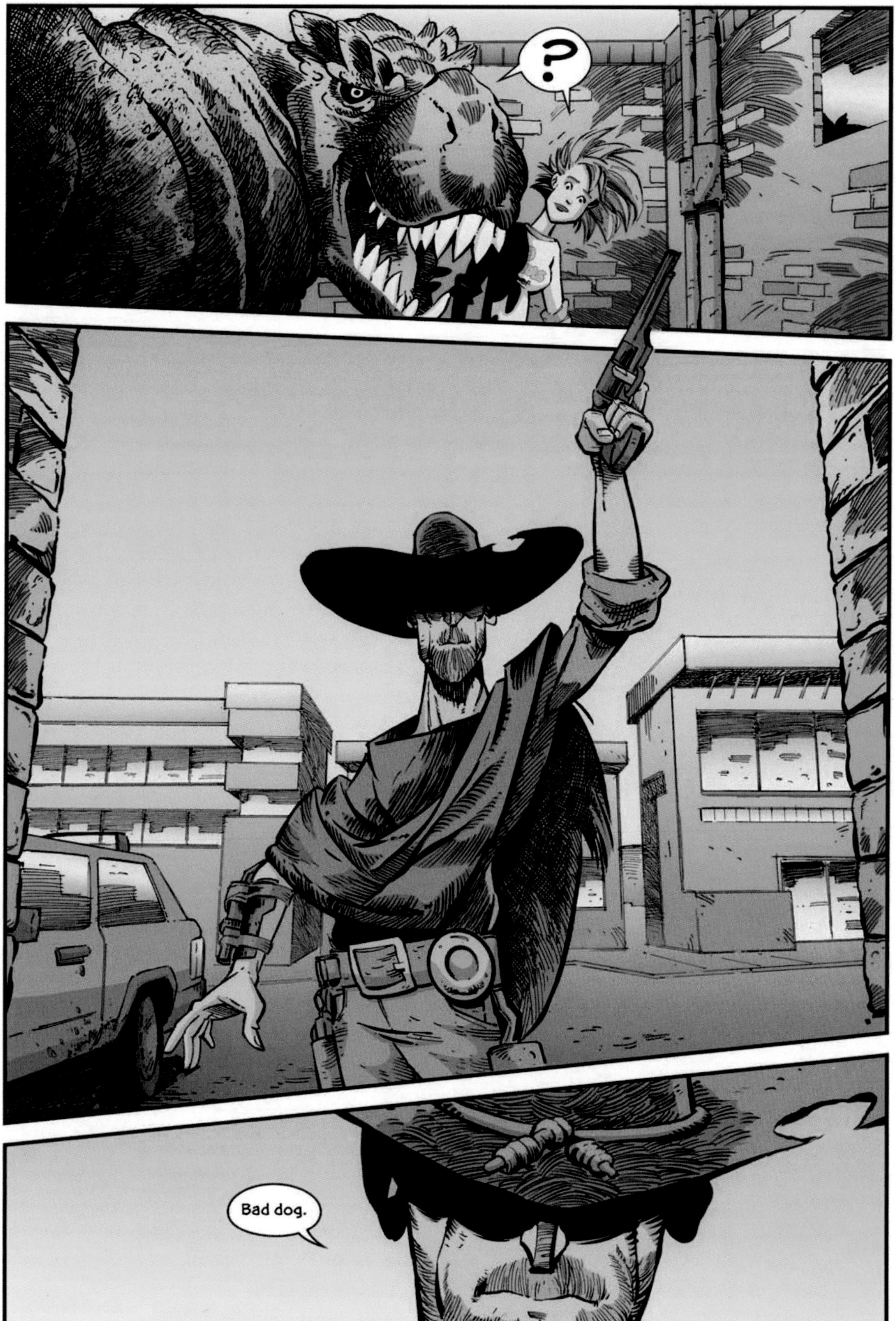
?
Bad dog.

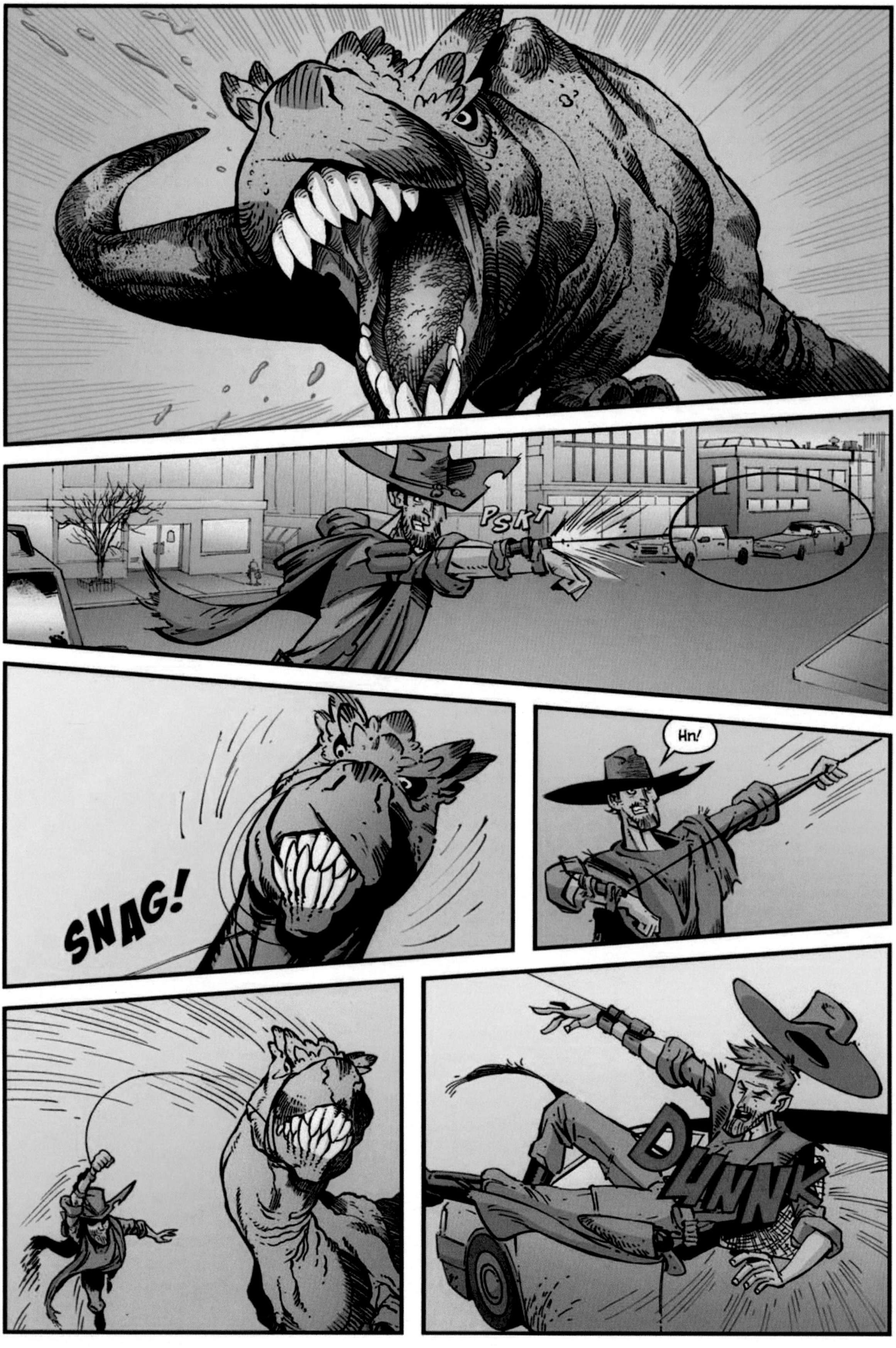
PSKT
SNAG!
Hn!
DUNNK

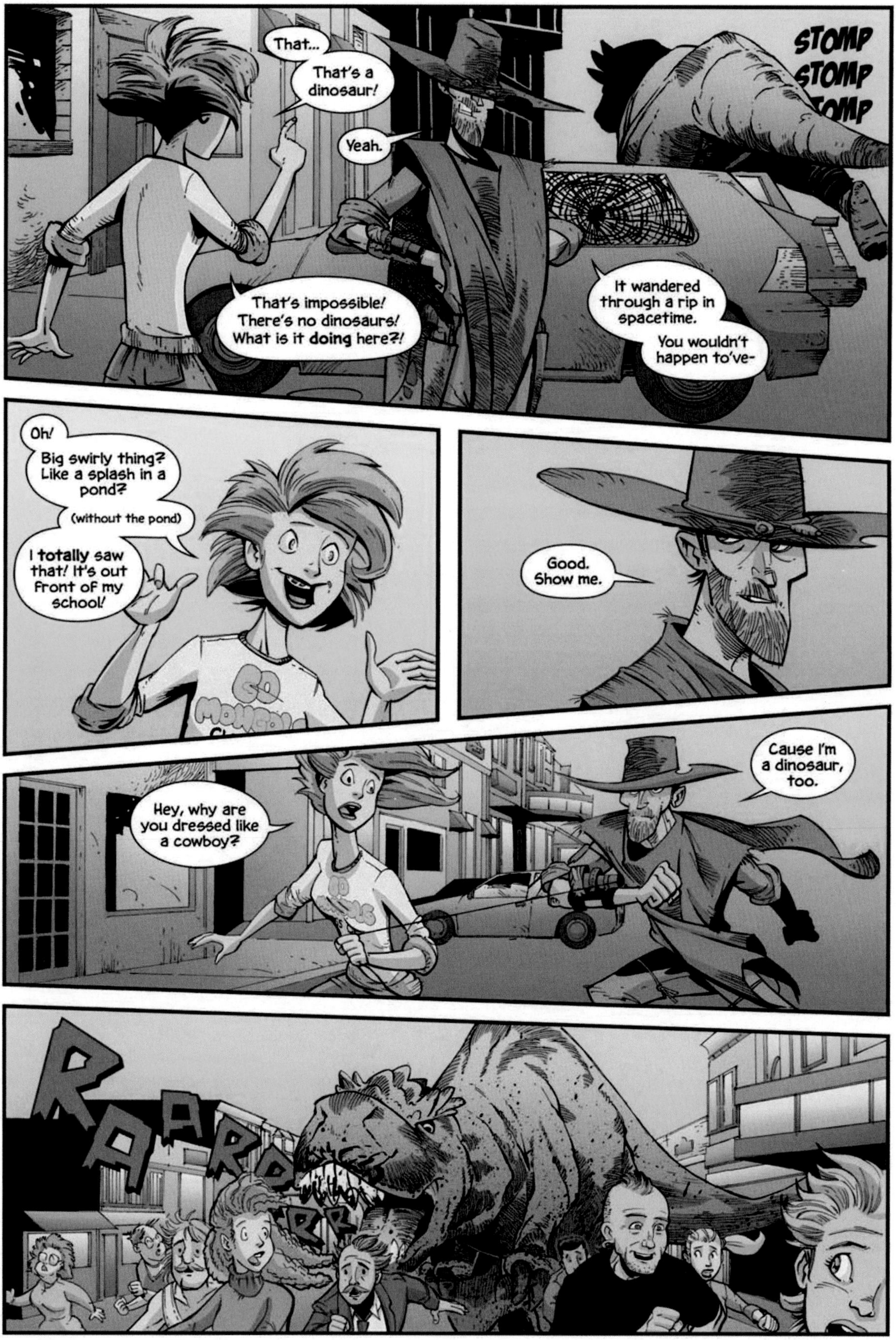
That...
That's a dinosaur!
Yeah.
STOMP
STOMP
That's impossible! There's no dinosaurs! What is it **doing** here?!
It wandered through a rip in spacetime.
You wouldn't happen to've-
Oh!
Big swirly thing? Like a splash in a pond?
(without the pond)
I **totally** saw that! It's out front of my school!
Good. Show me.
Hey, why are you dressed like a cowboy?
Cause I'm a dinosaur, too.

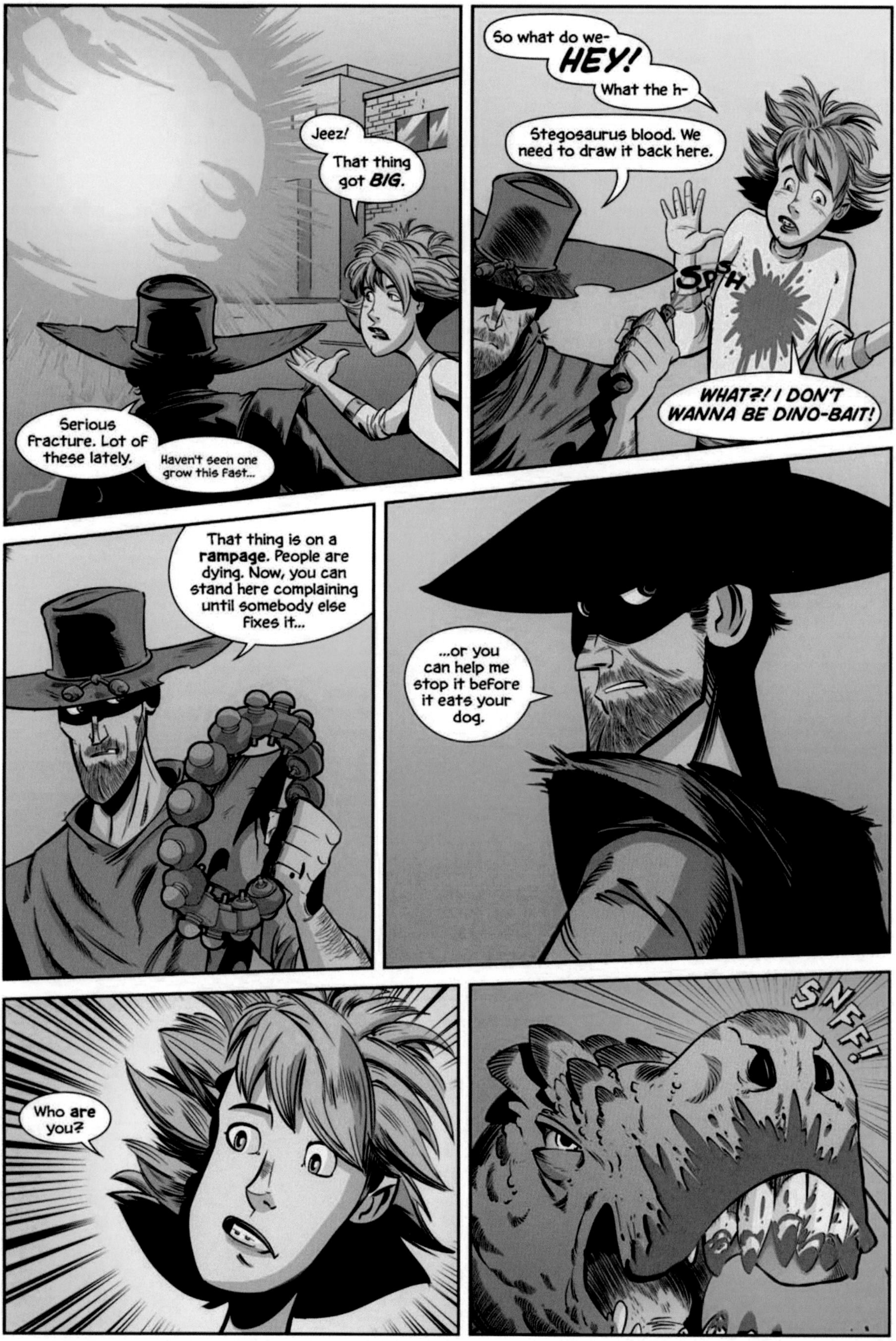
Jeez!
That thing got BIG.
Serious fracture. Lot of these lately.
Haven't seen one grow this fast...
So what do we-
HEY!
What the h-
Stegosaurus blood. We need to draw it back here.
SPSH
WHAT?! I DON'T WANNA BE DINO-BAIT!
That thing is on a rampage. People are dying. Now, you can stand here complaining until somebody else fixes it...
...or you can help me stop it before it eats your dog.
Who are you?
SNFF!

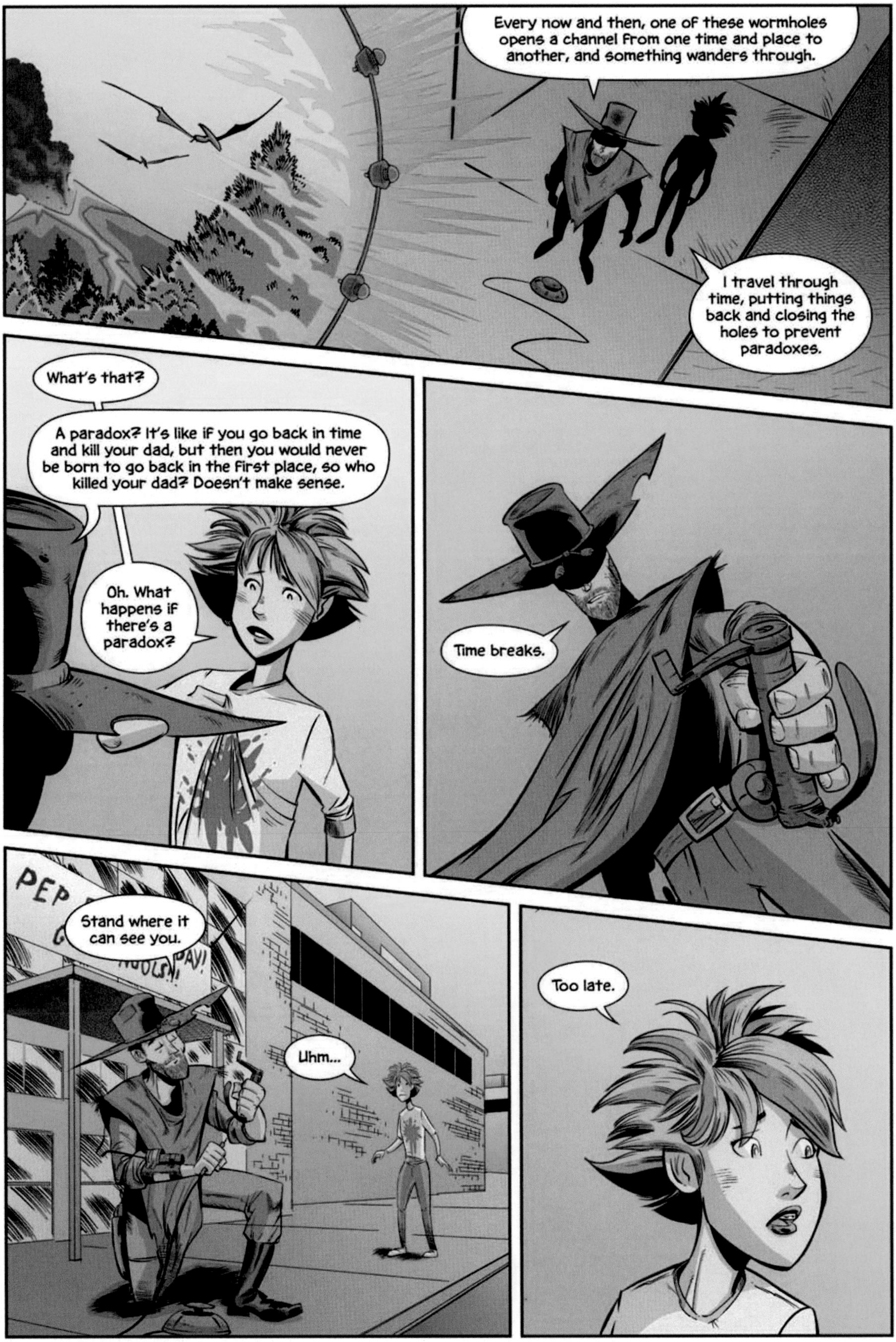
Every now and then, one of these wormholes opens a channel from one time and place to another, and something wanders through.
I travel through time, putting things back and closing the holes to prevent paradoxes.
What's that?
A paradox? It's like if you go back in time and kill your dad, but then you would never be born to go back in the first place, so who killed your dad? Doesn't make sense.
Oh. What happens if there's a paradox?
Time breaks.
Stand where it can see you.
Uhm...
Too late.

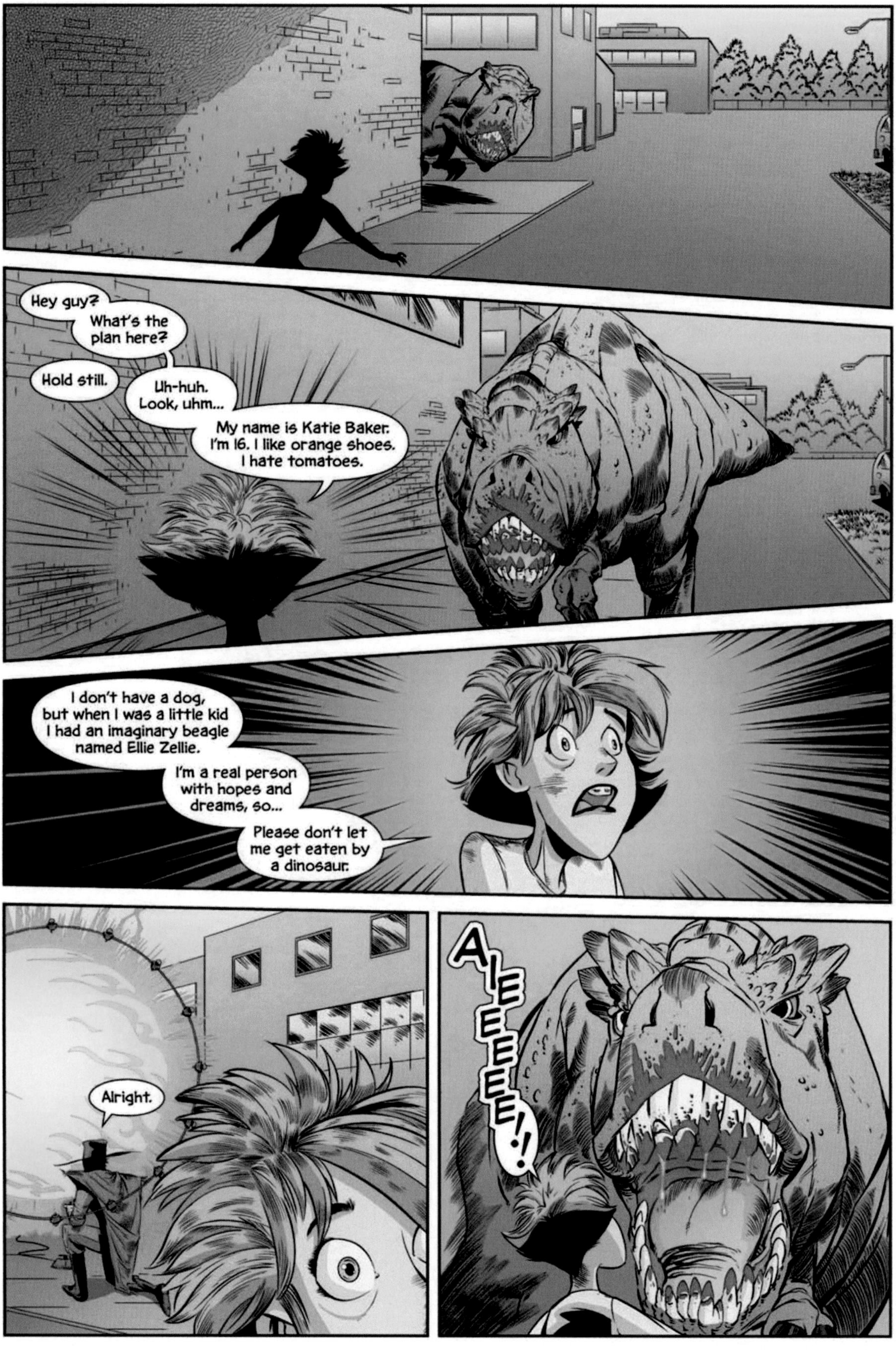
Hey guy?
What's the plan here?
Hold still.
Uh-huh. Look, uhm...
My name is Katie Baker. I'm 16. I like orange shoes. I hate tomatoes.
I don't have a dog, but when I was a little kid I had an imaginary beagle named Ellie Zellie.
I'm a real person with hopes and dreams, so...
Please don't let me get eaten by a dinosaur.
Alright.
AIEEEEE!!

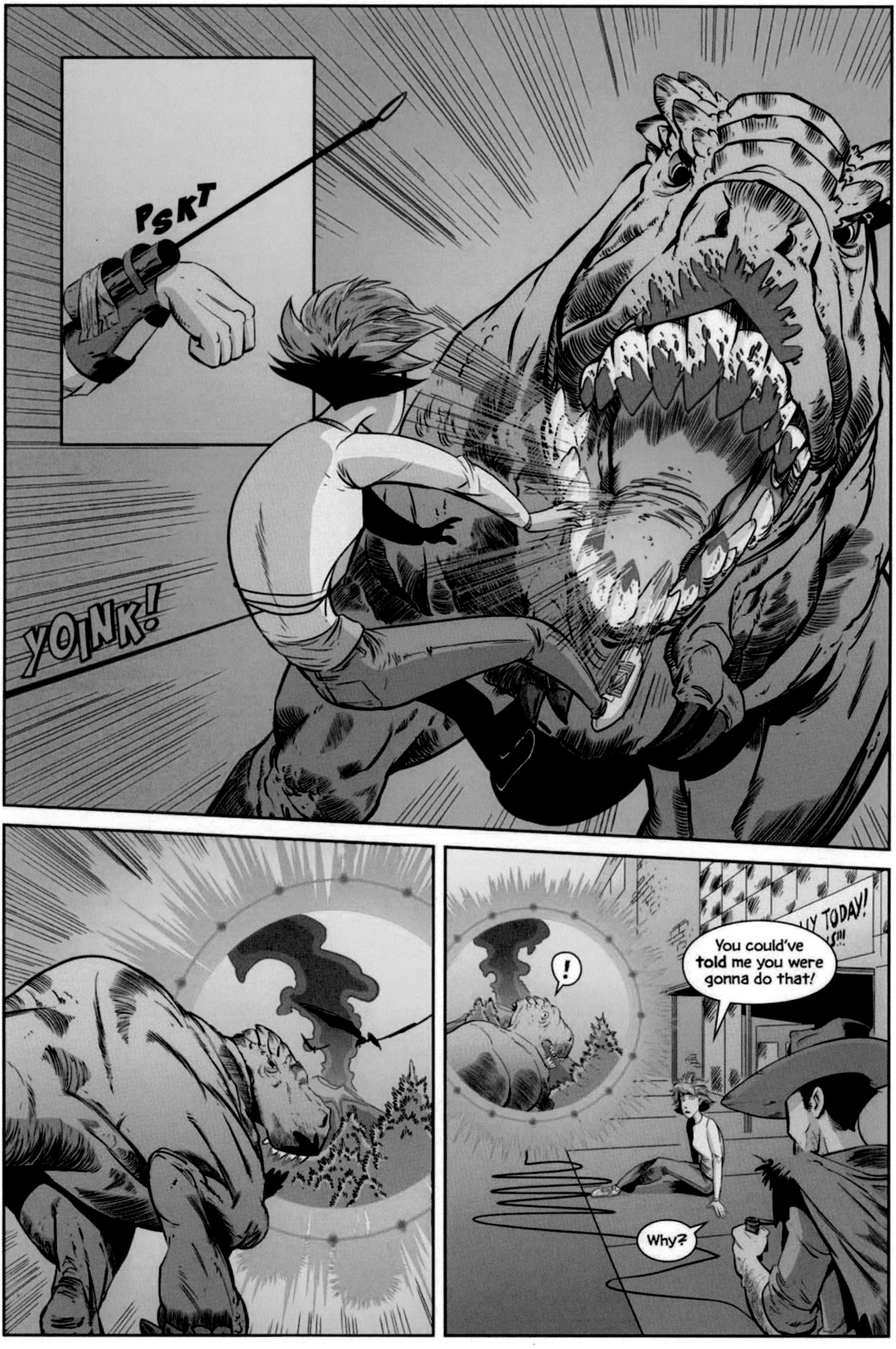
PSKT
YOINK!
!
You could've **told** me you were gonna do that!
Why?

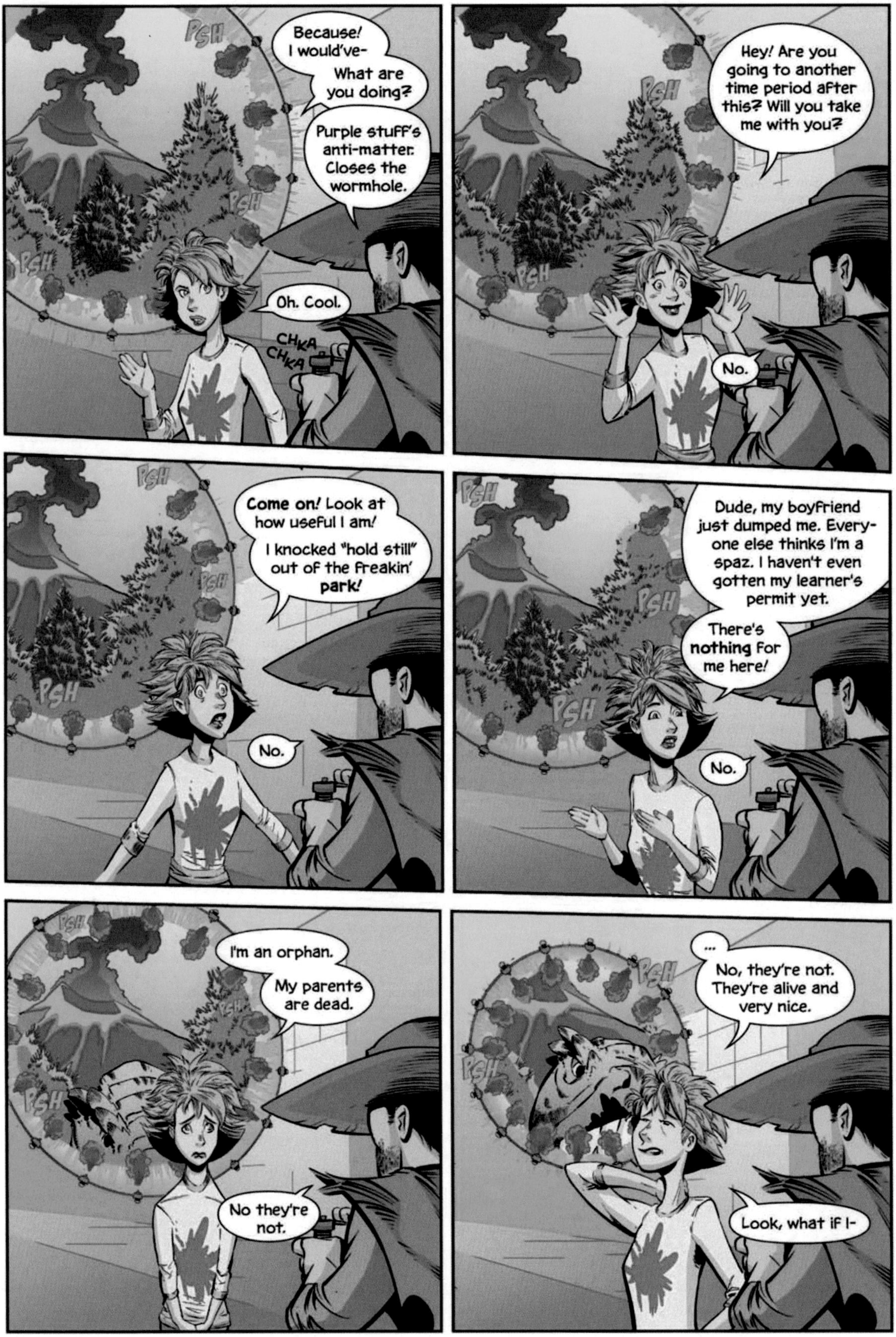
PSH
Because! I would've-
What are you doing?
Purple stuff's anti-matter. Closes the wormhole.
PSH
PSH
Oh. Cool.
CHKA CHKA
PSH
Hey! Are you going to another time period after this? Will you take me with you?
PSH
No.
PSH
Come on! Look at how useful I am!
I knocked "hold still" out of the freakin' park!
PSH
PSH
No.
PSH
Dude, my boyfriend just dumped me. Everyone else thinks I'm a spaz. I haven't even gotten my learner's permit yet.
There's nothing for me here!
PSH
PSH
No.
PSH
I'm an orphan.
My parents are dead.
PSH
PSH
No they're not.
...
No, they're not. They're alive and very nice.
PSH
PSH
Look, what if I-

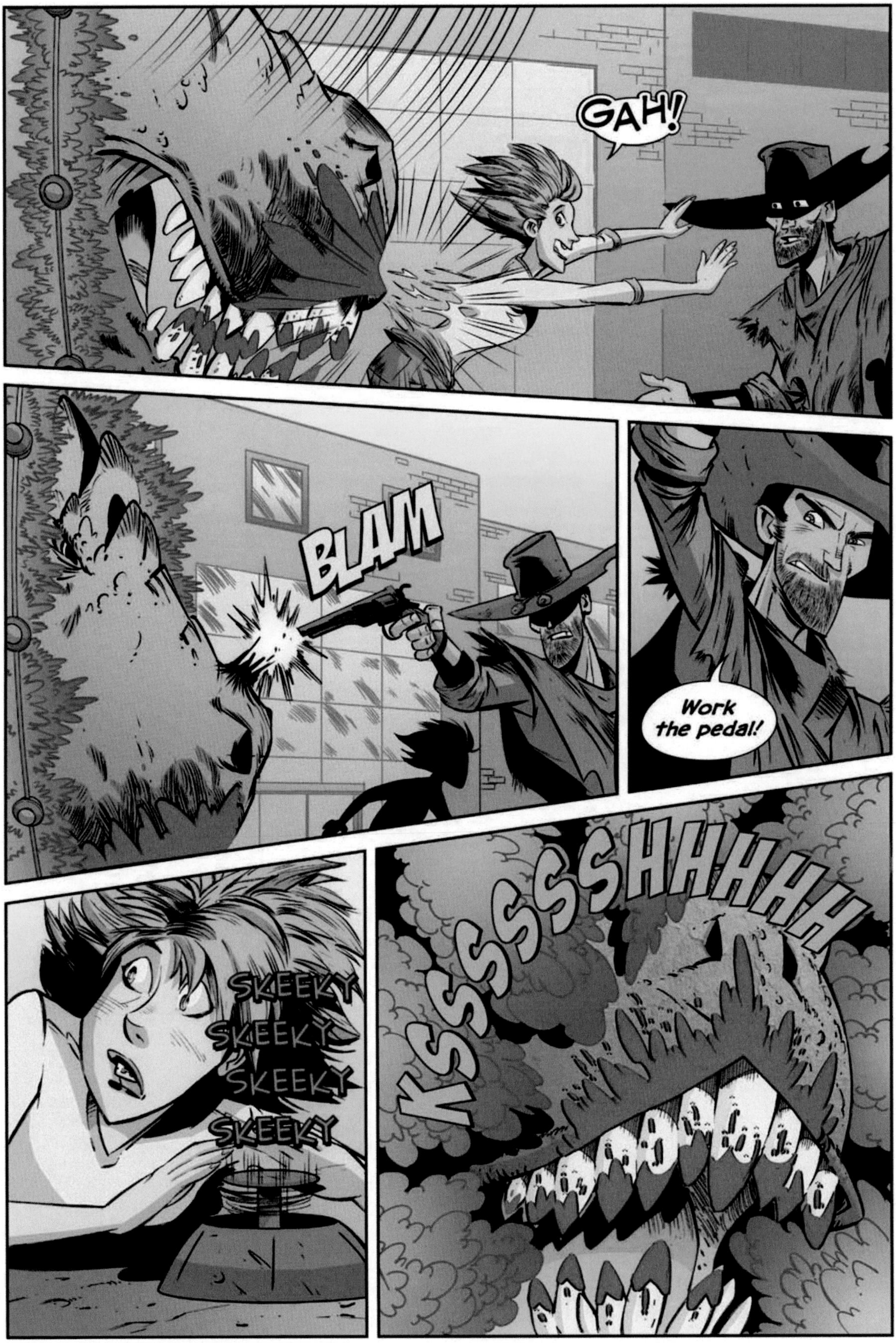
GAH!
BLAM
Work the pedal!
SKEEKY
SKEEKY
SKEEKY
SKEEKY
KSSSSSSHHHHHH

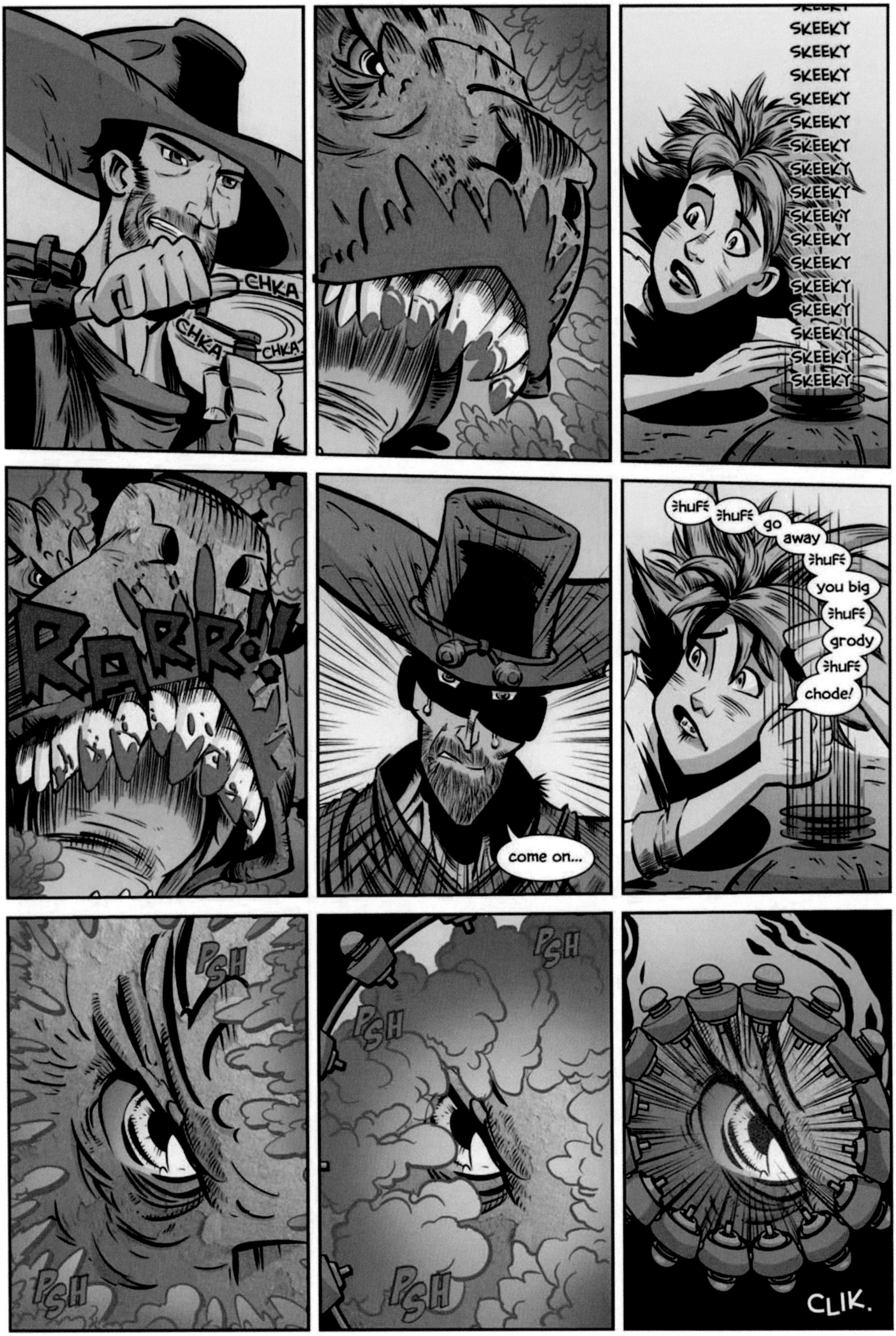
CHKA
CHKA
CHKA
SKEEKY
SKEEKY
SKEEKY
SKEEKY
SKEEKY
SKEEKY
SKEEKY
SKEEKY
SKEEKY
SKEEKY
SKEEKY
SKEEKY
SKEEKY
SKEEKY
SKEEKY
SKEEKY
RARR!!
come on...
huf
huf
go away
huf
you big
huf
grody
huf
chode!
PSH
PSH
PSH
PSH
CLIK.

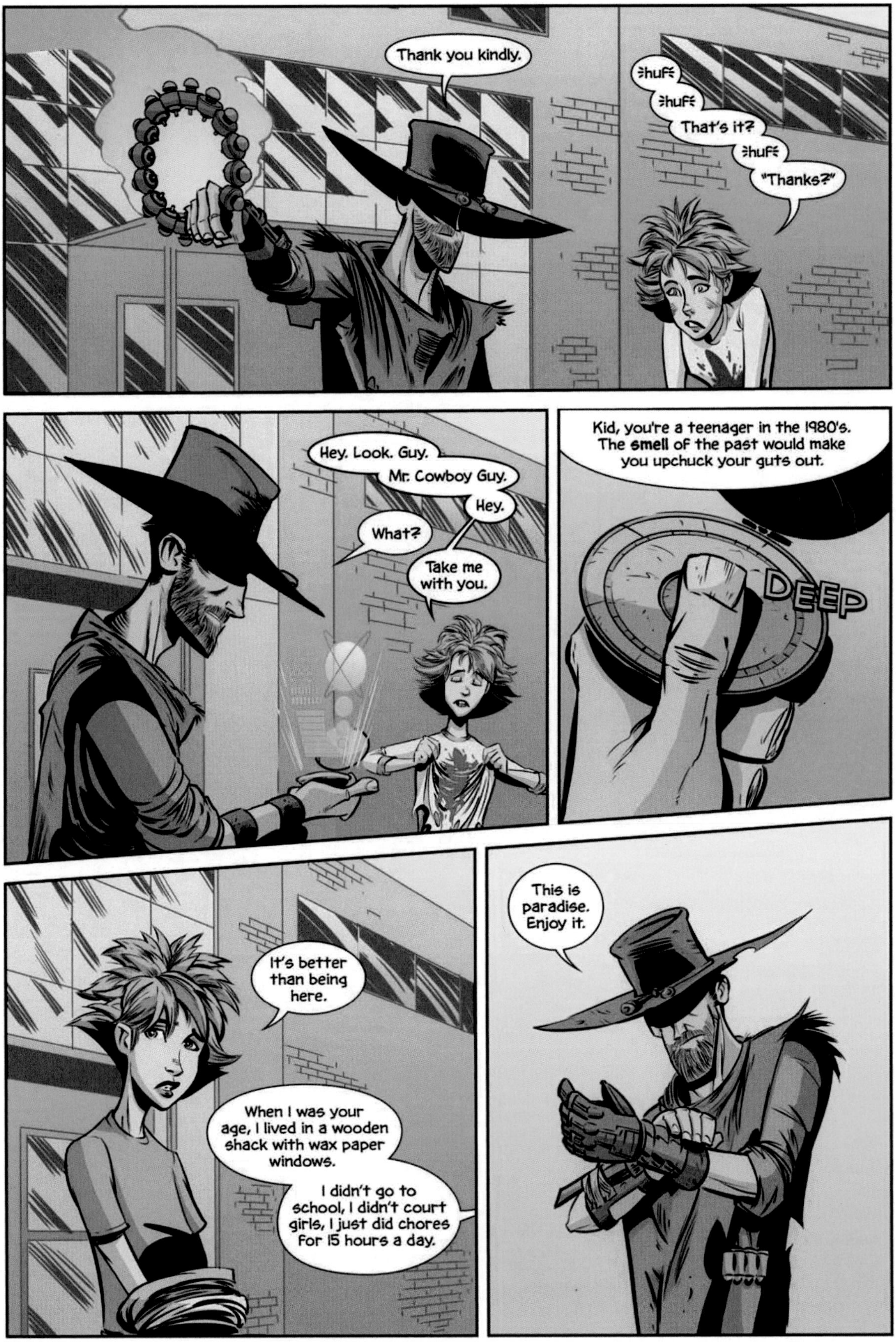
Thank you kindly.
≡huf≡
≡huf≡
That's it?
≡huf≡
"Thanks?"
Hey. Look. Guy.
Mr. Cowboy Guy.
Hey.
What?
Take me with you.
Kid, you're a teenager in the 1980's. The **smell** of the past would make you upchuck your guts out.
DEEP
It's better than being here.
When I was your age, I lived in a wooden shack with wax paper windows.
I didn't go to school, I didn't court girls, I just did chores for 15 hours a day.
This is paradise. Enjoy it.

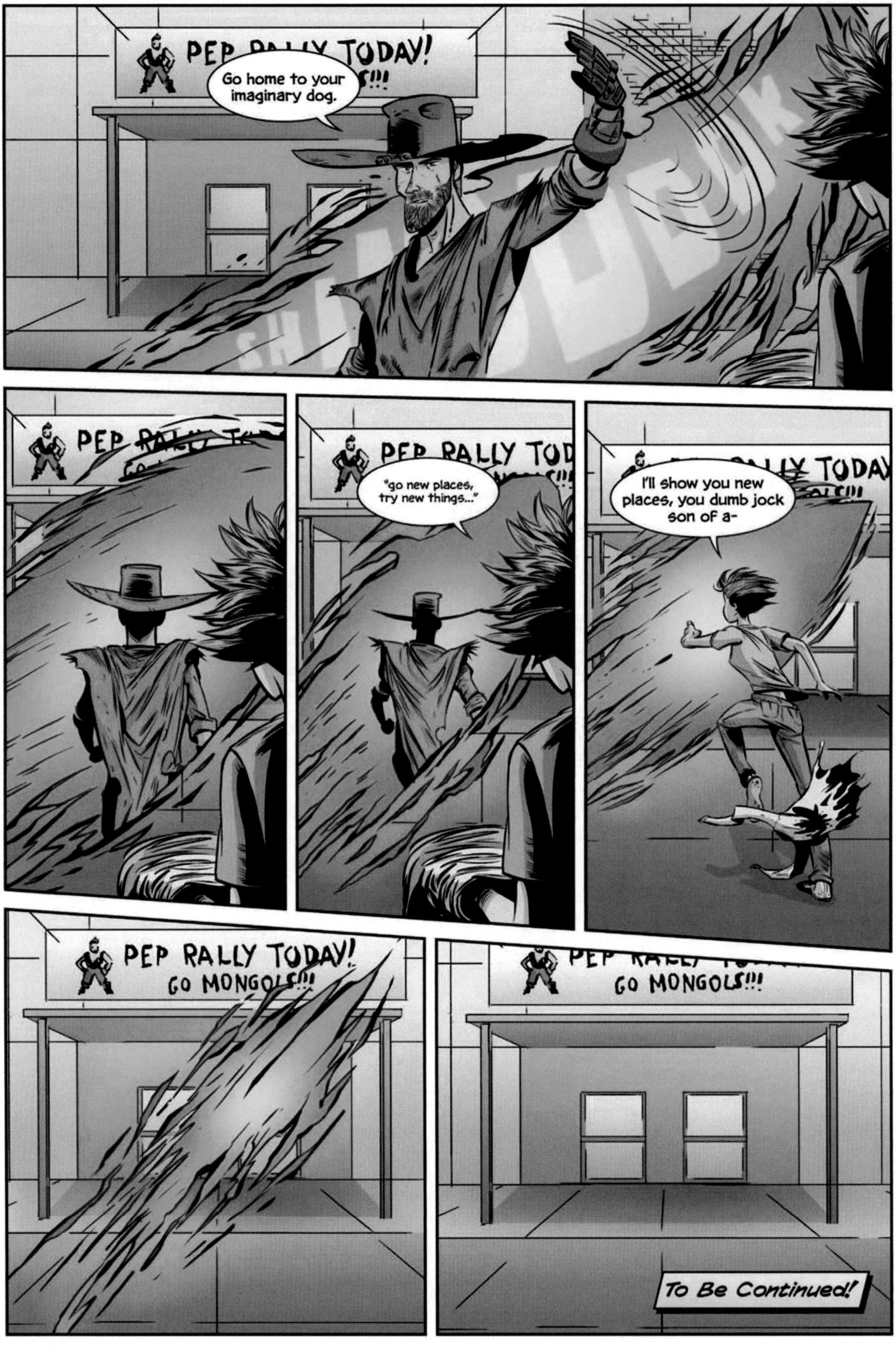
PEP RALLY TODAY!
Go home to your imaginary dog.
SHADDDK
PEP RALLY TODAY
"go new places, try new things..."
I'll show you new places, you dumb jock son of a-
PEP RALLY TODAY!
GO MONGOLS!!!
GO MONGOLS!!!
To Be Continued!

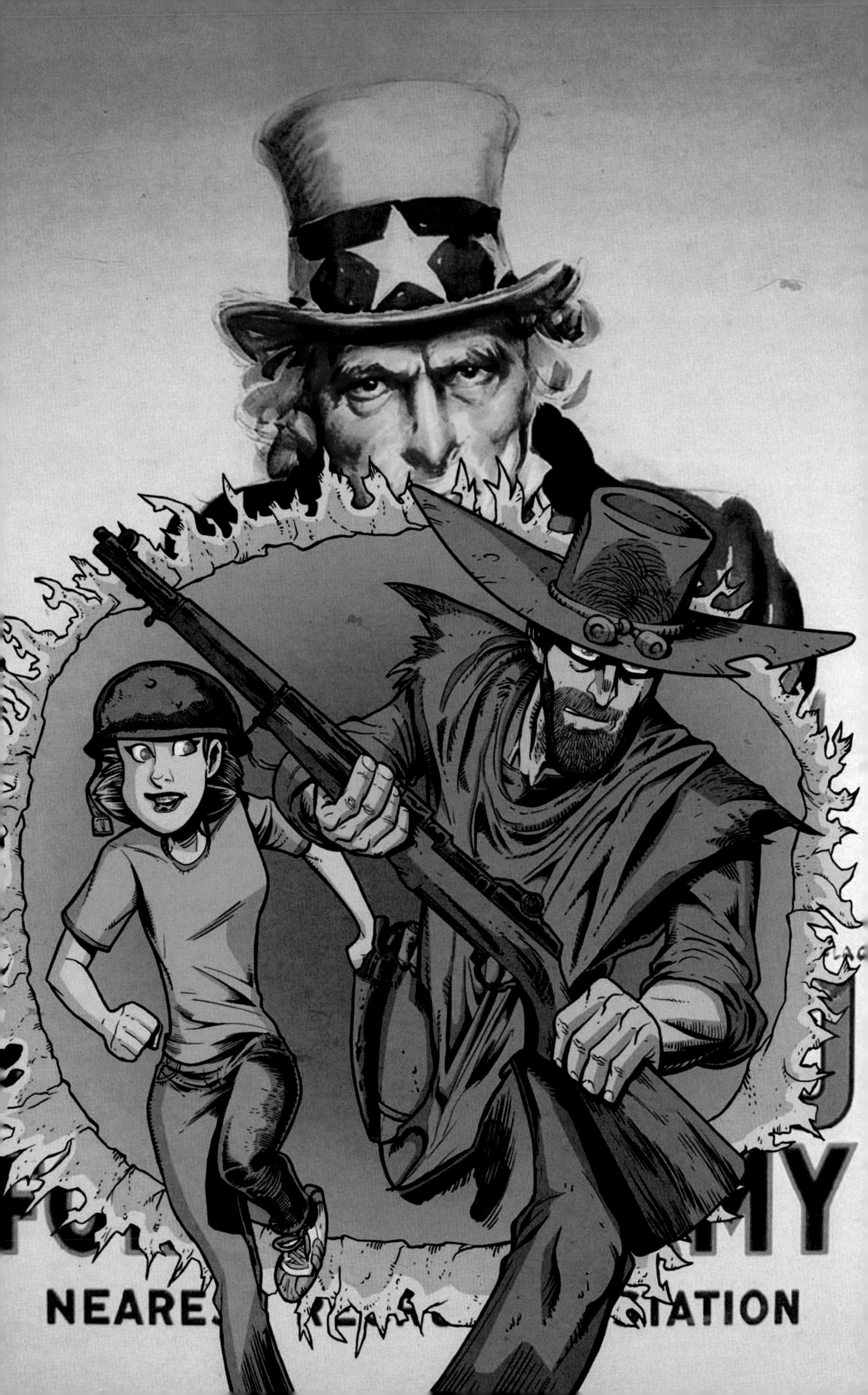
MY
NEARES
TATION

ISSUE TWO

"AGENTS...AT WAR!"

BOOM

Brat-tat-tat-tat

BOOM

BOOM

SHOOOK

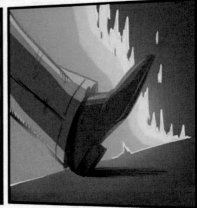

Pah!

Ok! Guy! Don't freak out, but I followed you into...

...a house?

That's so lame.

ARE YOU OUT OF YOUR DAMN BLASTED MIND?!

I'm gonna help you close wormholes?

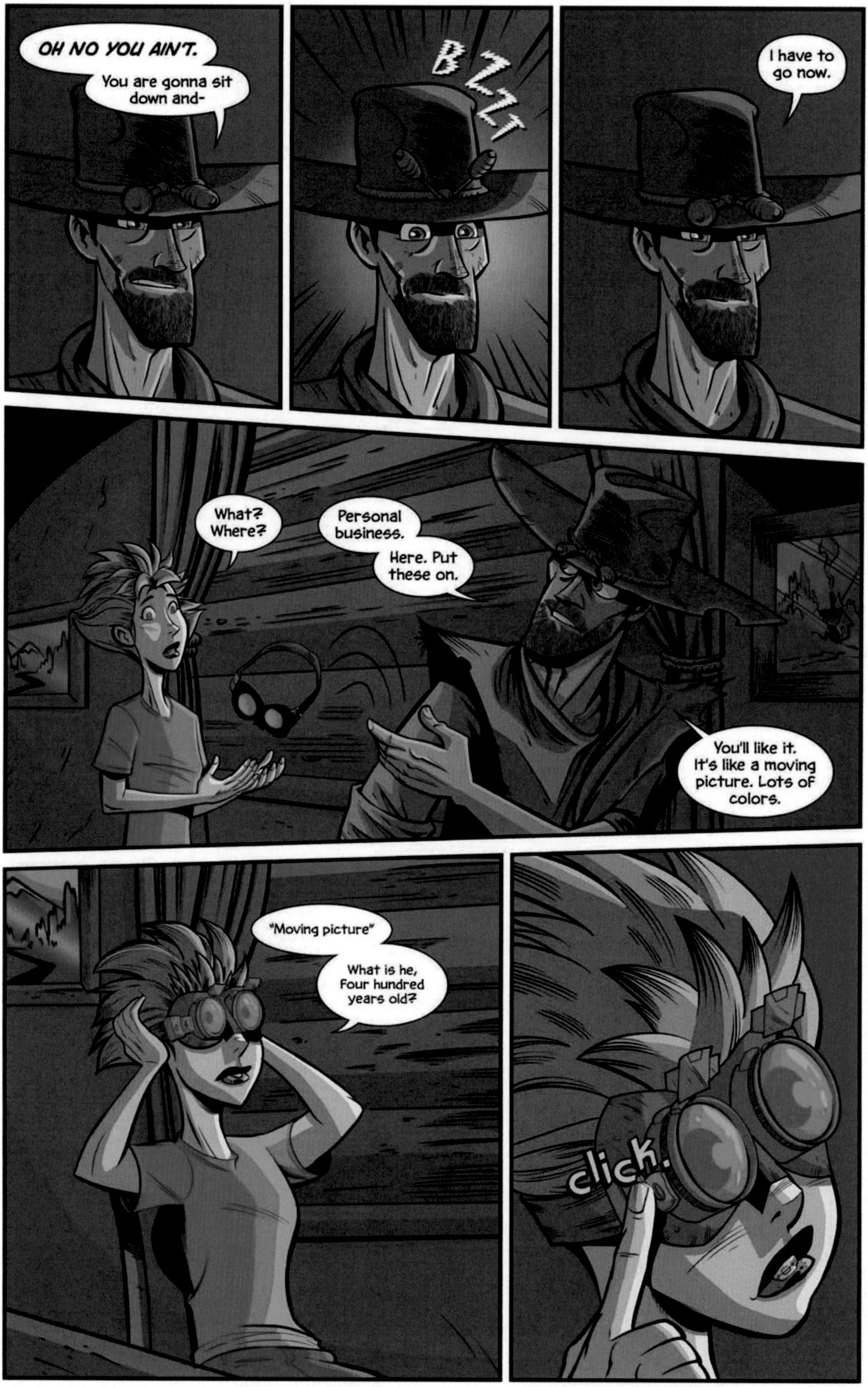
OH NO YOU AIN'T.
You are gonna sit down and-
BZZZT
I have to go now.
What? Where?
Personal business.
Here. Put these on.
You'll like it. It's like a moving picture. Lots of colors.
"Moving picture"
What is he, four hundred years old?
click.

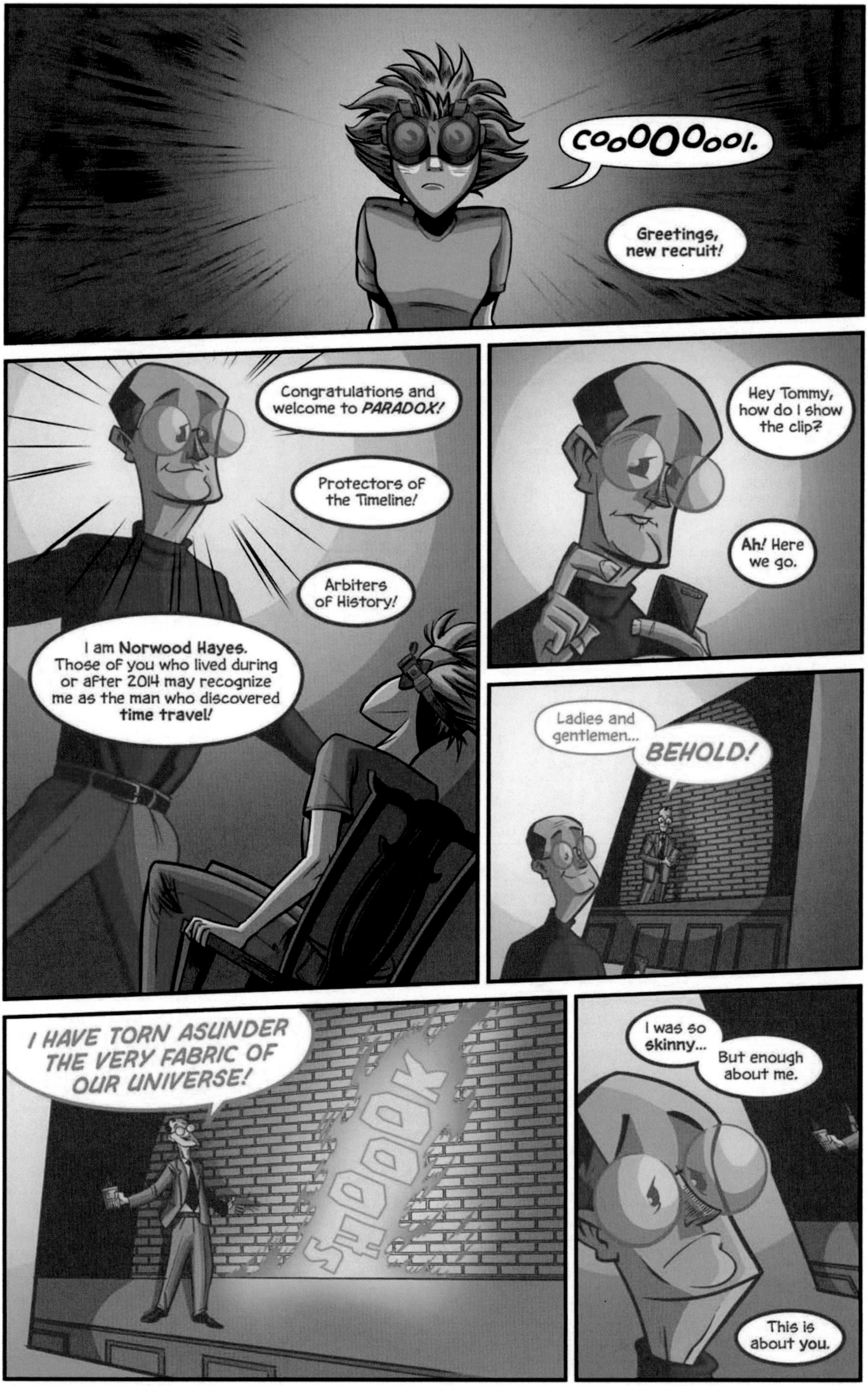
COoOOOool.
Greetings, new recruit!
Congratulations and welcome to PARADOX!
Protectors of the Timeline!
Arbiters of History!
I am Norwood Hayes. Those of you who lived during or after 2014 may recognize me as the man who discovered time travel!
Hey Tommy, how do I show the clip?
Ah! Here we go.
Ladies and gentlemen...
BEHOLD!
I HAVE TORN ASUNDER THE VERY FABRIC OF OUR UNIVERSE!
SHOOK
I was so skinny...
But enough about me.
This is about you.

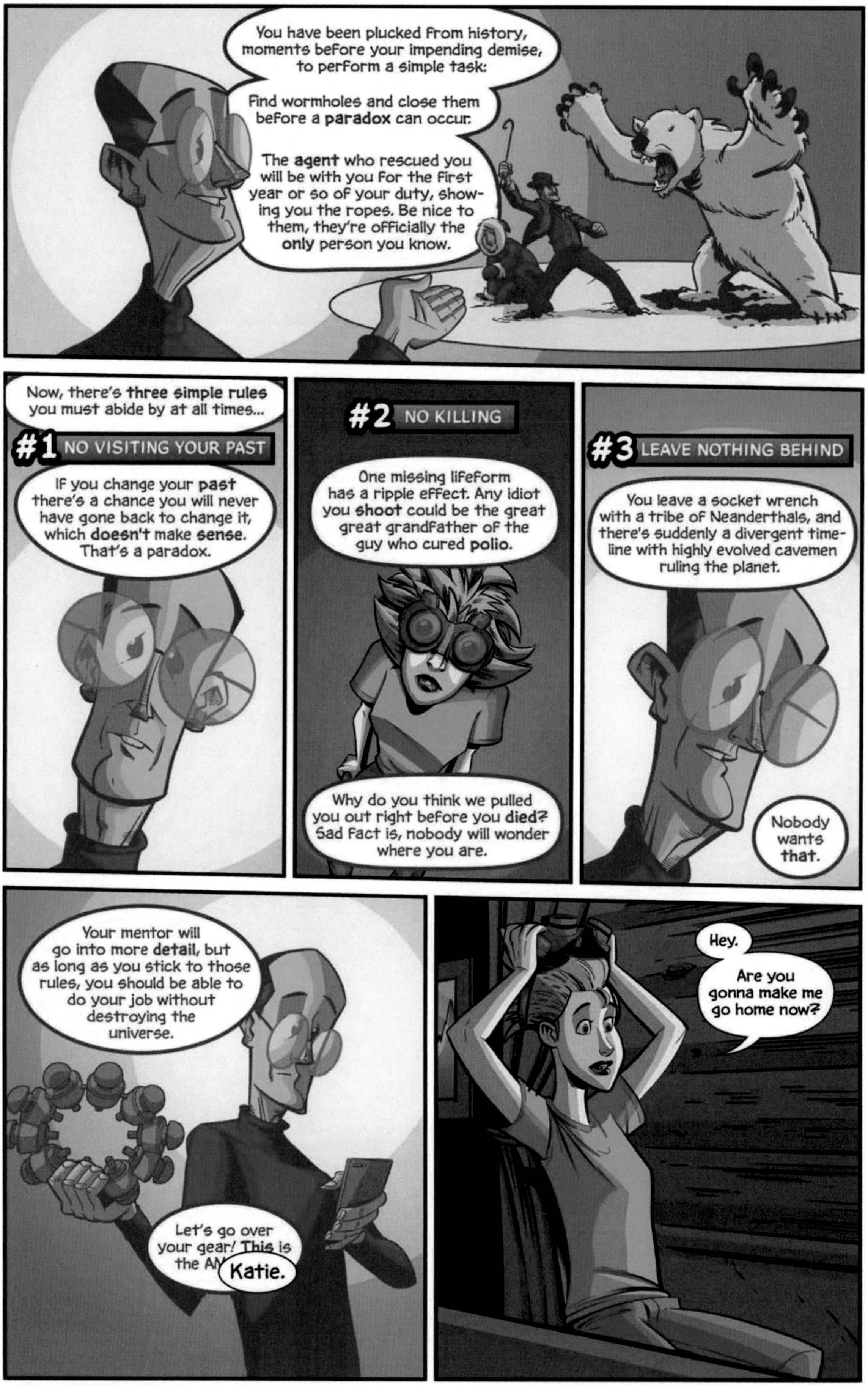

You have been plucked from history, moments before your impending demise, to perform a simple task:
Find wormholes and close them before a paradox can occur.
The agent who rescued you will be with you for the first year or so of your duty, showing you the ropes. Be nice to them, they're officially the only person you know.
Now, there's three simple rules you must abide by at all times...
#1 NO VISITING YOUR PAST
If you change your past there's a chance you will never have gone back to change it, which doesn't make sense. That's a paradox.
#2 NO KILLING
One missing lifeform has a ripple effect. Any idiot you shoot could be the great great grandfather of the guy who cured polio.
Why do you think we pulled you out right before you died? Sad fact is, nobody will wonder where you are.
#3 LEAVE NOTHING BEHIND
You leave a socket wrench with a tribe of Neanderthals, and there's suddenly a divergent time-line with highly evolved cavemen ruling the planet.
Nobody wants that.
Your mentor will go into more detail, but as long as you stick to those rules, you should be able to do your job without destroying the universe.
Let's go over your gear! This is the AN
Katie.
Hey.
Are you gonna make me go home now?

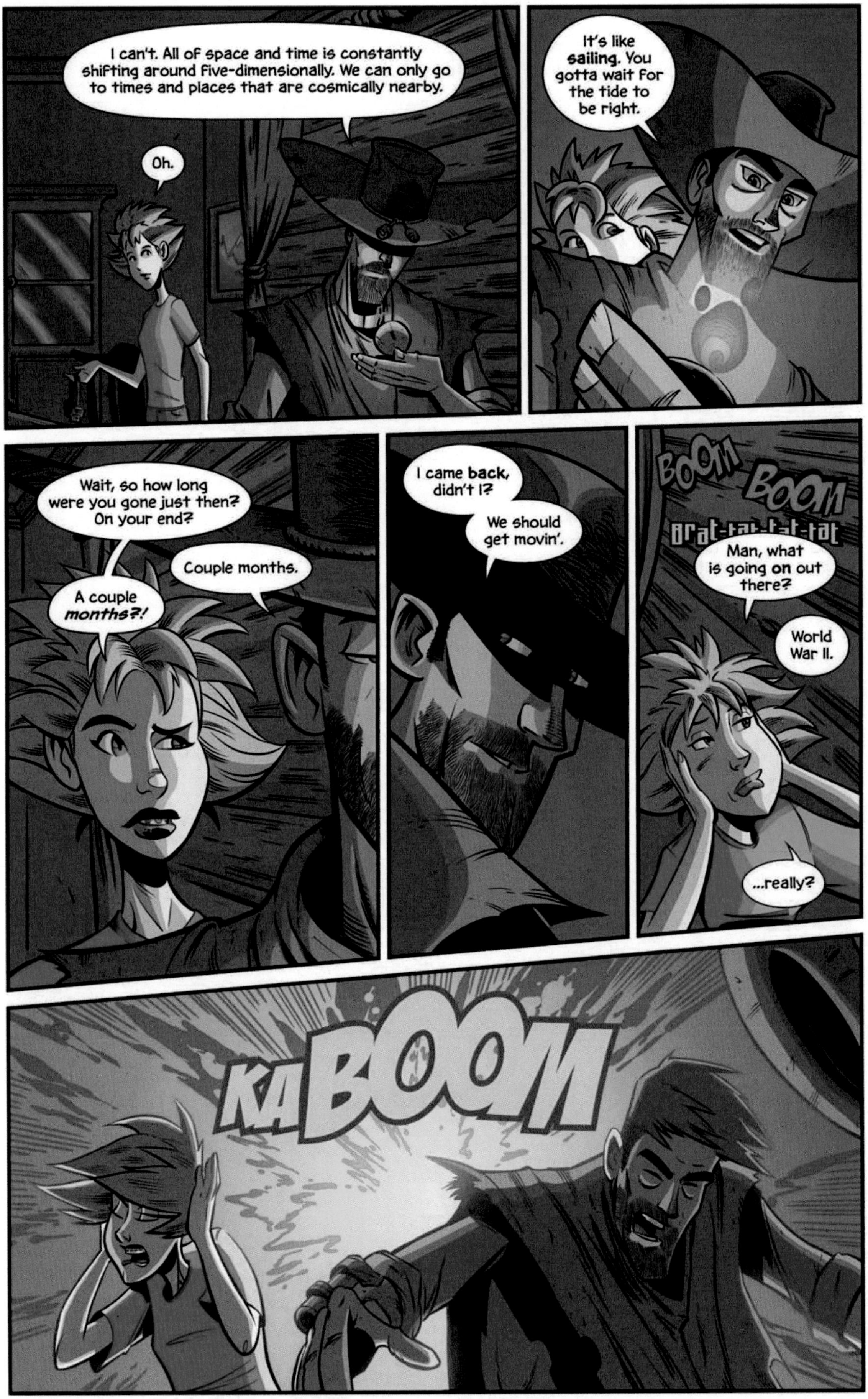
I can't. All of space and time is constantly shifting around five-dimensionally. We can only go to times and places that are cosmically nearby.
Oh.
It's like **sailing**. You gotta wait for the tide to be right.
Wait, so how long were you gone just then? On your end?
Couple months.
A couple *months?!*
I came **back**, didn't I?
We should get movin'.
BOOM
BOOM
BRAT-TAT-TAT-TAT
Man, what is going **on** out there?
World War II.
...really?
KABOOM

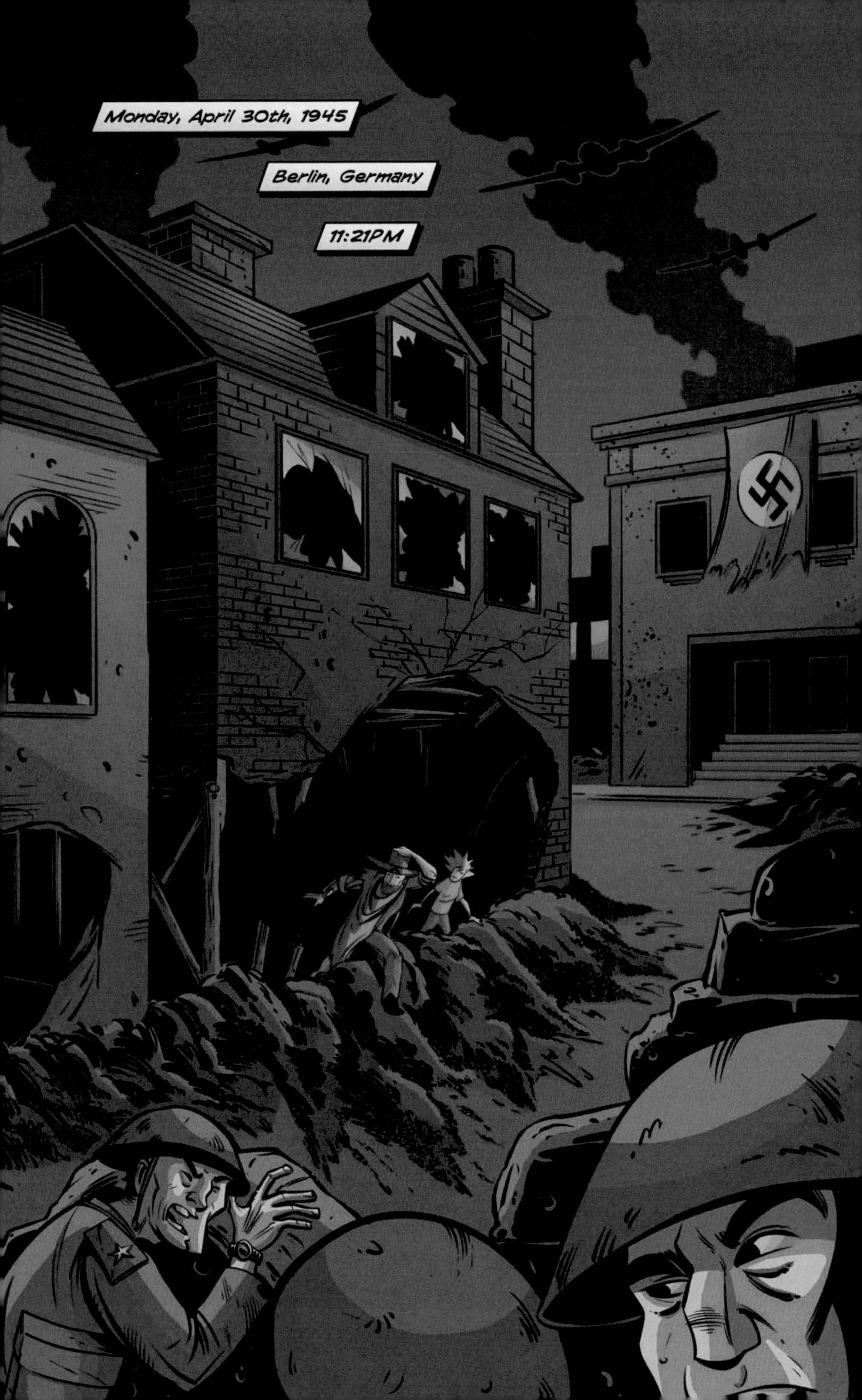
Monday, April 30th, 1945
Berlin, Germany
11:21PM

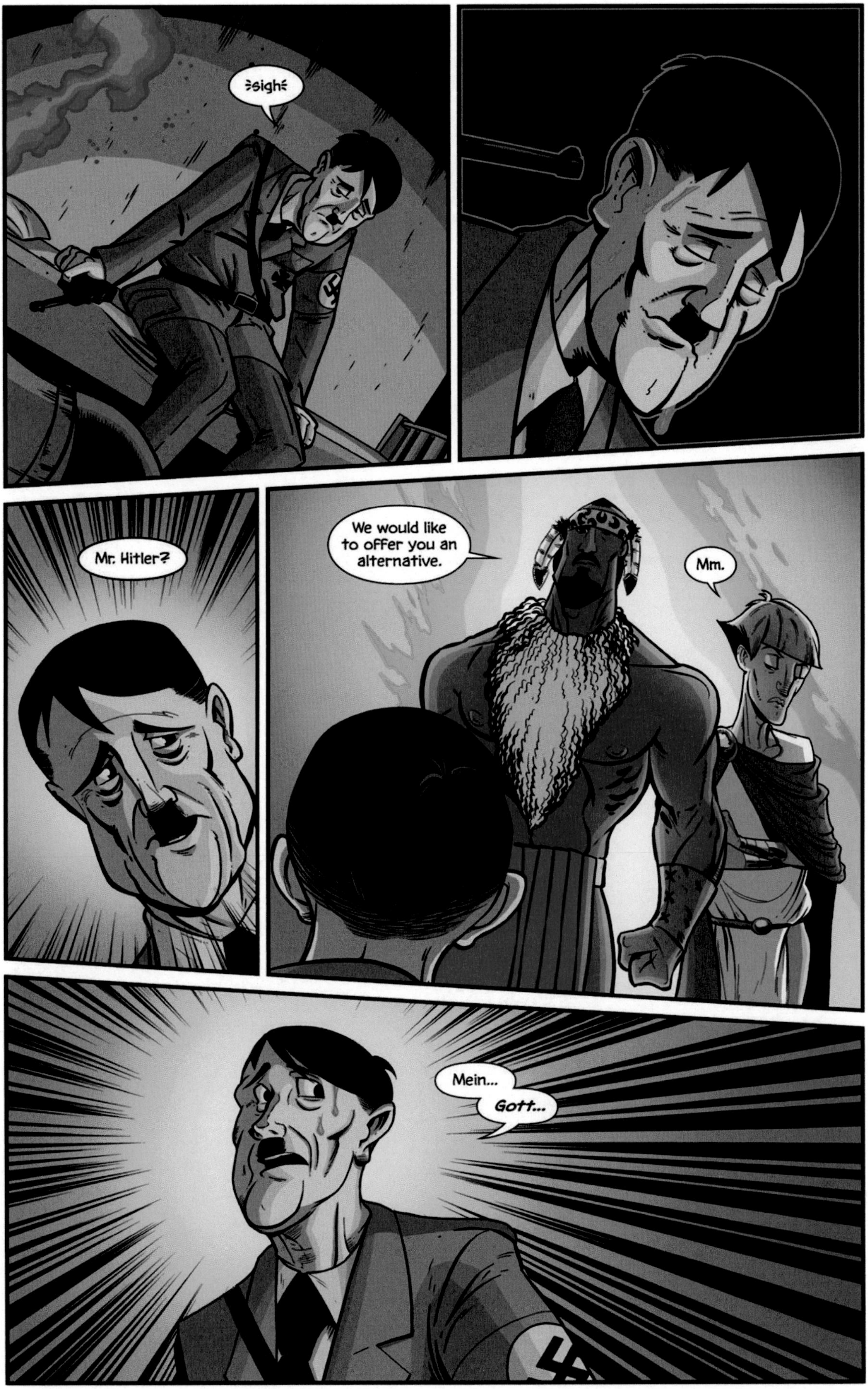

sigh
Mr. Hitler?
We would like to offer you an alternative.
Mm.
Mein...
Gott...

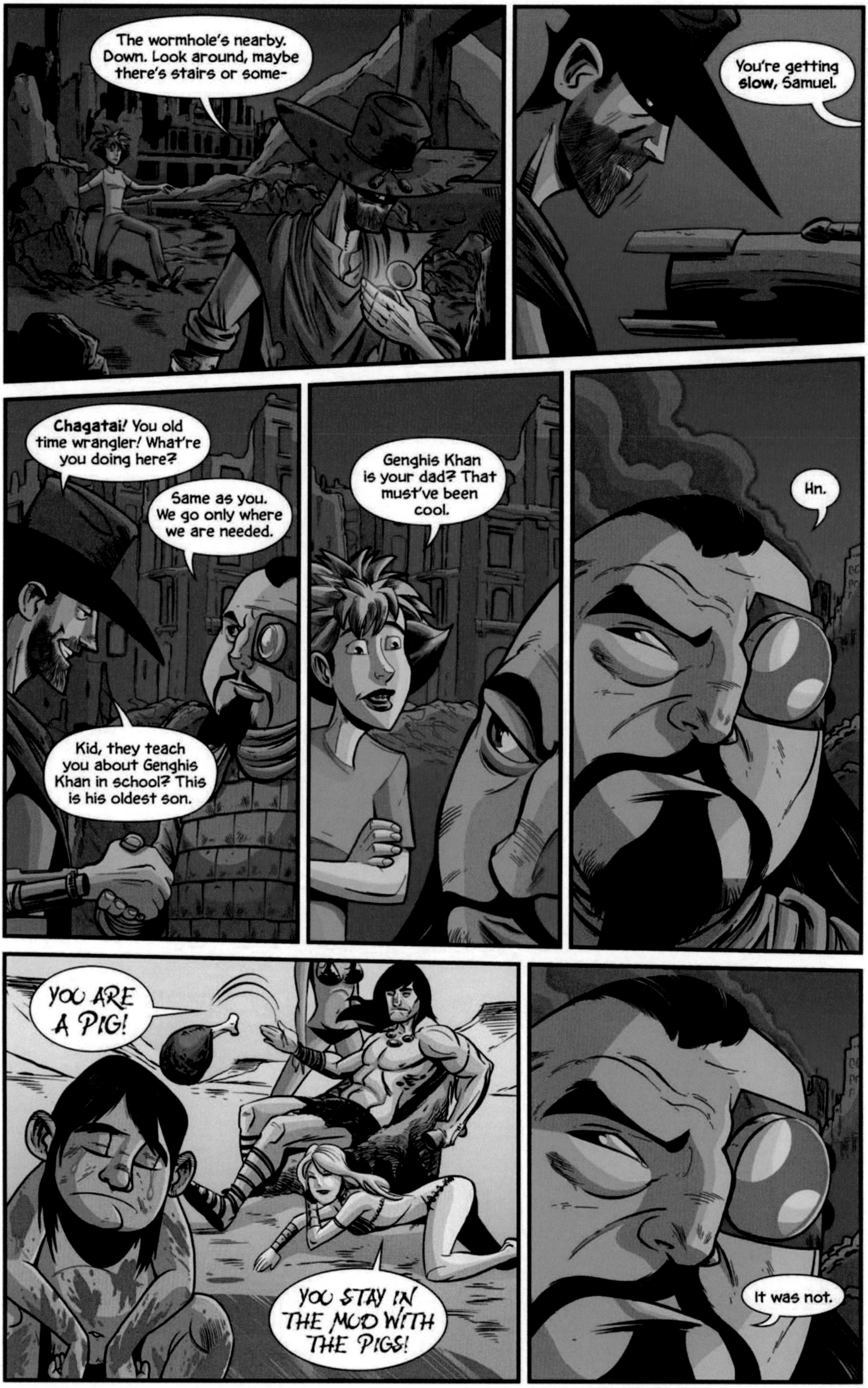
The wormhole's nearby. Down. Look around, maybe there's stairs or some-
You're getting slow, Samuel.
Chagatai! You old time wrangler! What're you doing here?
Same as you. We go only where we are needed.
Kid, they teach you about Genghis Khan in school? This is his oldest son.
Genghis Khan is your dad? That must've been cool.
Hn.
YOU ARE A PIG!
YOU STAY IN THE MUD WITH THE PIGS!
It was not.

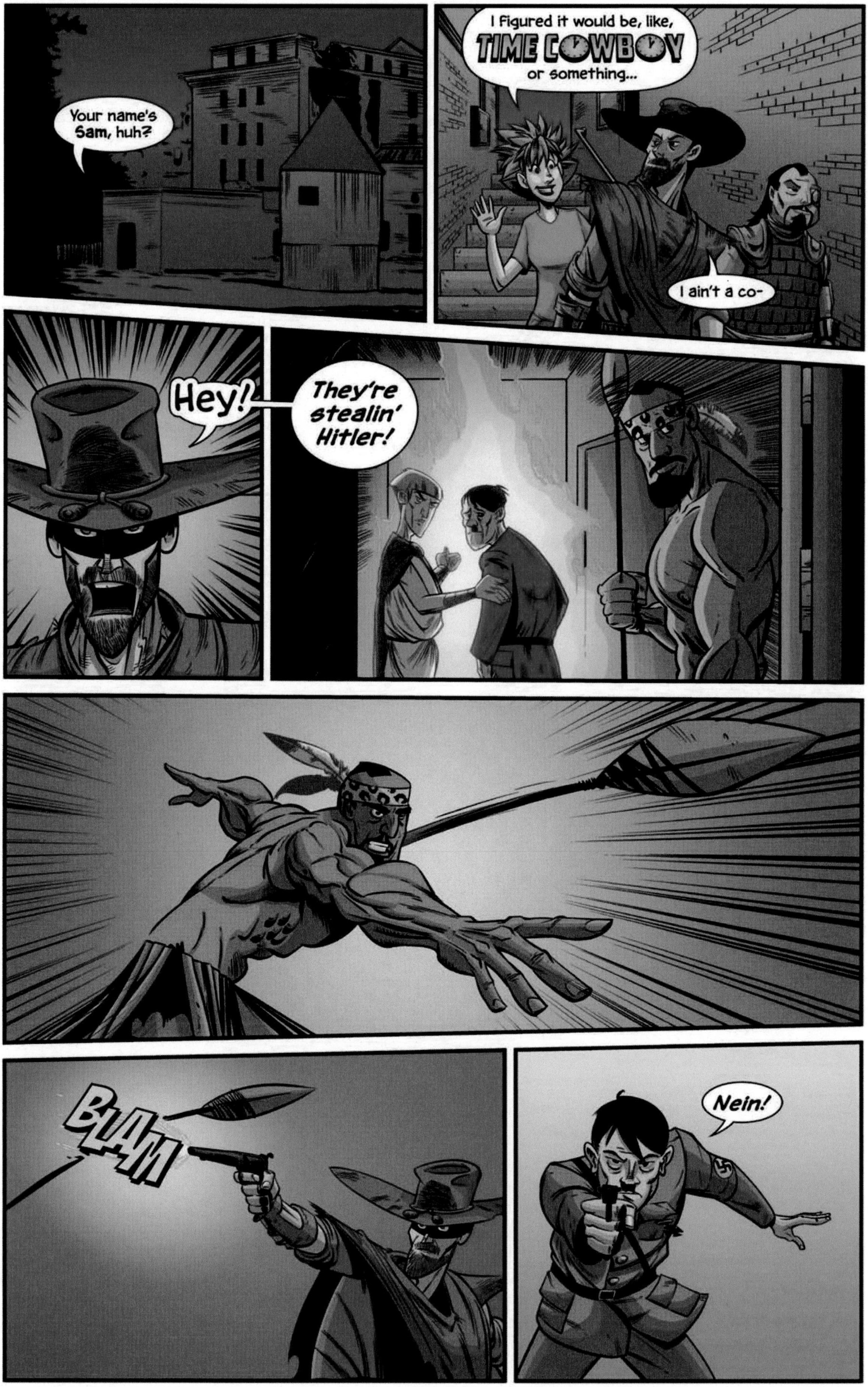
Your name's Sam, huh?
I figured it would be, like, TIME COWBOY or something...
I ain't a co-
Hey!
They're stealin' Hitler!
BLAM
Nein!

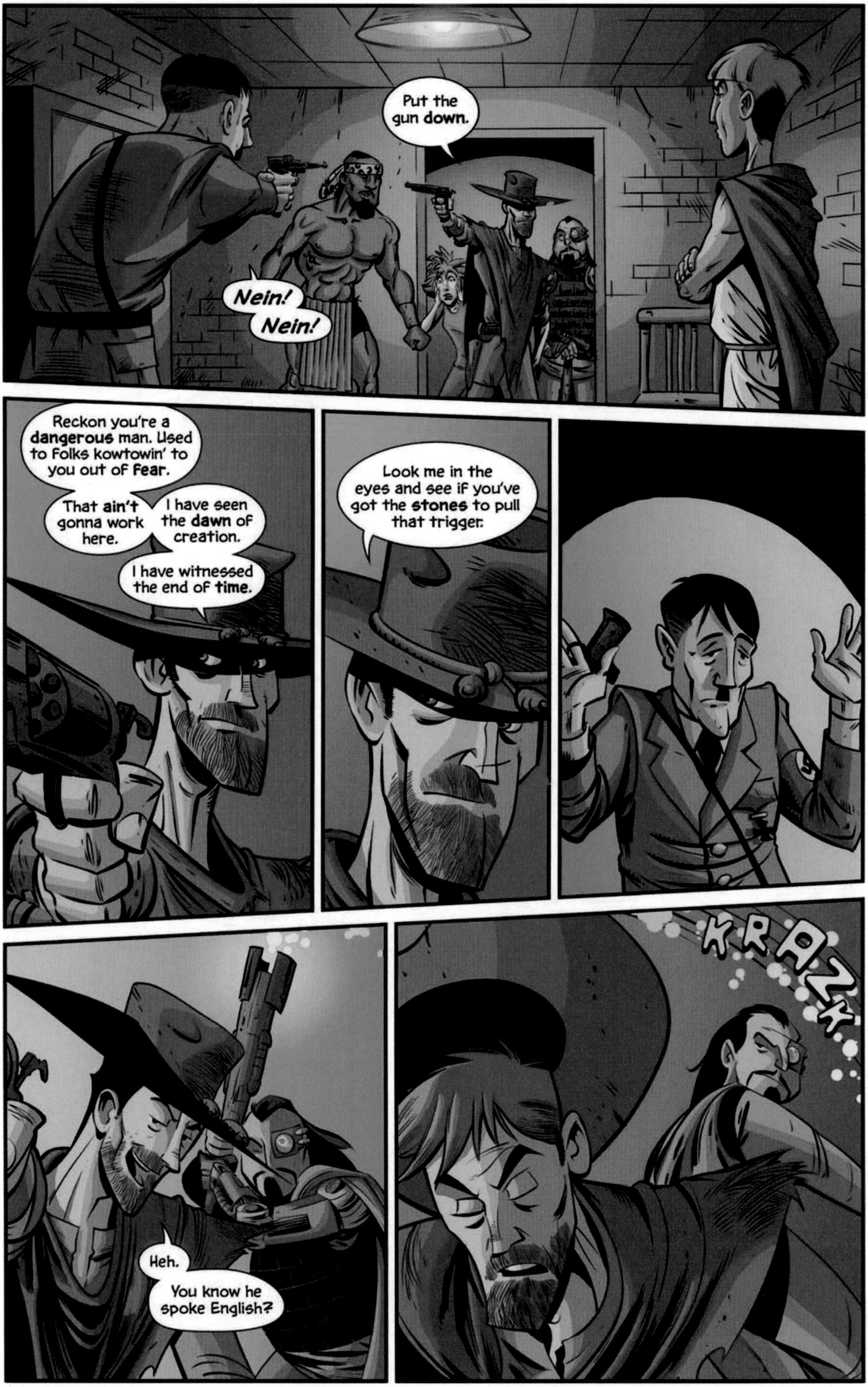
Put the gun down.
Nein! Nein!
Reckon you're a dangerous man. Used to folks kowtowin' to you out of fear.
That ain't gonna work here.
I have seen the dawn of creation.
I have witnessed the end of time.
Look me in the eyes and see if you've got the stones to pull that trigger.
Heh.
You know he spoke English?
KRAZK

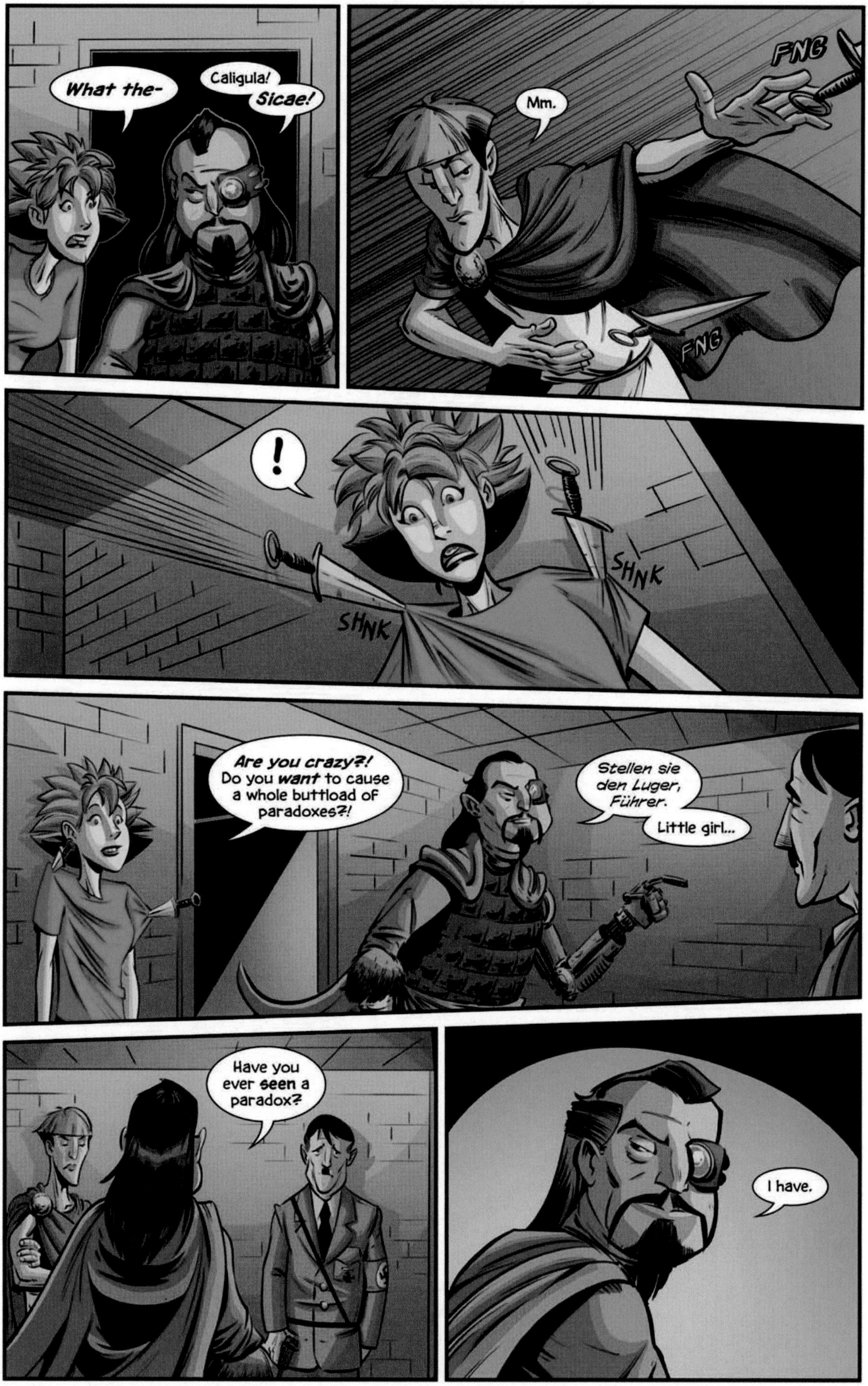
What the-
Caligula!
Sicae!
Mm.
FNG
FNG
!
SHNK
SHNK
Are you crazy?! Do you want to cause a whole buttload of paradoxes?!
Stellen sie den Luger, Führer.
Little girl...
Have you ever seen a paradox?
I have.

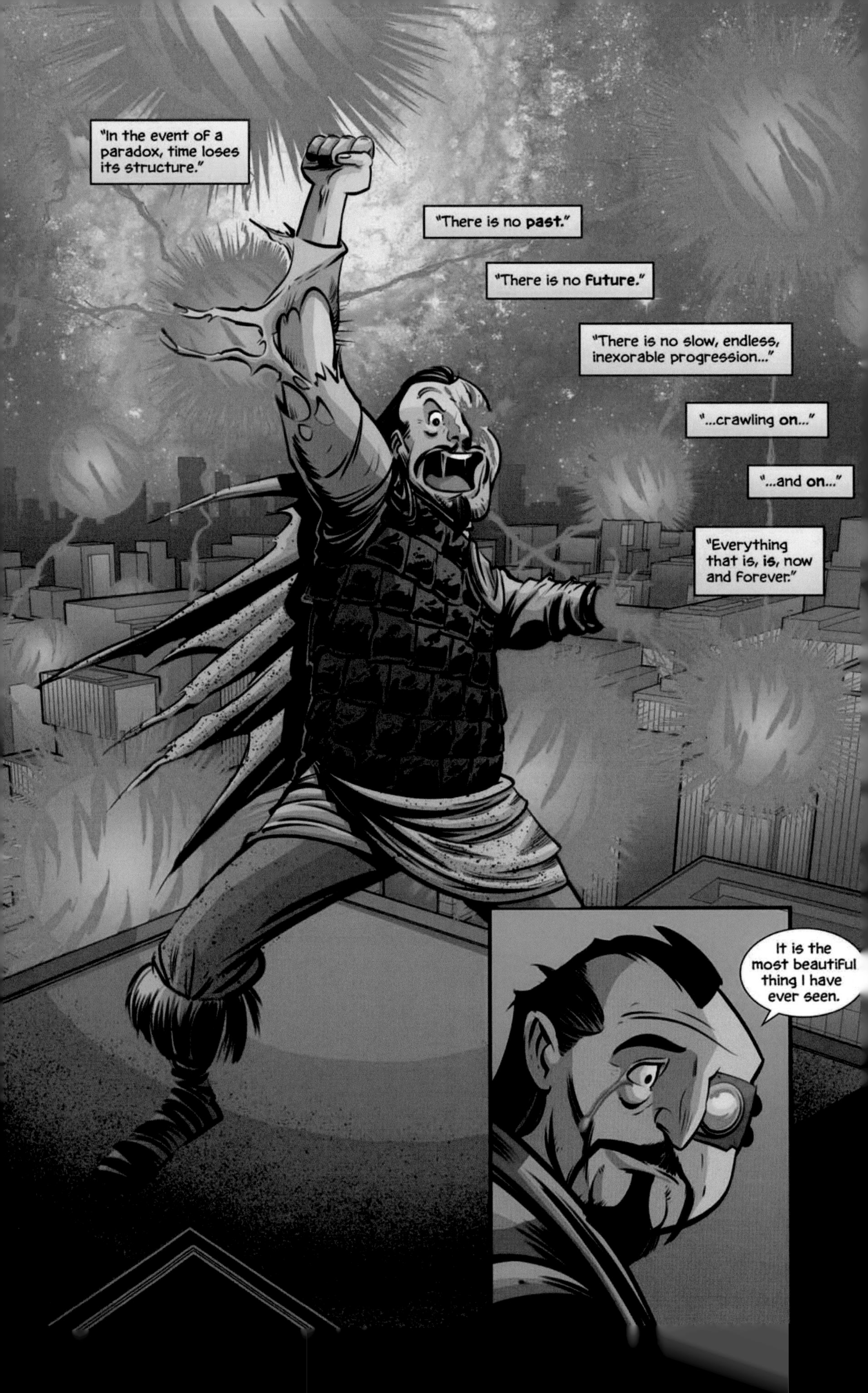

"In the event of a paradox, time loses its structure."
"There is no past."
"There is no future."
"There is no slow, endless, inexorable progression..."
"...crawling on..."
"...and on..."
"Everything that is, is, now and forever."
It is the most beautiful thing I have ever seen.

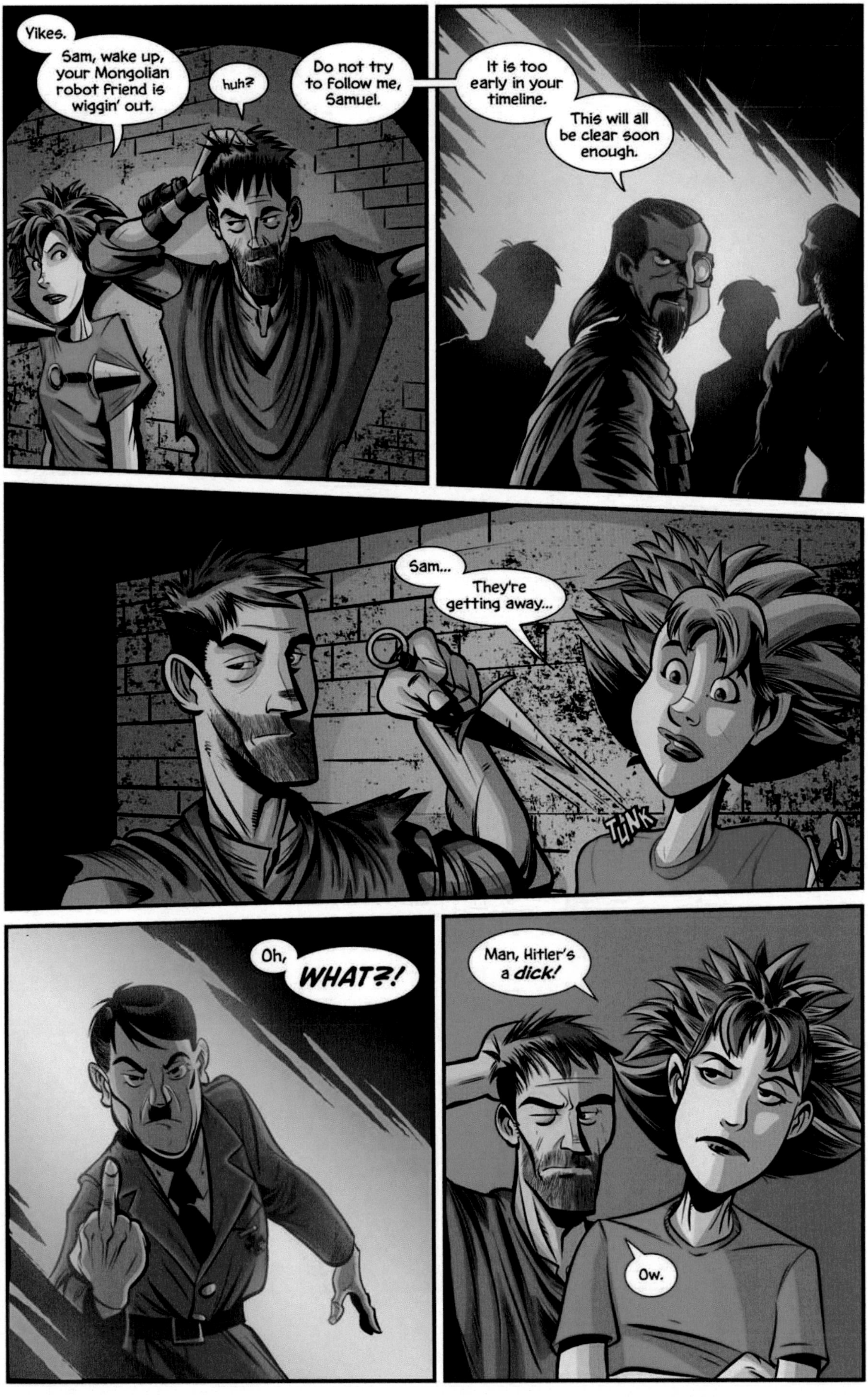
Yikes.
Sam, wake up, your Mongolian robot friend is wiggin' out.
huh?
Do not try to follow me, Samuel.
It is too early in your timeline.
This will all be clear soon enough.
Sam...
They're getting away...
TINK
Oh,
WHAT?!
Man, Hitler's a dick!
Ow.

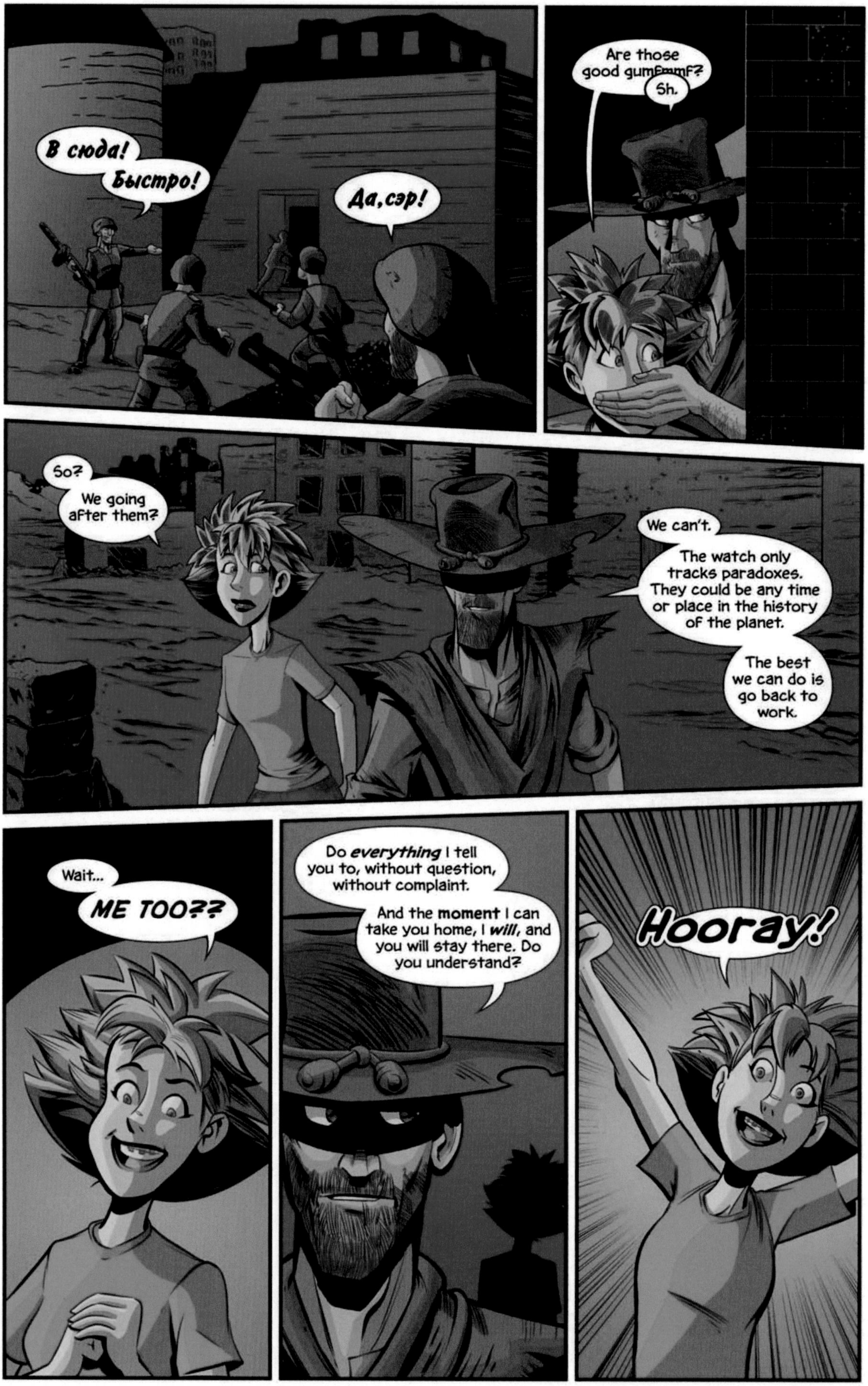
В сюда!
Быстро!
Да, сэр!
Are those good gumFmmF?
Sh.
So?
We going after them?
We can't.
The watch only tracks paradoxes. They could be any time or place in the history of the planet.
The best we can do is go back to work.
Wait...
ME TOO??
Do *everything* I tell you to, without question, without complaint.
And the **moment** I can take you home, I *will*, and you will stay there. Do you understand?
Hooray!

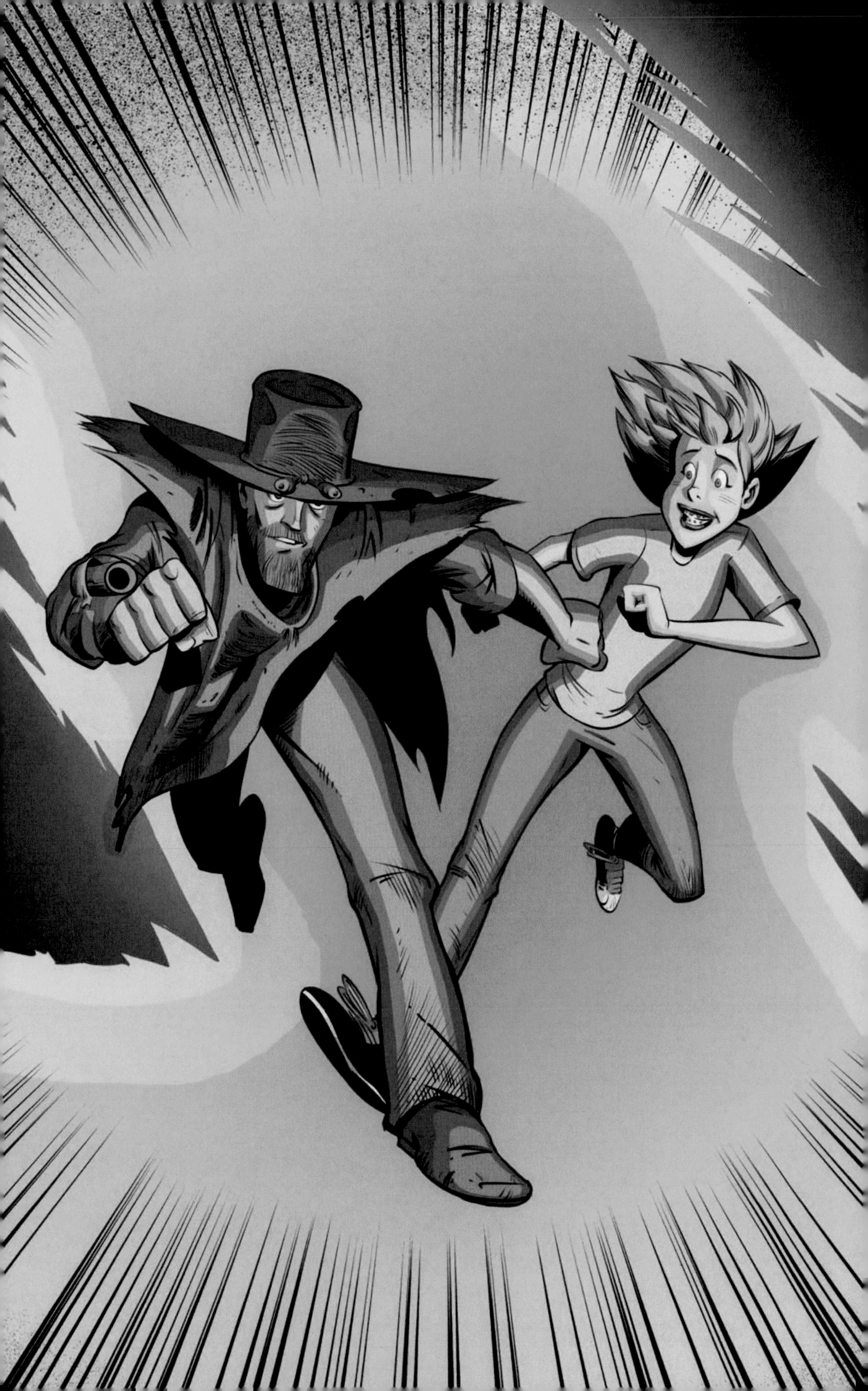

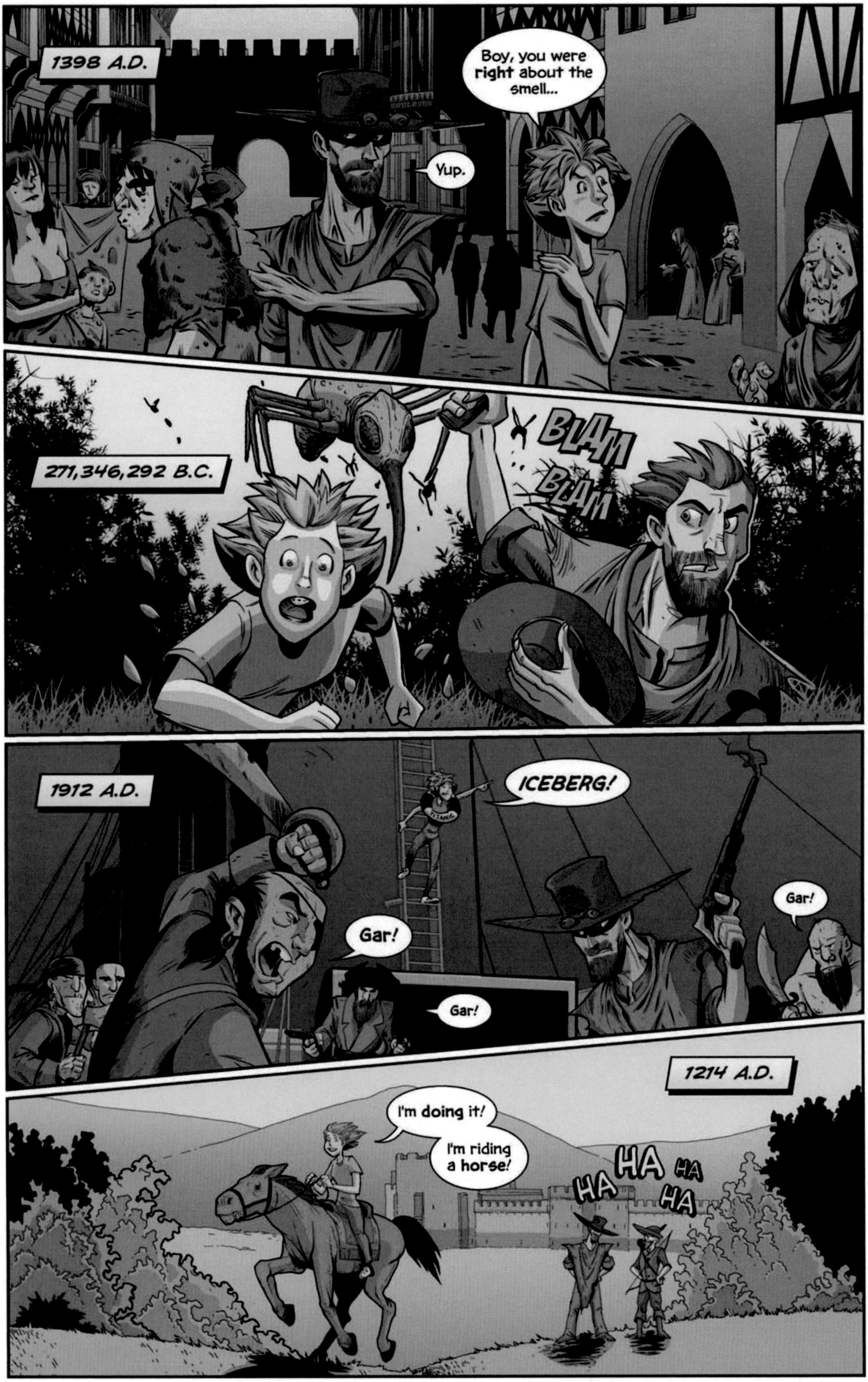
1398 A.D.
Boy, you were right about the smell...
Yup.
271,346,292 B.C.
BLAM
BLAM
1912 A.D.
ICEBERG!
Gar!
Gar!
Gar!
1214 A.D.
I'm doing it!
I'm riding a horse!
HA HA HA HA

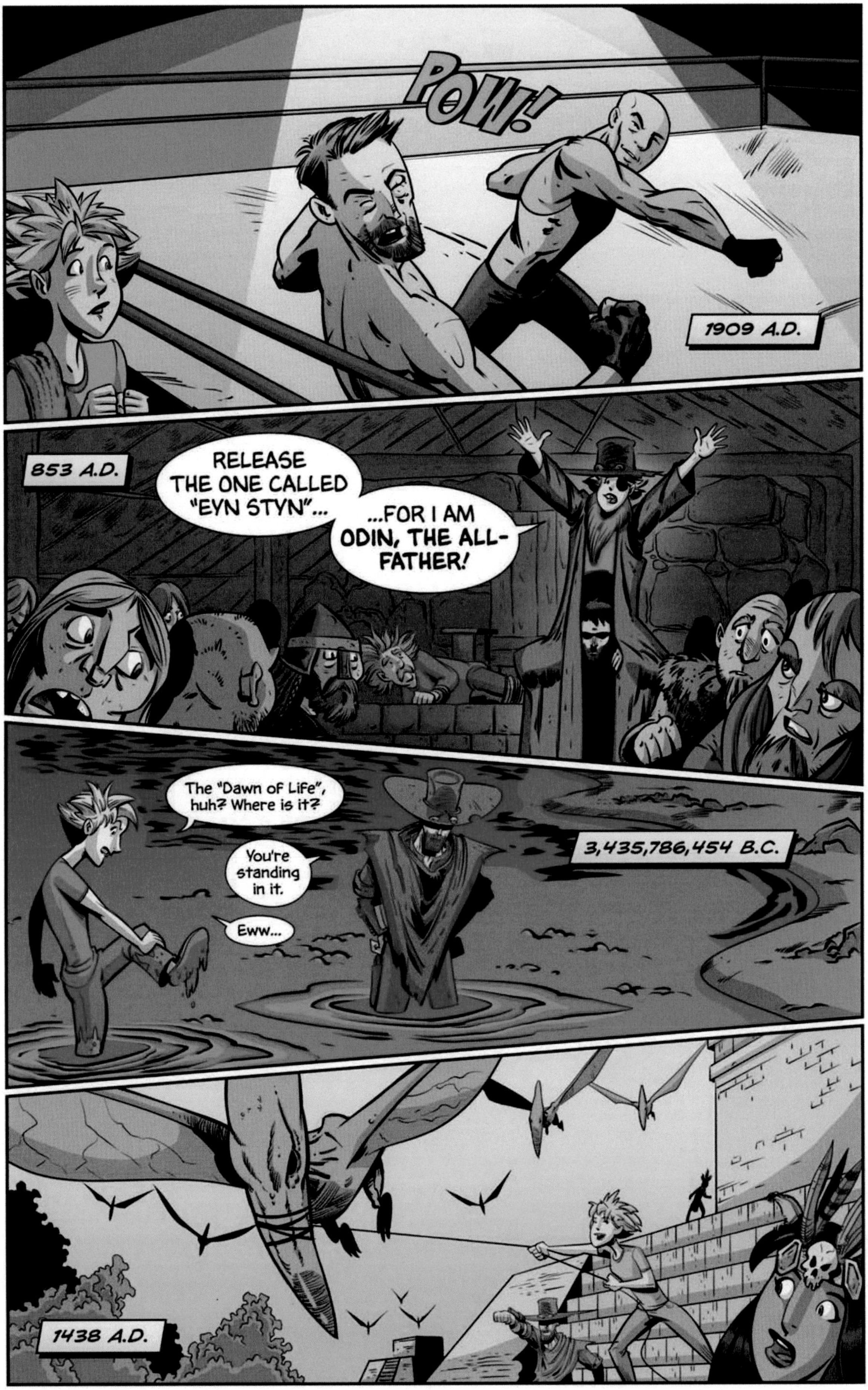
POW!
1909 A.D.
853 A.D.
RELEASE THE ONE CALLED "EYN STYN"...
...FOR I AM ODIN, THE ALL-FATHER!
The "Dawn of Life", huh? Where is it?
3,435,786,454 B.C.
You're standing in it.
Eww...
1438 A.D.

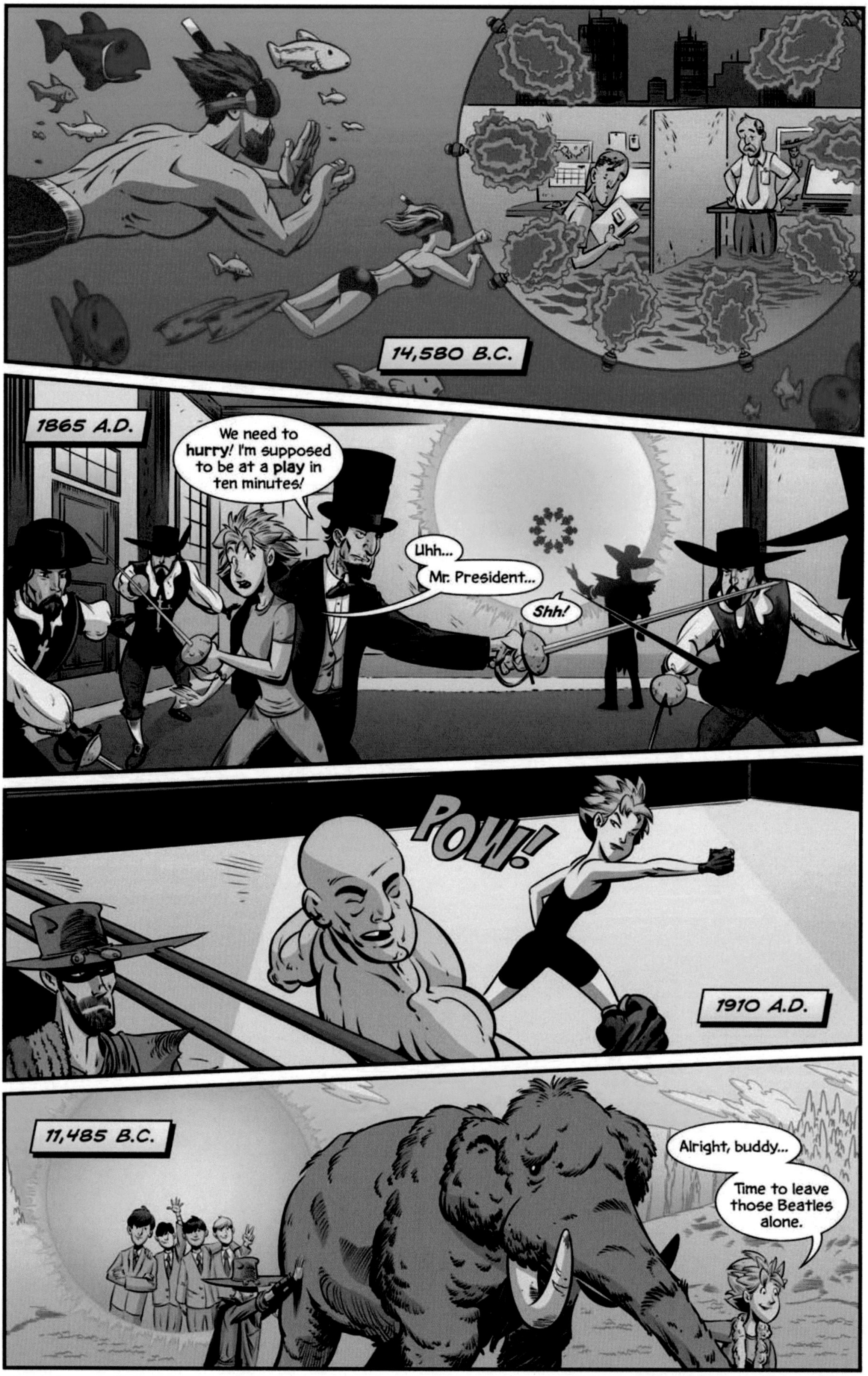
14,580 B.C.
1865 A.D.
We need to hurry! I'm supposed to be at a play in ten minutes!
Uhh...
Mr. President...
Shh!
POW!
1910 A.D.
11,485 B.C.
Alright, buddy...
Time to leave those Beatles alone.

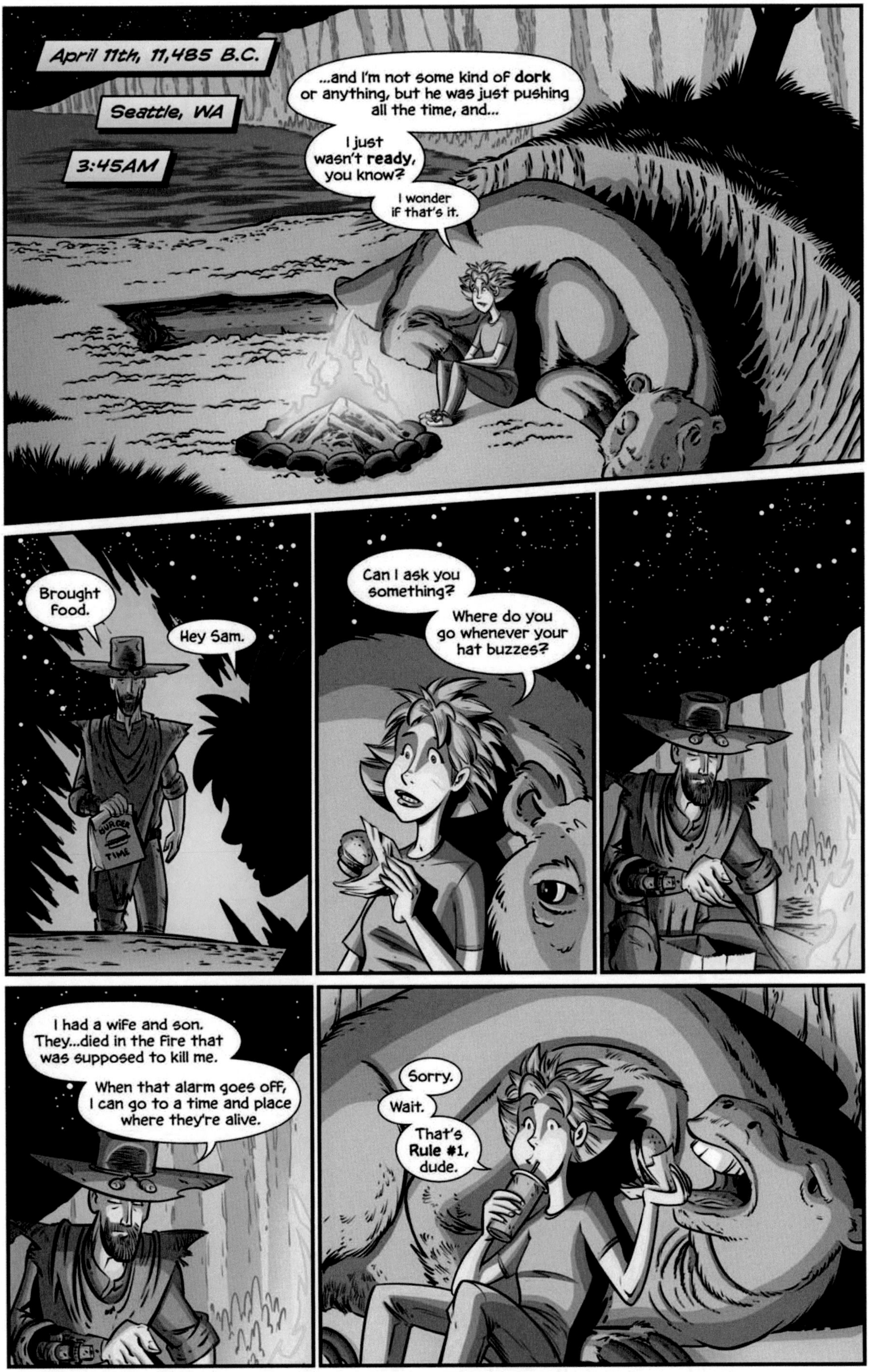
April 11th, 11,485 B.C.
Seattle, WA
3:45AM
...and I'm not some kind of **dork** or anything, but he was just pushing all the time, and...
I just wasn't **ready**, you know?
I wonder if that's it.
Brought food.
Hey Sam.
BURGER TIME
Can I ask you something?
Where do you go whenever your hat buzzes?
I had a wife and son. They...died in the fire that was supposed to kill me.
When that alarm goes off, I can go to a time and place where they're alive.
Sorry.
Wait.
That's **Rule #1**, dude.

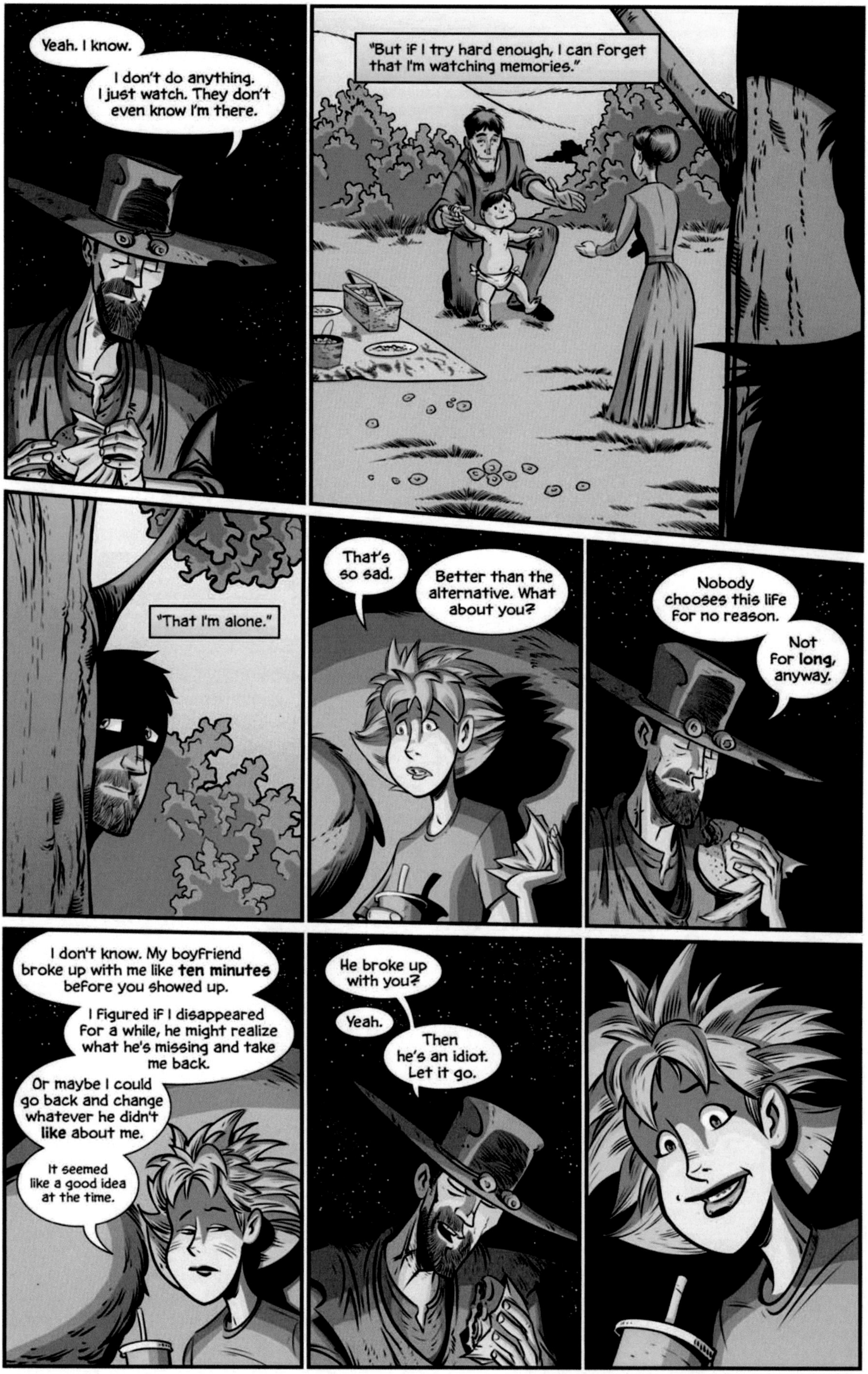
Yeah. I know.
I don't do anything. I just watch. They don't even know I'm there.
"But if I try hard enough, I can forget that I'm watching memories."
"That I'm alone."
That's so sad.
Better than the alternative. What about you?
Nobody chooses this life for no reason.
Not for **long**, anyway.
I don't know. My boyfriend broke up with me like **ten minutes** before you showed up.
I figured if I disappeared for a while, he might realize what he's missing and take me back.
Or maybe I could go back and change whatever he didn't **like** about me.
It seemed like a good idea at the time.
He broke up with you?
Yeah.
Then he's an idiot. Let it go.

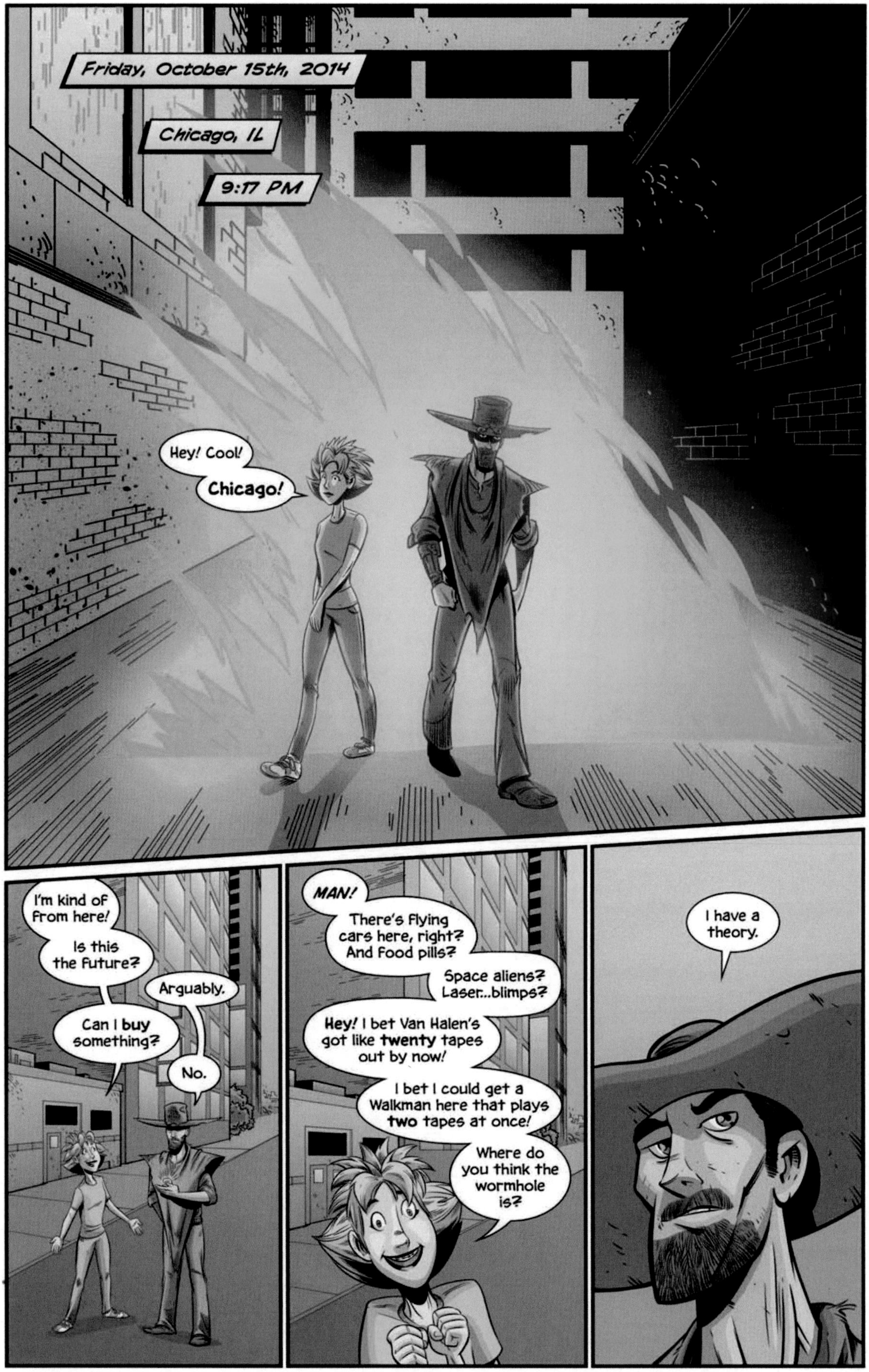
Friday, October 15th, 2014
Chicago, IL
9:17 PM
Hey! Cool!
Chicago!
I'm kind of from here!
Is this the future?
Arguably.
Can I buy something?
No.
MAN!
There's flying cars here, right? And food pills?
Space aliens? Laser...blimps?
Hey! I bet Van Halen's got like twenty tapes out by now!
I bet I could get a Walkman here that plays two tapes at once!
Where do you think the wormhole is?
I have a theory.

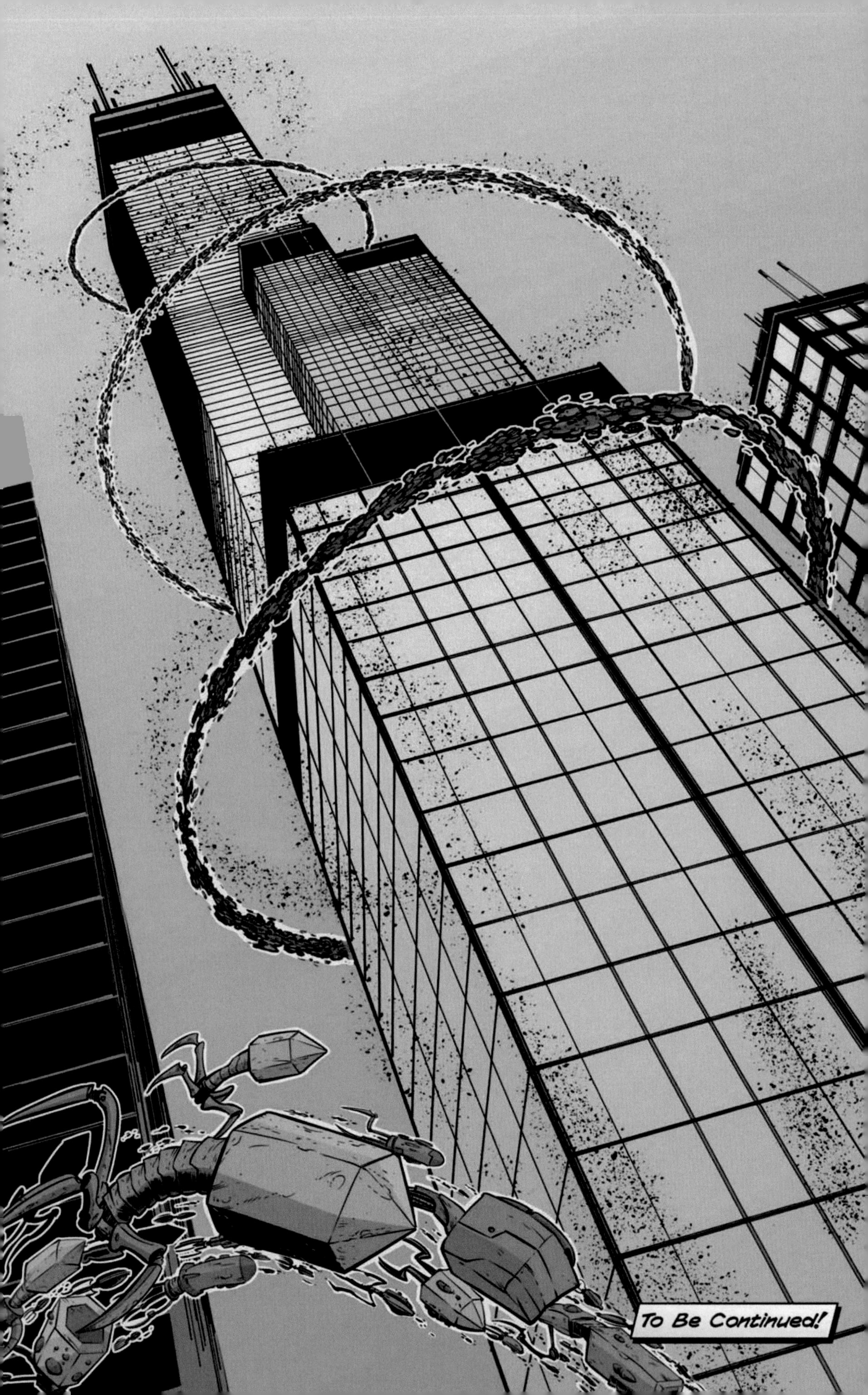
To Be Continued!

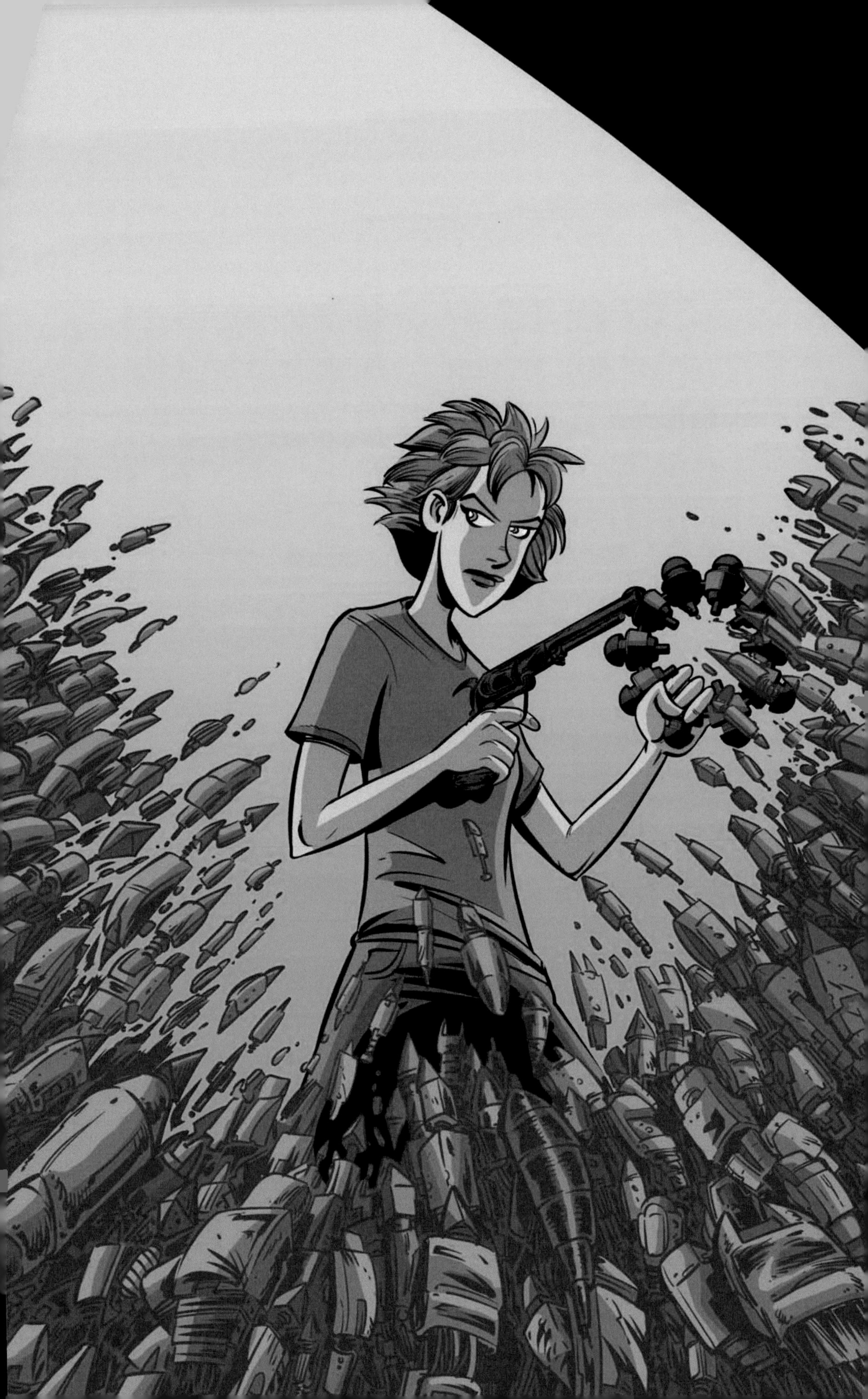

ISSUE THREE

"THE BIONIC PLAGUE"

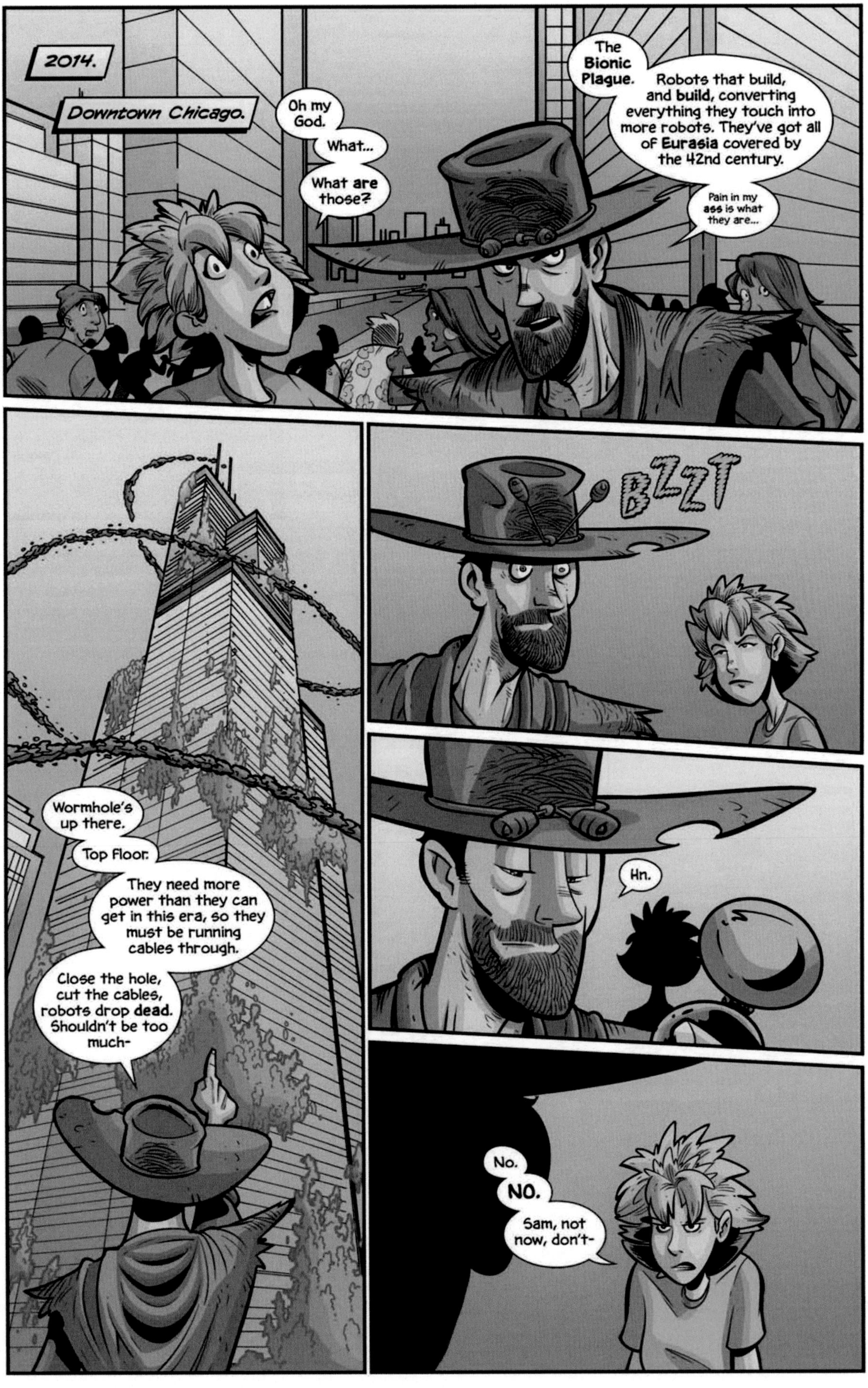
2014.
Downtown Chicago.
Oh my God.
What...
What are those?
The Bionic Plague.
Robots that build, and build, converting everything they touch into more robots. They've got all of Eurasia covered by the 42nd century.
Pain in my ass is what they are...
Wormhole's up there.
Top Floor.
They need more power than they can get in this era, so they must be running cables through.
Close the hole, cut the cables, robots drop dead. Shouldn't be too much-
BZZT
Hn.
No.
NO.
Sam, not now, don't-

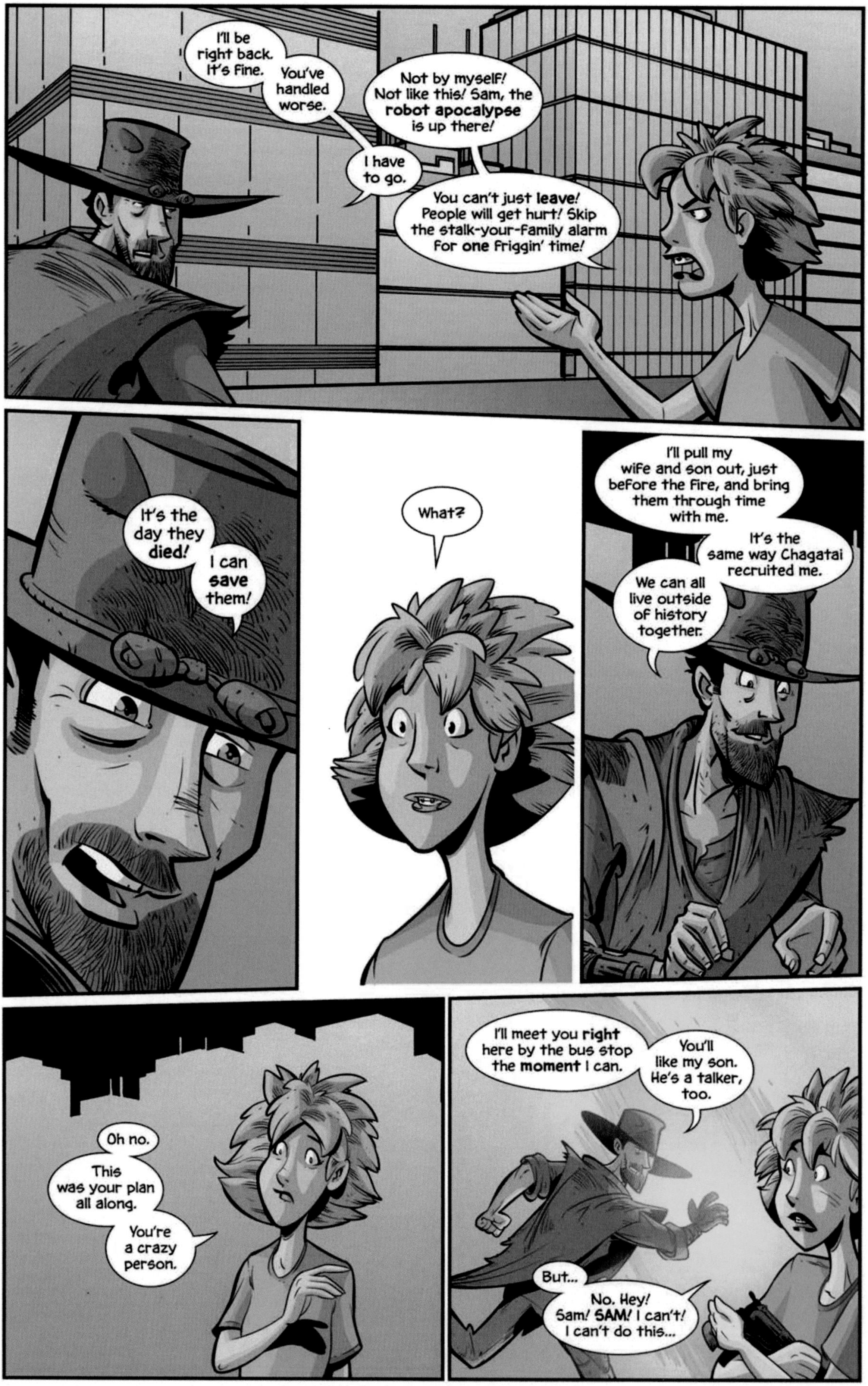
I'll be right back. It's fine.
You've handled worse.
Not by myself! Not like this! Sam, the **robot apocalypse** is up there!
I have to go.
You can't just **leave**! People will get hurt! Skip the stalk-your-family alarm for **one** friggin' time!
It's the day they **died**!
I can **save** them!
What?
I'll pull my wife and son out, just before the fire, and bring them through time with me.
It's the same way Chagatai recruited me.
We can all live outside of history together.
Oh no.
This was your plan all along.
You're a crazy person.
I'll meet you **right** here by the bus stop the **moment** I can.
You'll like my son. He's a talker, too.
But...
No. Hey! Sam! **SAM!** I can't! I can't do this...

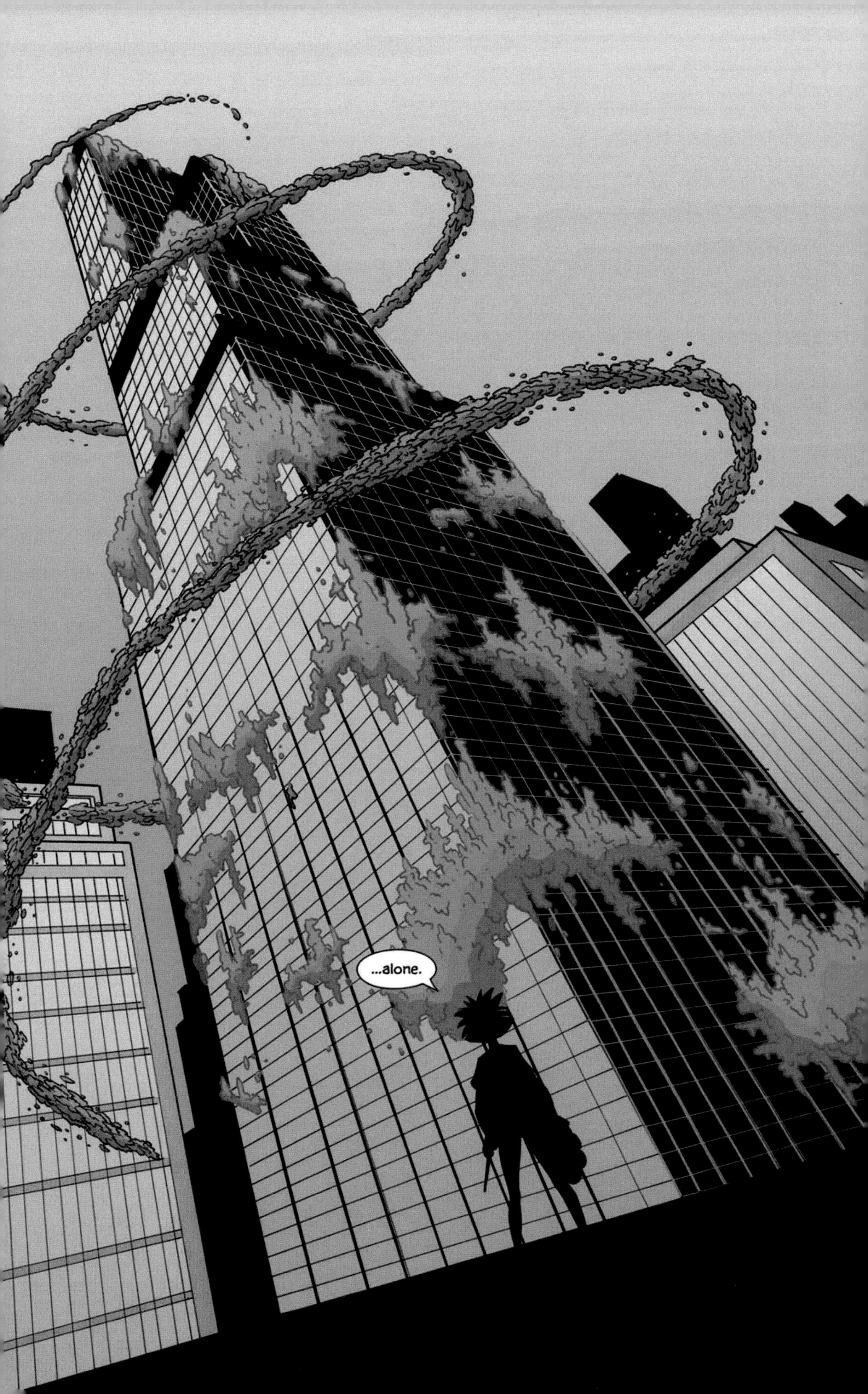
...alone.

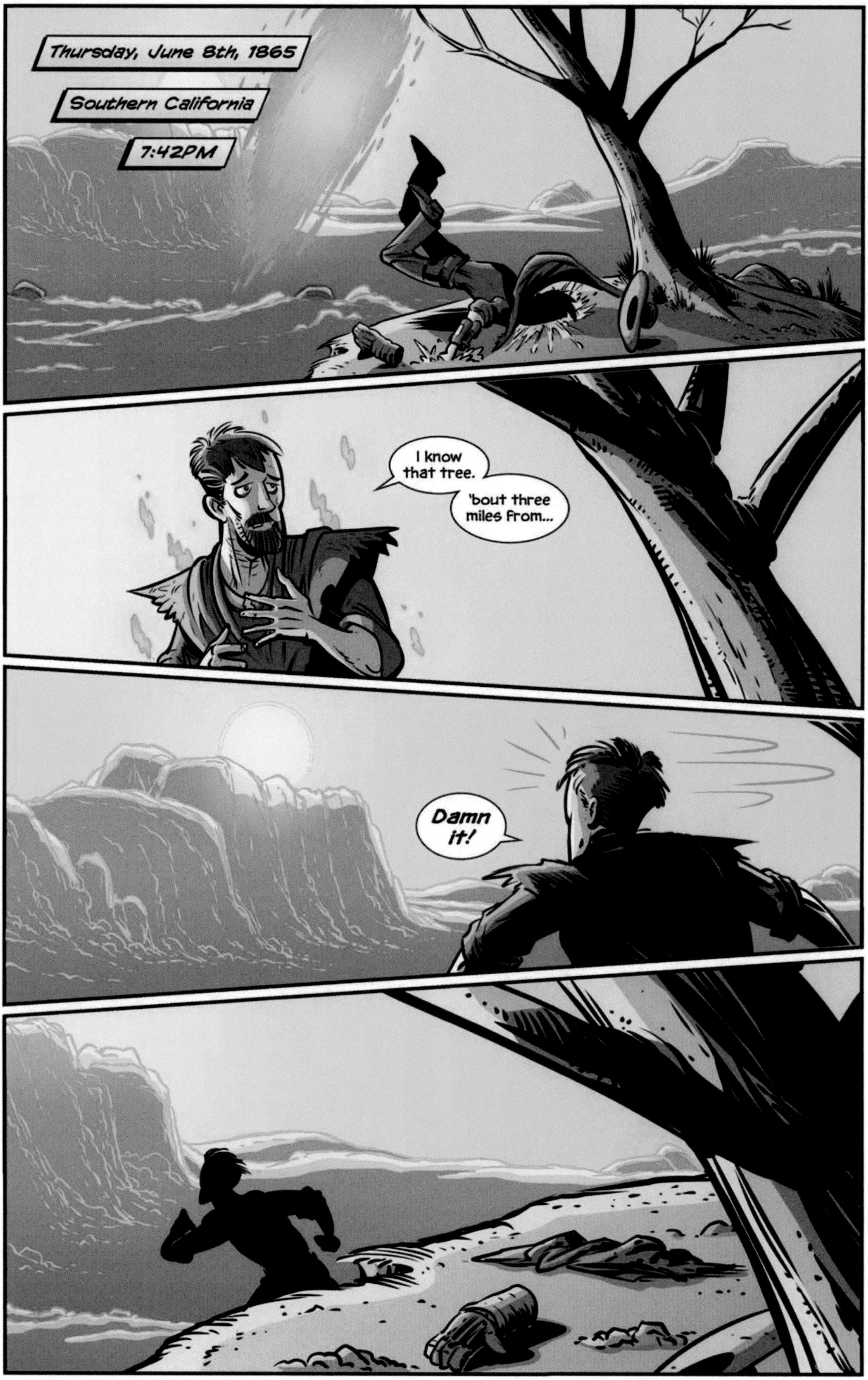
Thursday, June 8th, 1865
Southern California
7:42PM
I know that tree.
'bout three miles from...
Damn it!

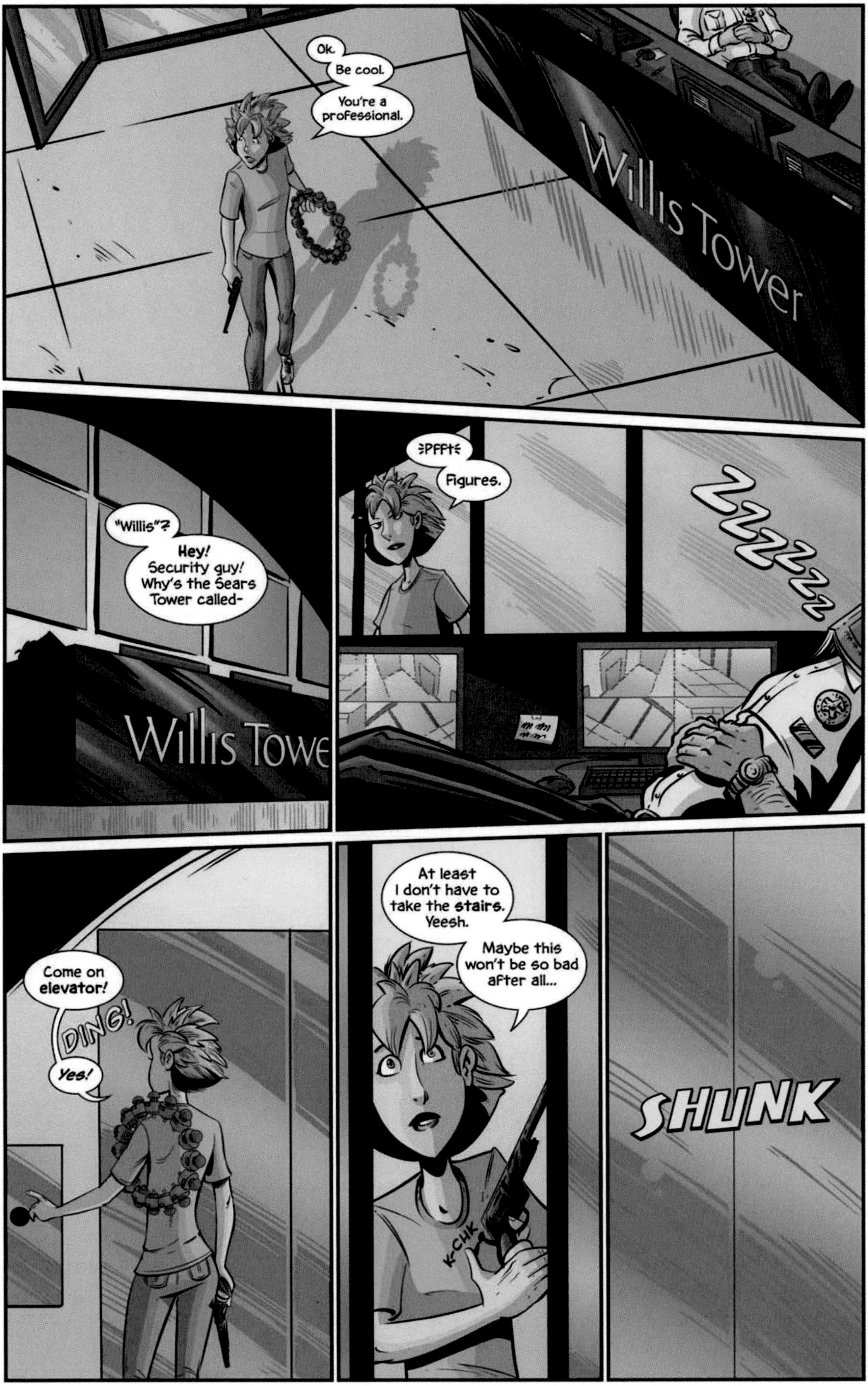
Ok.
Be cool.
You're a professional.
Willis Tower
"Willis"?
Hey! Security guy! Why's the Sears Tower called-
Willis Towe
Pfft
Figures.
ZZZZZZ
Come on elevator!
DING!
Yes!
At least I don't have to take the stairs. Yeesh.
Maybe this won't be so bad after all...
CHK
SHUNK

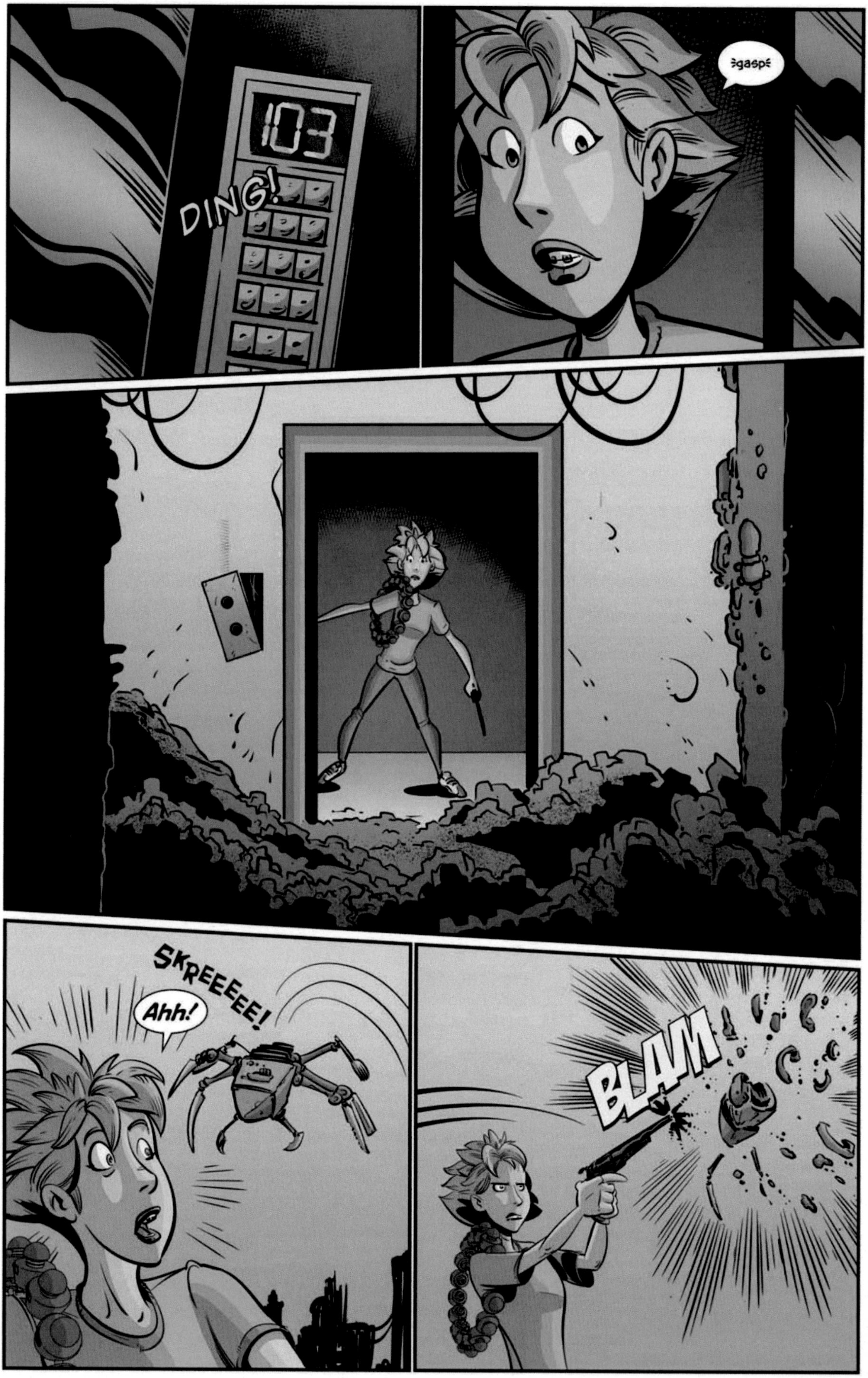

103
DING!
gasp
SKREEEEEE!
Ahh!
BLAM

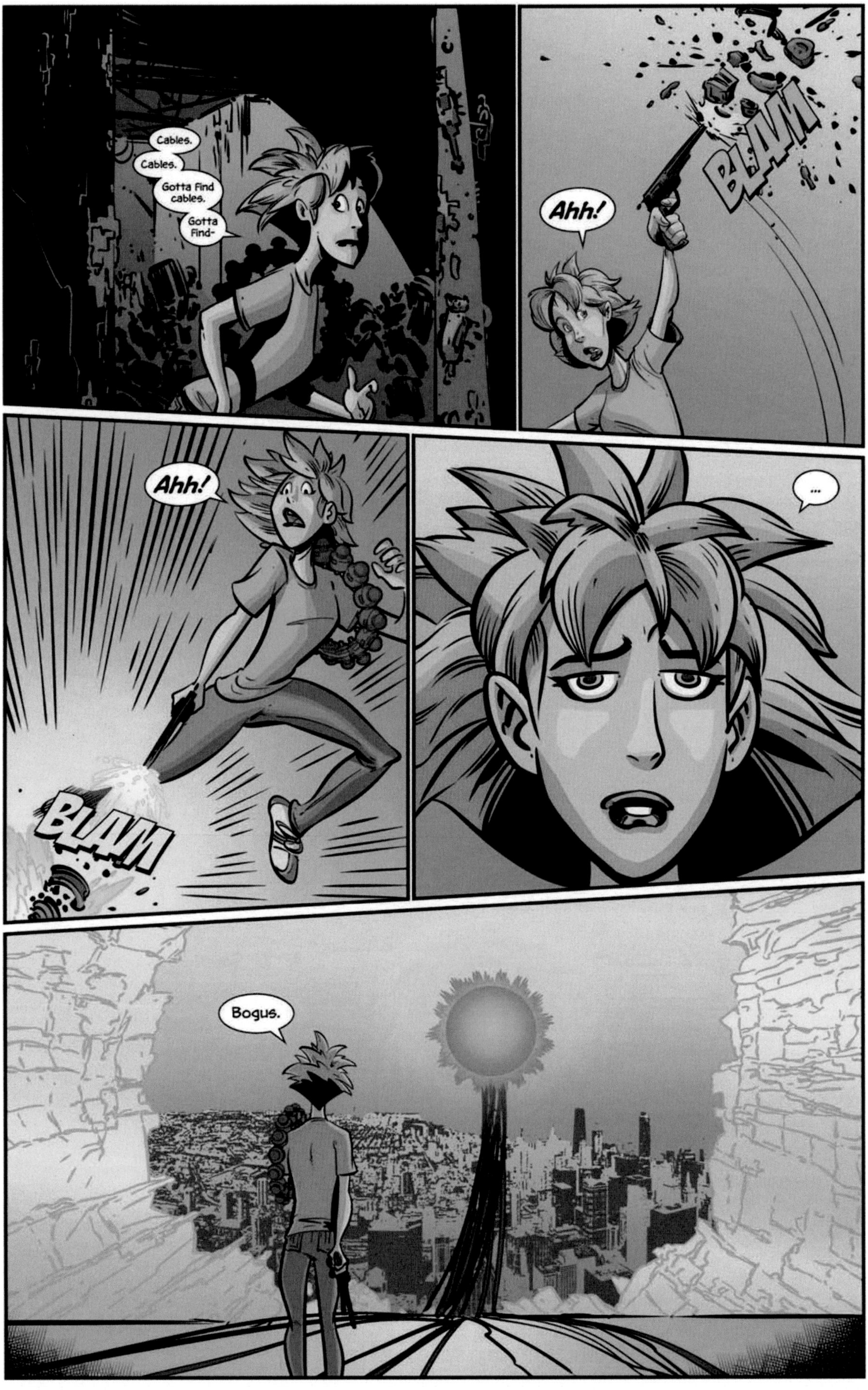
Cables.
Cables.
Gotta find cables.
Gotta find-
Ahh!
BLAM
Ahh!
BLAM
...
Bogus.

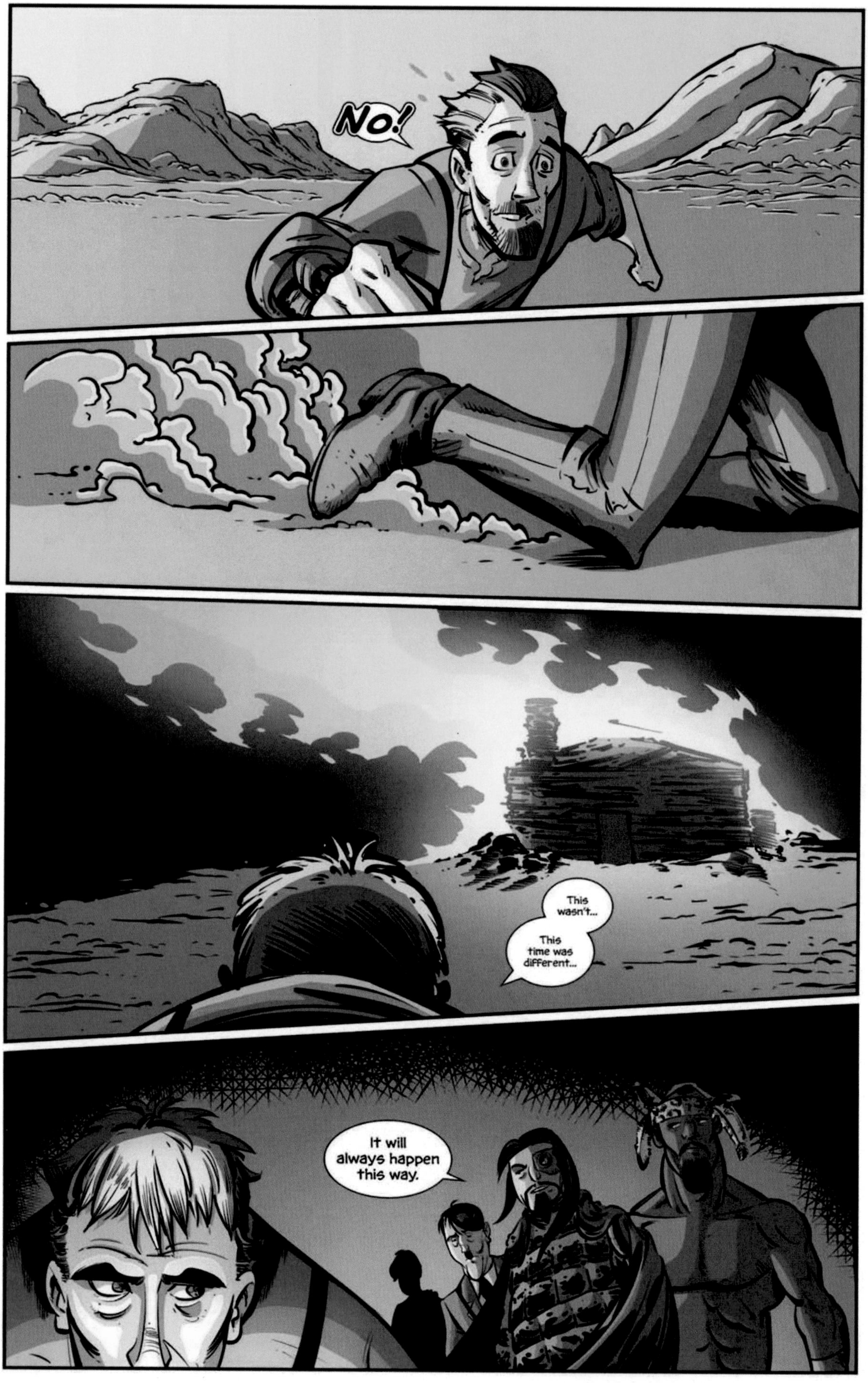
NO!
This wasn't...
This time was different...
It will always happen this way.

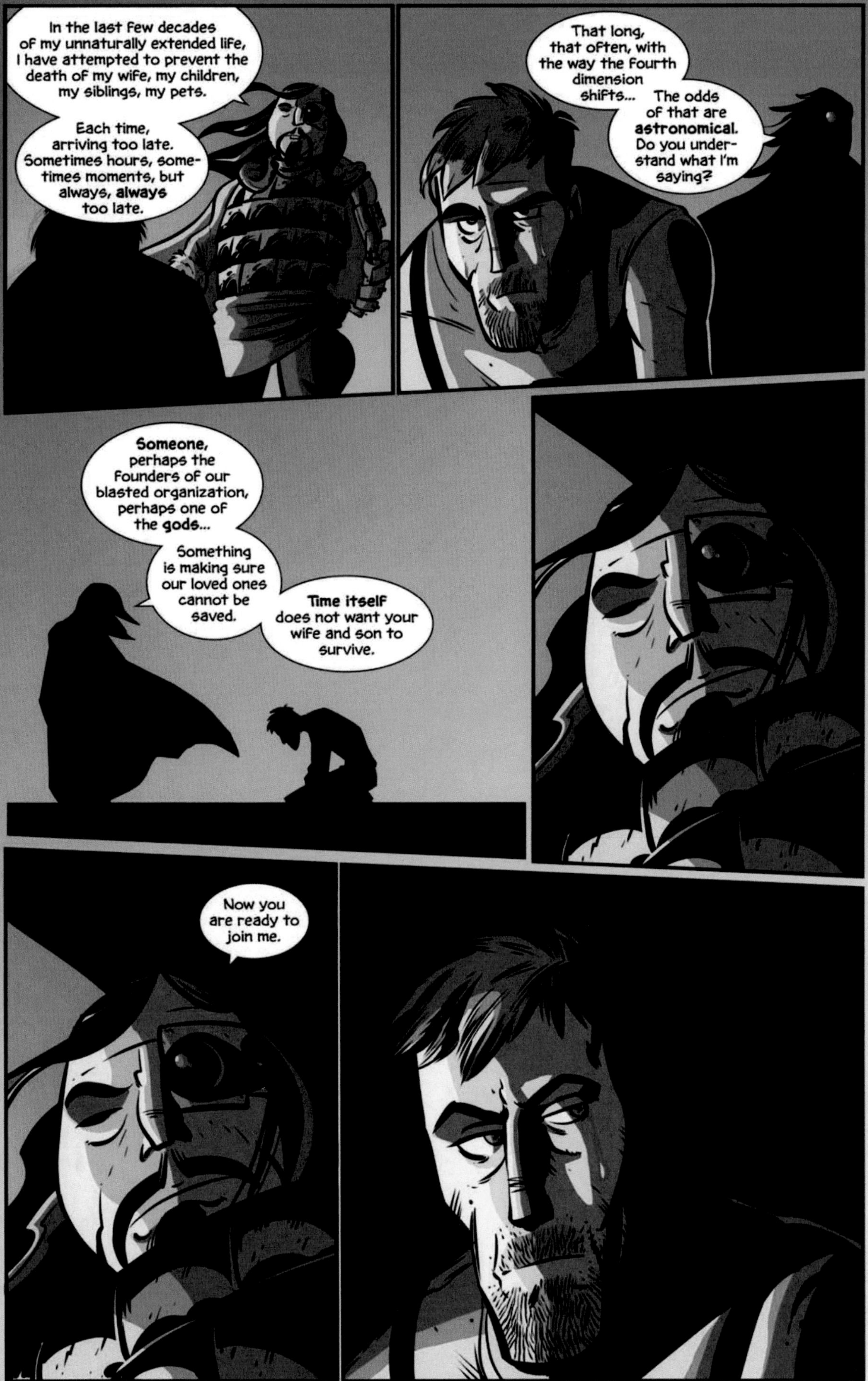
In the last few decades of my unnaturally extended life, I have attempted to prevent the death of my wife, my children, my siblings, my pets.
Each time, arriving too late. Sometimes hours, sometimes moments, but always, always too late.
That long, that often, with the way the fourth dimension shifts...
The odds of that are astronomical. Do you understand what I'm saying?
Someone, perhaps the founders of our blasted organization, perhaps one of the gods...
Something is making sure our loved ones cannot be saved.
Time itself does not want your wife and son to survive.
Now you are ready to join me.

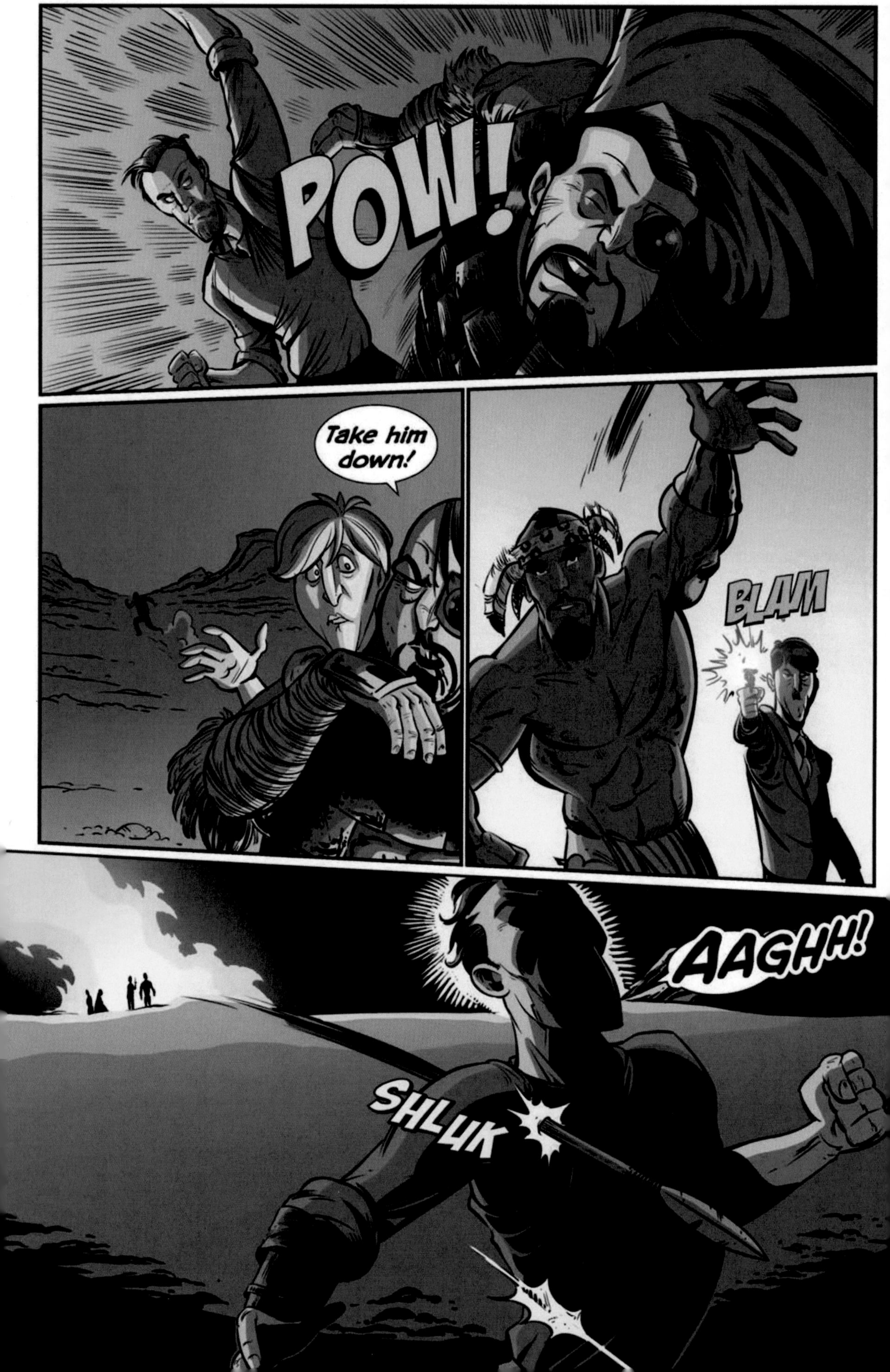
POW!
Take him down!
BLAM
AAGHH!
SHLUK

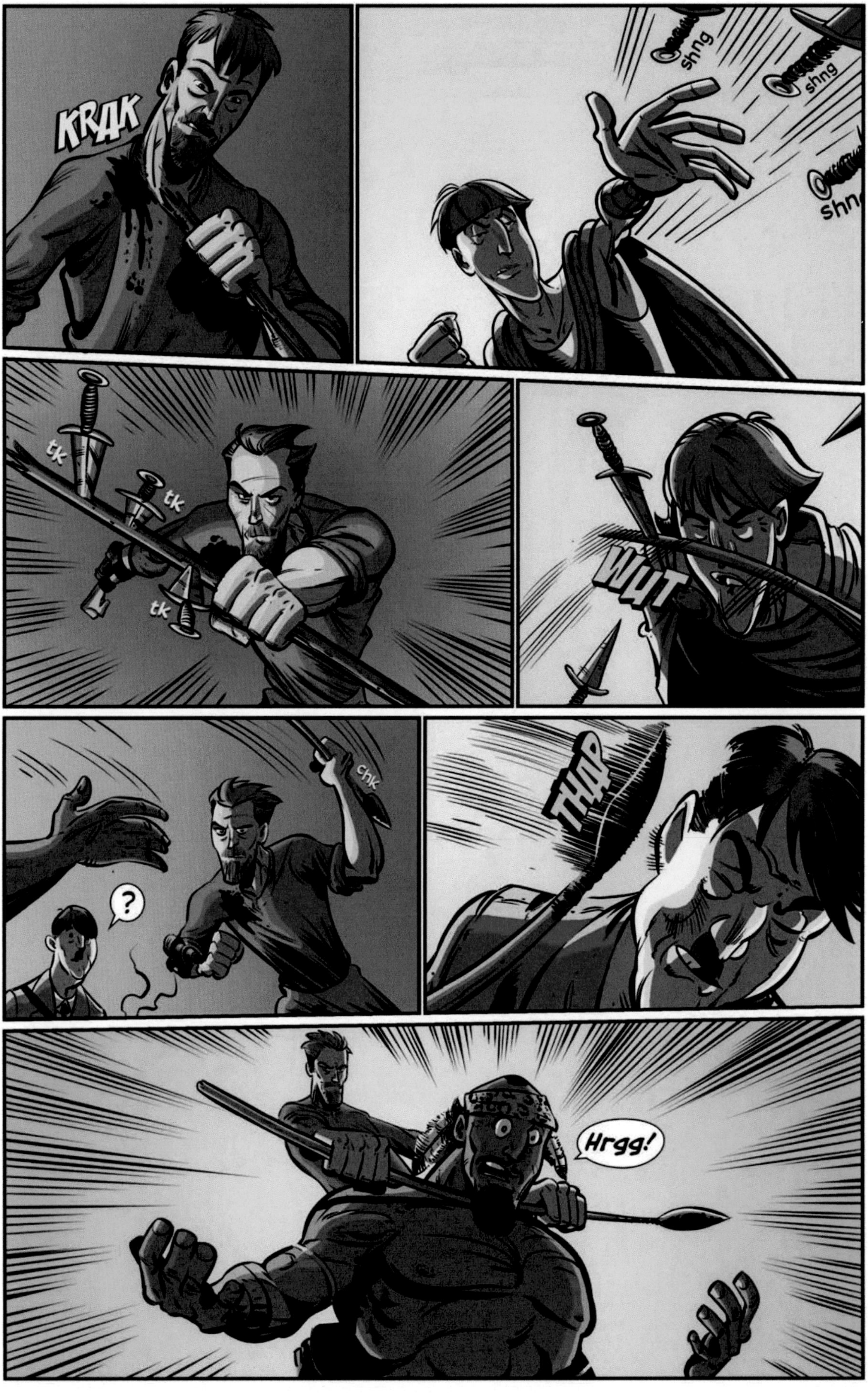
KRAK
shng
shng
shng
tk
tk
tk
WUT
chk
?
THAP
Hrgg!

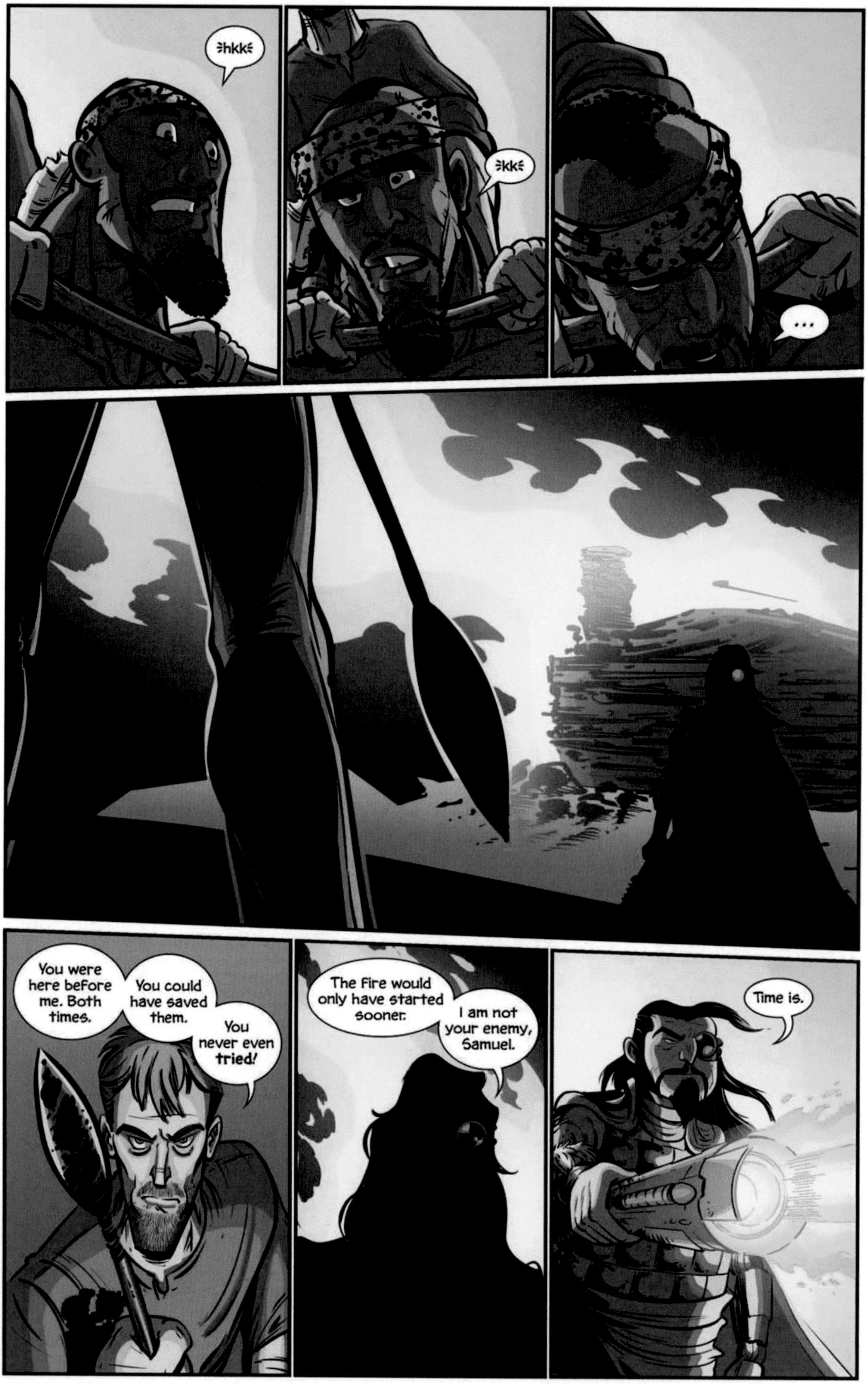
hkk
kk
...
You were here before me. Both times.
You could have saved them.
You never even **tried!**
The fire would only have started sooner.
I am not your enemy, Samuel.
Time is.

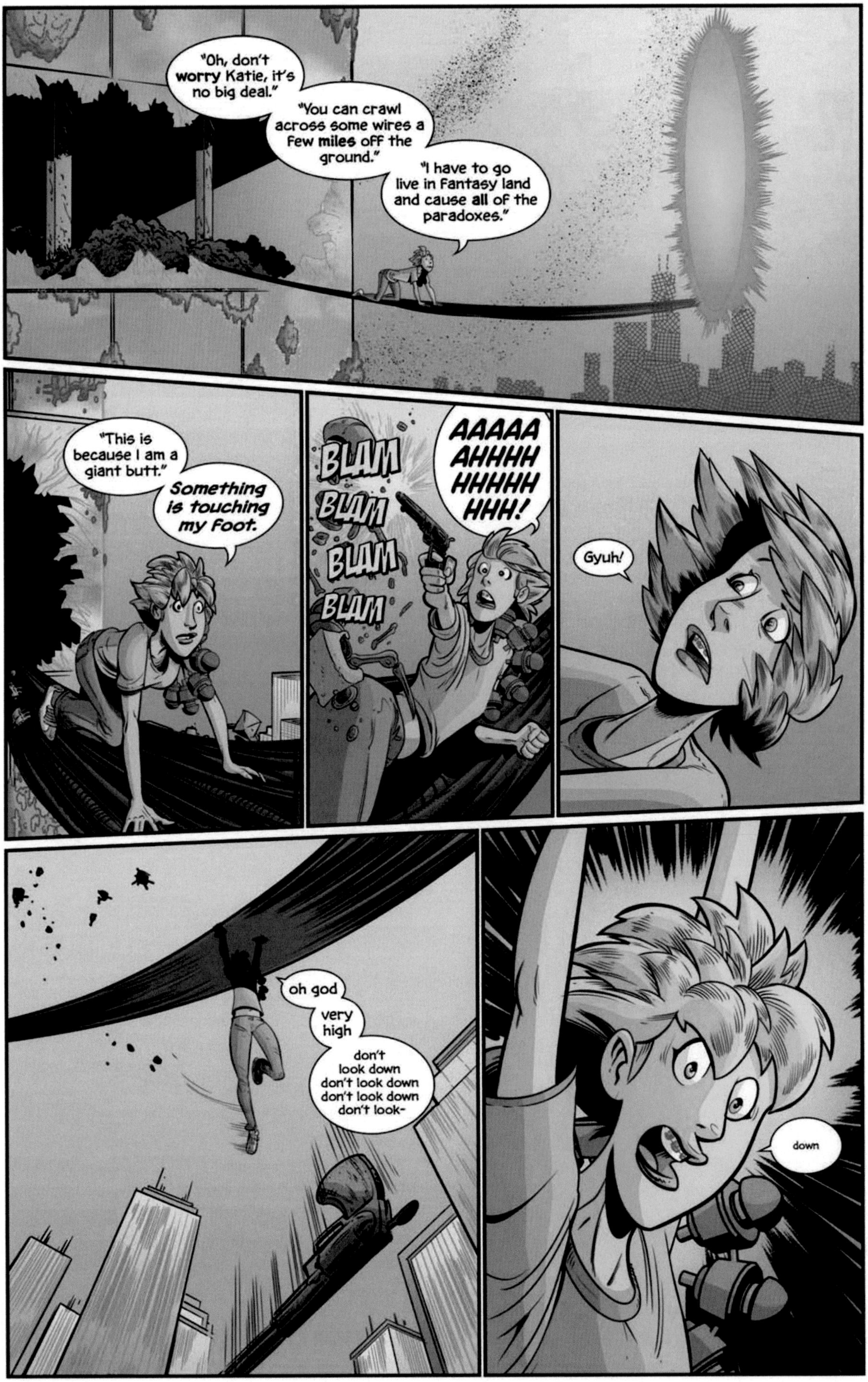
"Oh, don't worry Katie, it's no big deal."
"You can crawl across some wires a few miles off the ground."
"I have to go live in Fantasy land and cause all of the paradoxes."
"This is because I am a giant butt."
Something is touching my foot.
BLAM
BLAM
BLAM
BLAM
AAAAAAHHHHHHHHHHHHH!
Gyuh!
oh god
very high
don't look down
don't look down
don't look down
don't look-
down

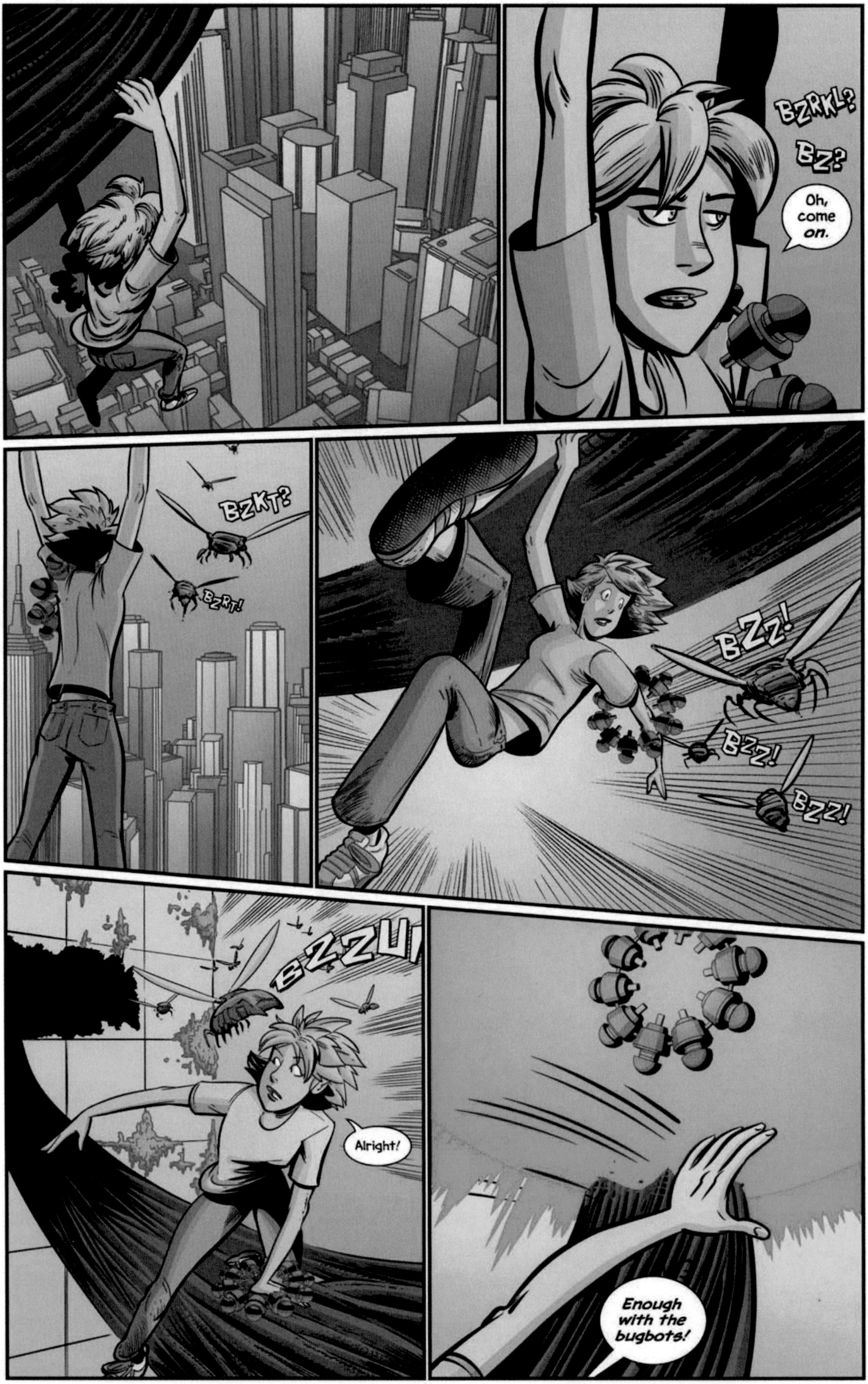
BZRKL?
BZ?
Oh, come on.
BZKT?
BZRT!
BZZ!
BZZ!
BZZ!
BZZU
Alright!
Enough with the bugbots!

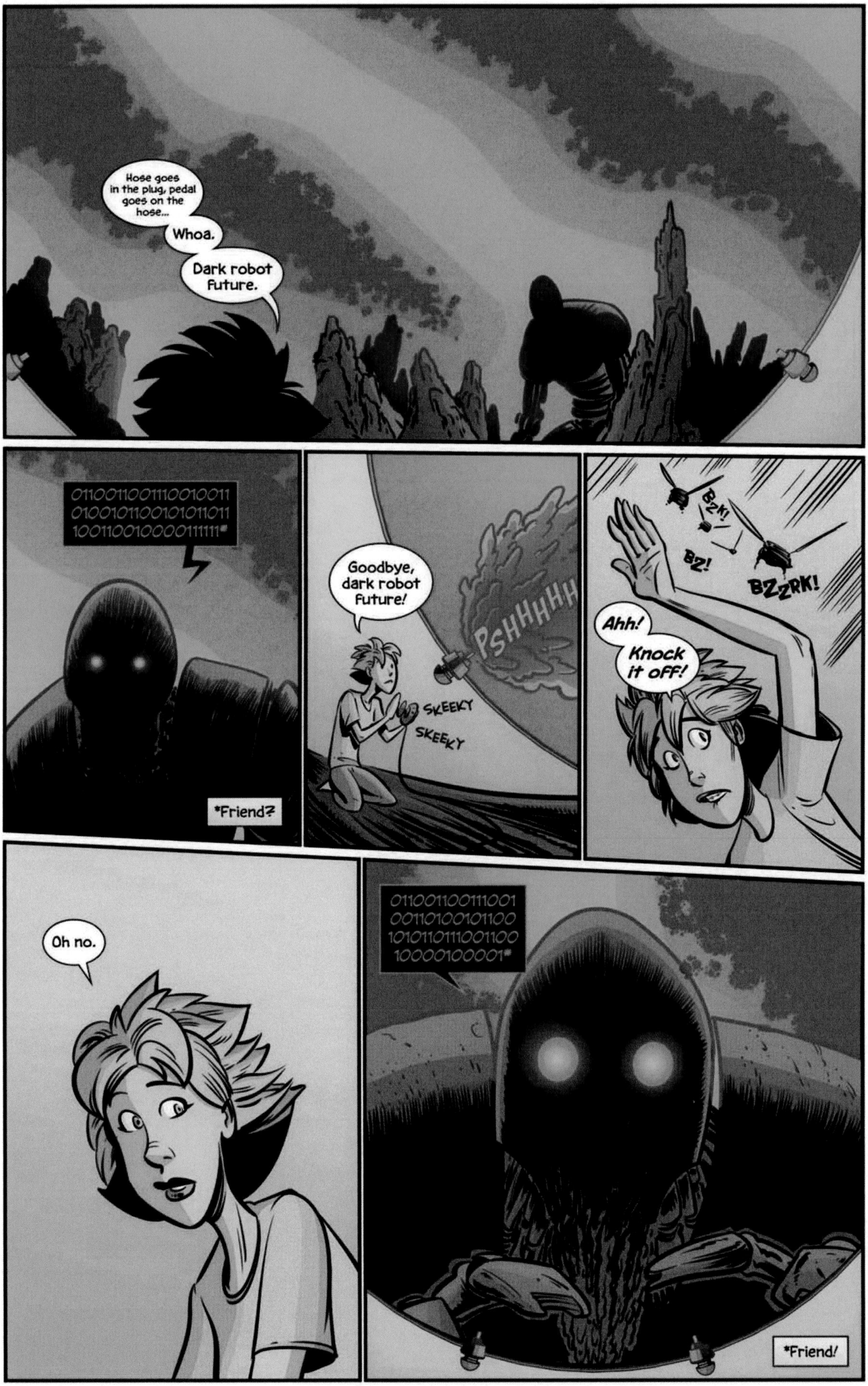
Hose goes in the plug, pedal goes on the hose...
Whoa.
Dark robot future.
01001100111001001101001011001010110111001100100001111111*
*Friend?
Goodbye, dark robot future!
PSHHHHH
SKEEKY
SKEEKY
BZK!
BZ!
BZZRK!
Ahh!
Knock it off!
Oh no.
0110011001110010011010010110010101101110011001000010000100001*
*Friend!

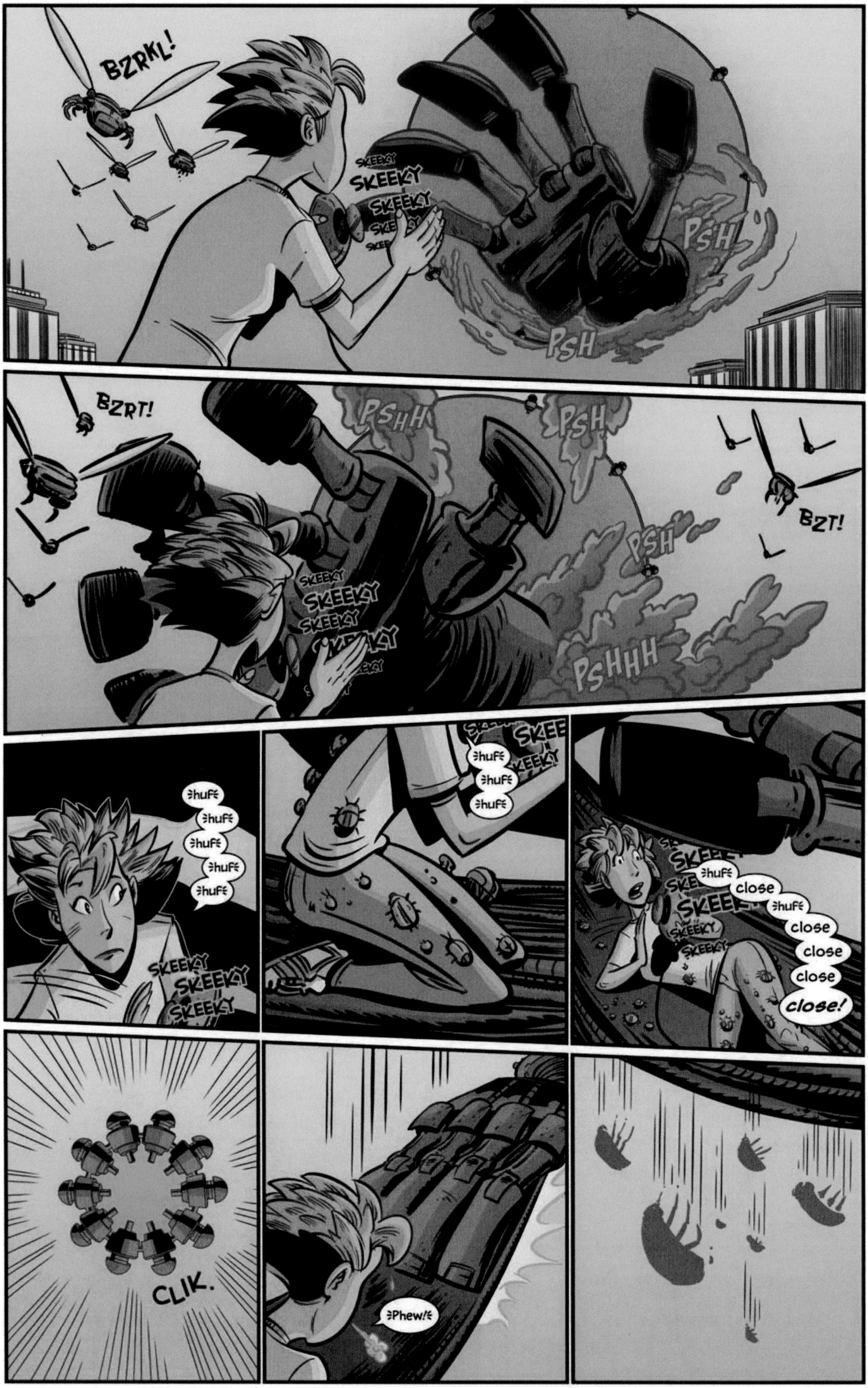
BZRKL!
SKEEKY
SKEEKY
SKEEKY
PSH
PSH
BZRT!
PSHH
PSH
BZT!
PSH
SKEEKY
SKEEKY
SKEEKY
PSHHH
huf
huf
huf
huf
huf
SKEEKY
SKEEKY
SKEEKY
huf
huf
huf
huf
close
huf
close
close
close
close!
CLIK.
Phew!

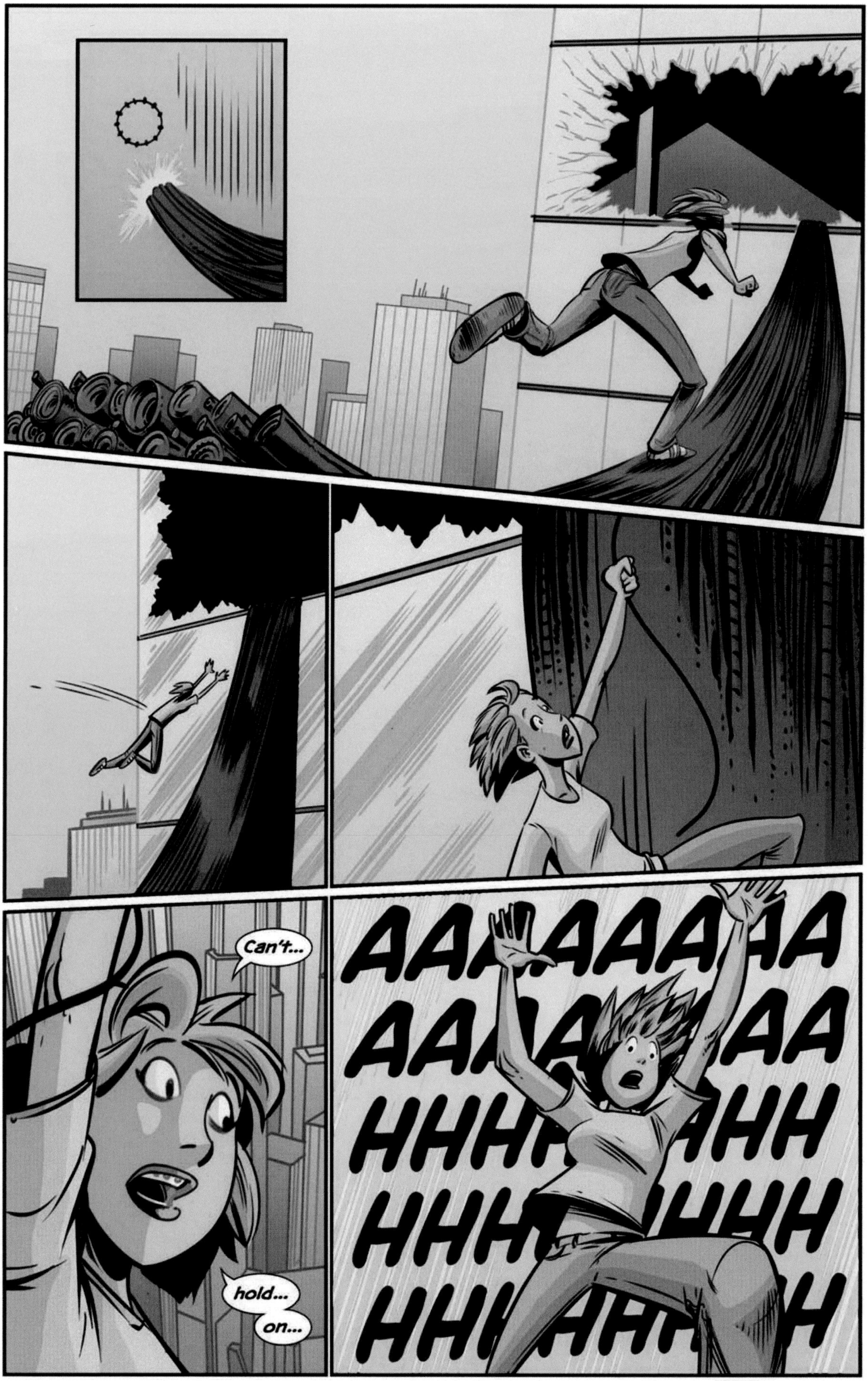
Can't...
hold...
on...
AAAAAAAAA
AAAAAAAAA
HHHHHHHHH
HHHHHHHHH
HHHHHHHHH

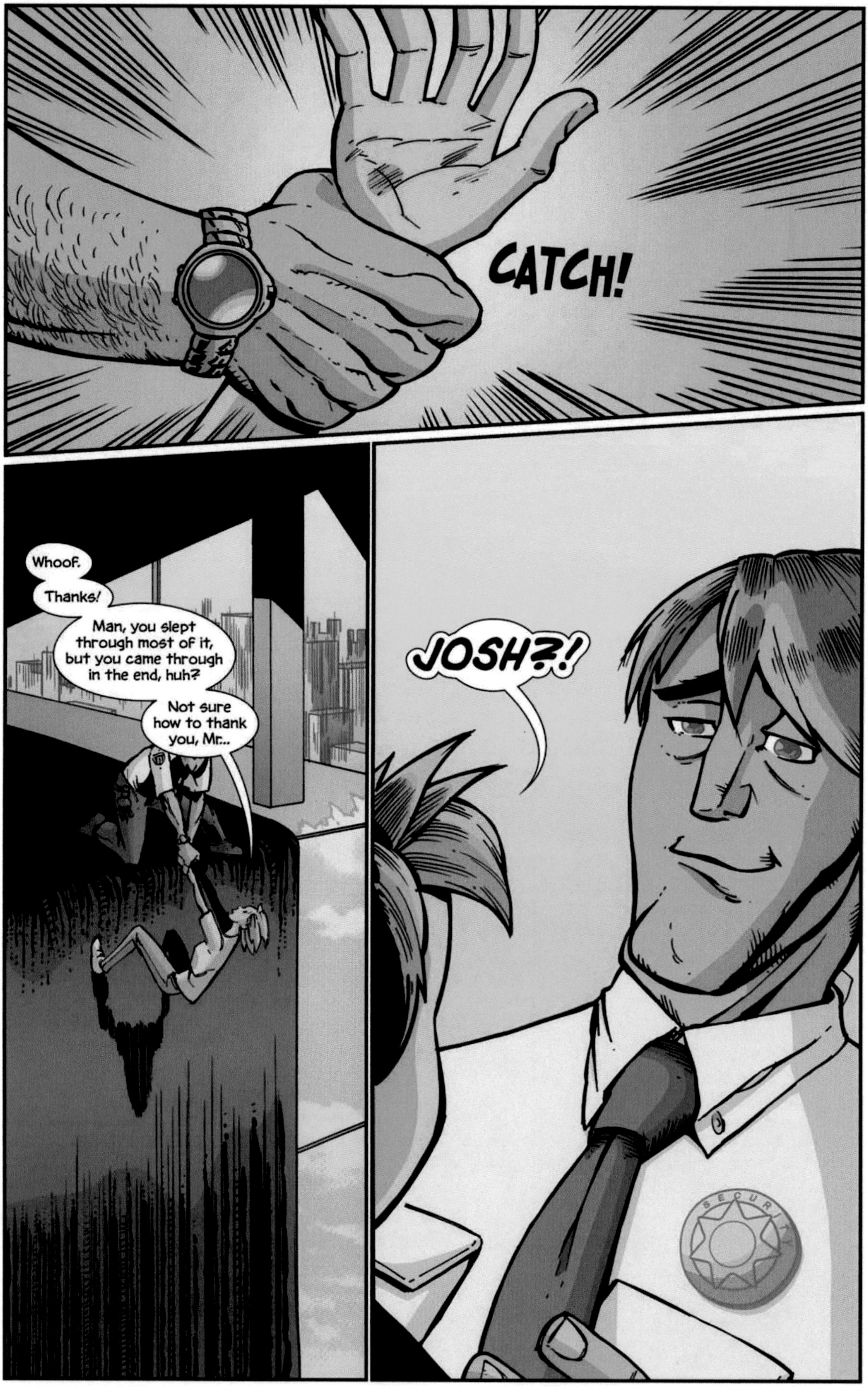
CATCH!
Whoof.
Thanks!
Man, you slept through most of it, but you came through in the end, huh?
Not sure how to thank you, Mr...
JOSH?!

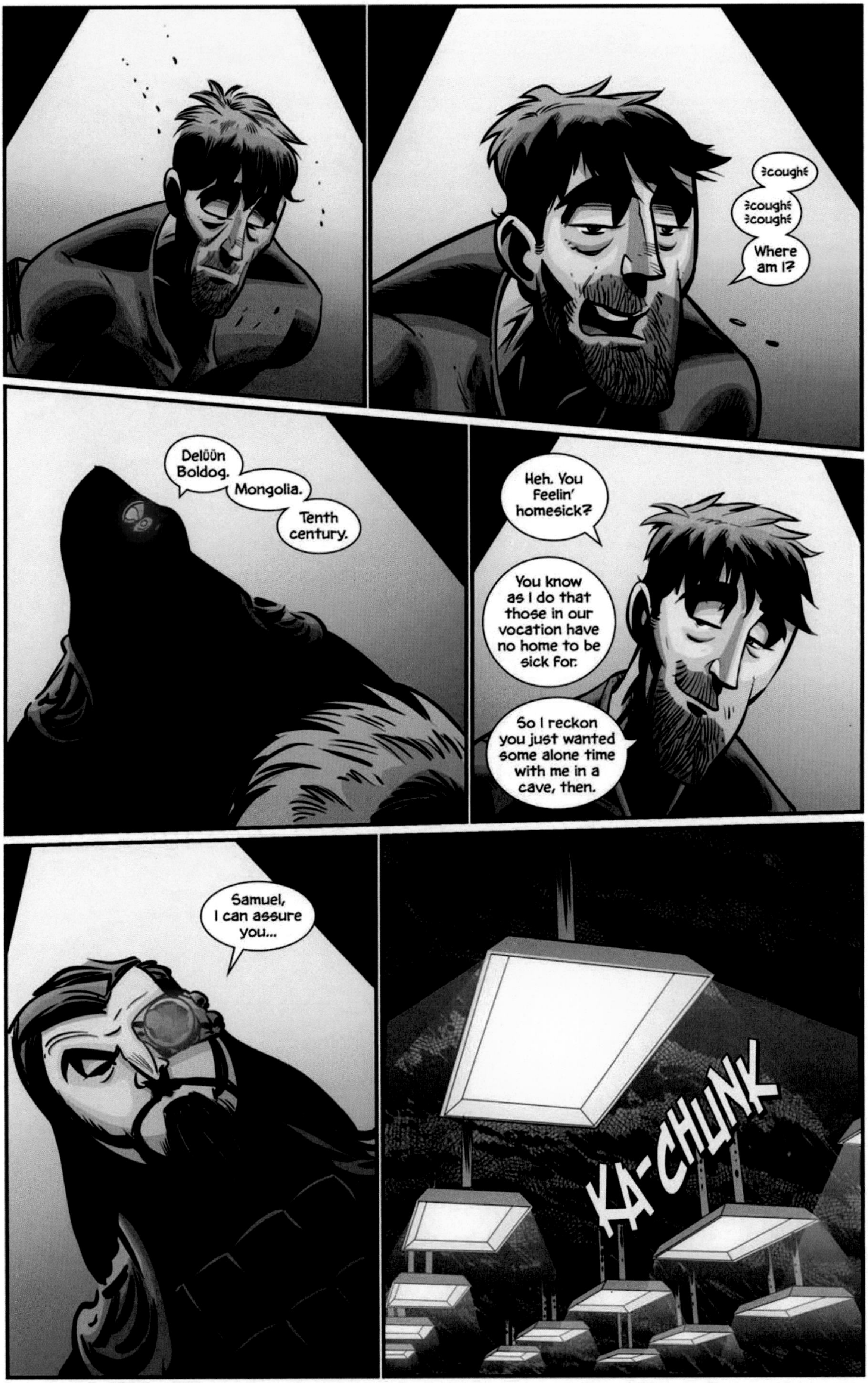

cough
cough
cough
Where am I?
Delüün Boldog.
Mongolia.
Tenth century.
Heh. You Feelin' homesick?
You know as I do that those in our vocation have no home to be sick for.
So I reckon you just wanted some alone time with me in a cave, then.
Samuel, I can assure you...
KA-CHUNK

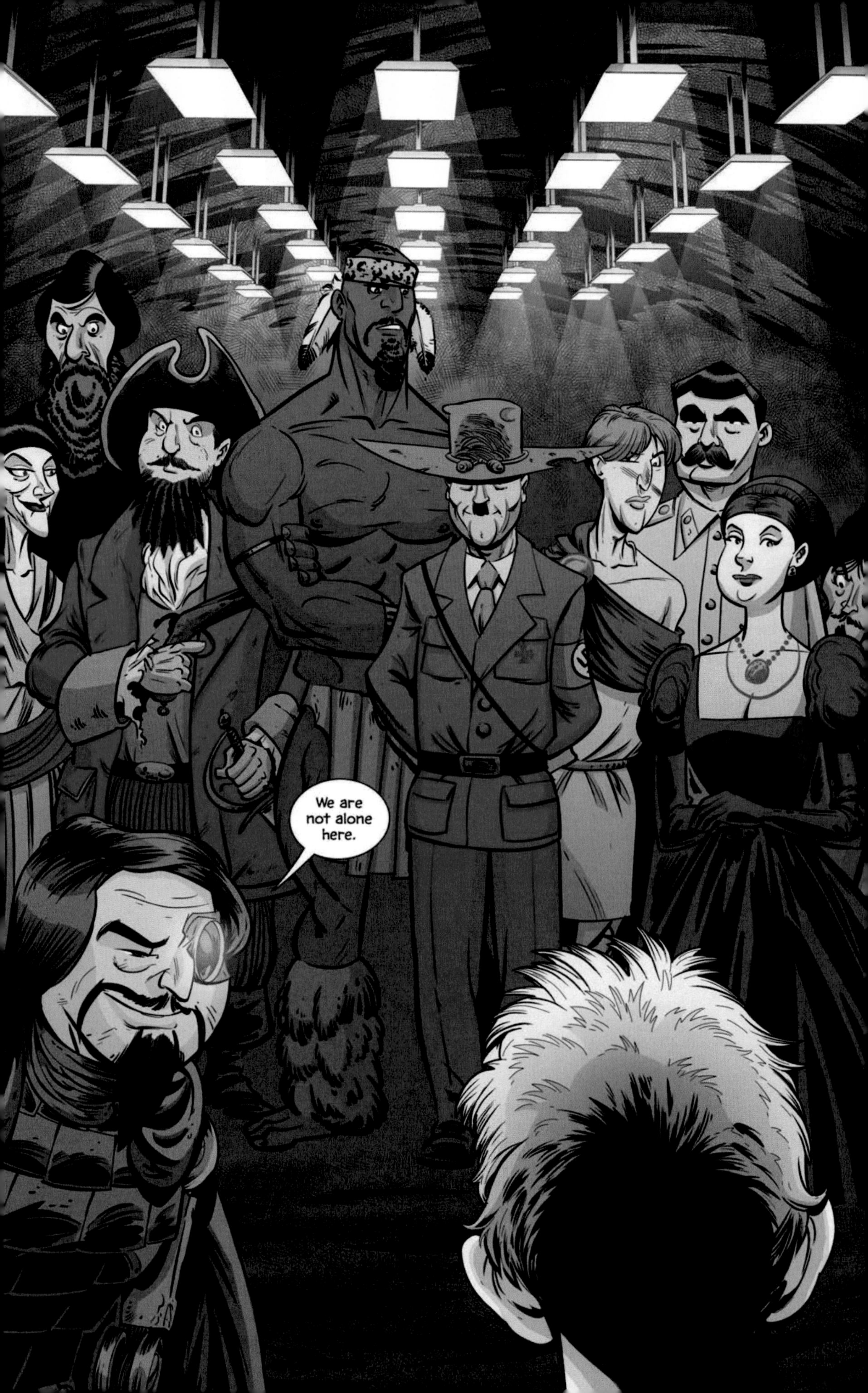
We are not alone here.

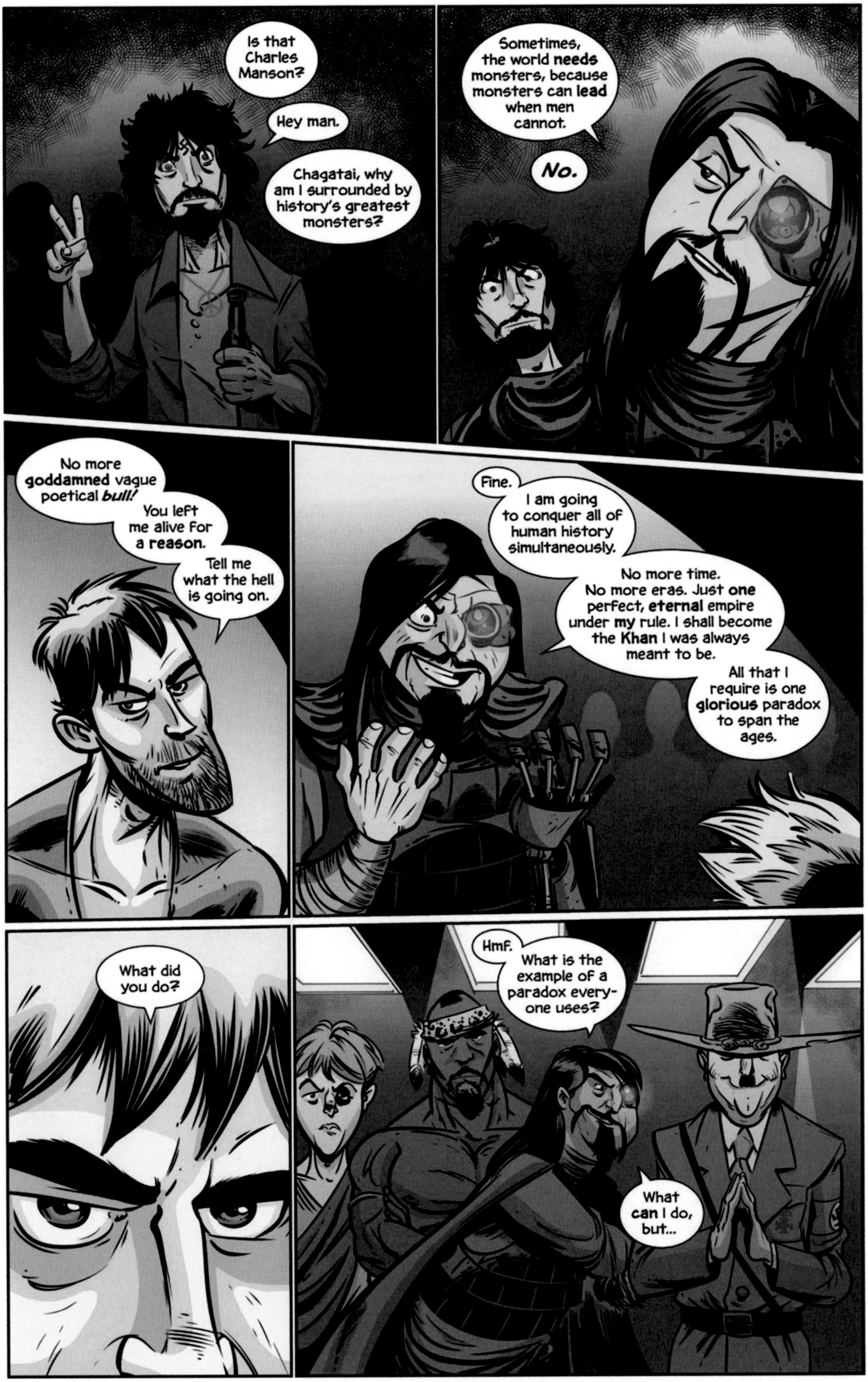
Is that Charles Manson?
Hey man.
Chagatai, why am I surrounded by history's greatest monsters?
Sometimes, the world **needs** monsters, because monsters can **lead** when men cannot.
No.
No more **goddamned** vague poetical ***bull!***
You left me alive for a **reason.**
Tell me what the hell is going on.
Fine.
I am going to conquer all of human history simultaneously.
No more time. No more eras. Just **one** perfect, **eternal** empire under **my** rule. I shall become the **Khan** I was always meant to be.
All that I require is one **glorious** paradox to span the ages.
What did you do?
Hmf.
What is the example of a paradox every-one uses?
What **can** I do, but...

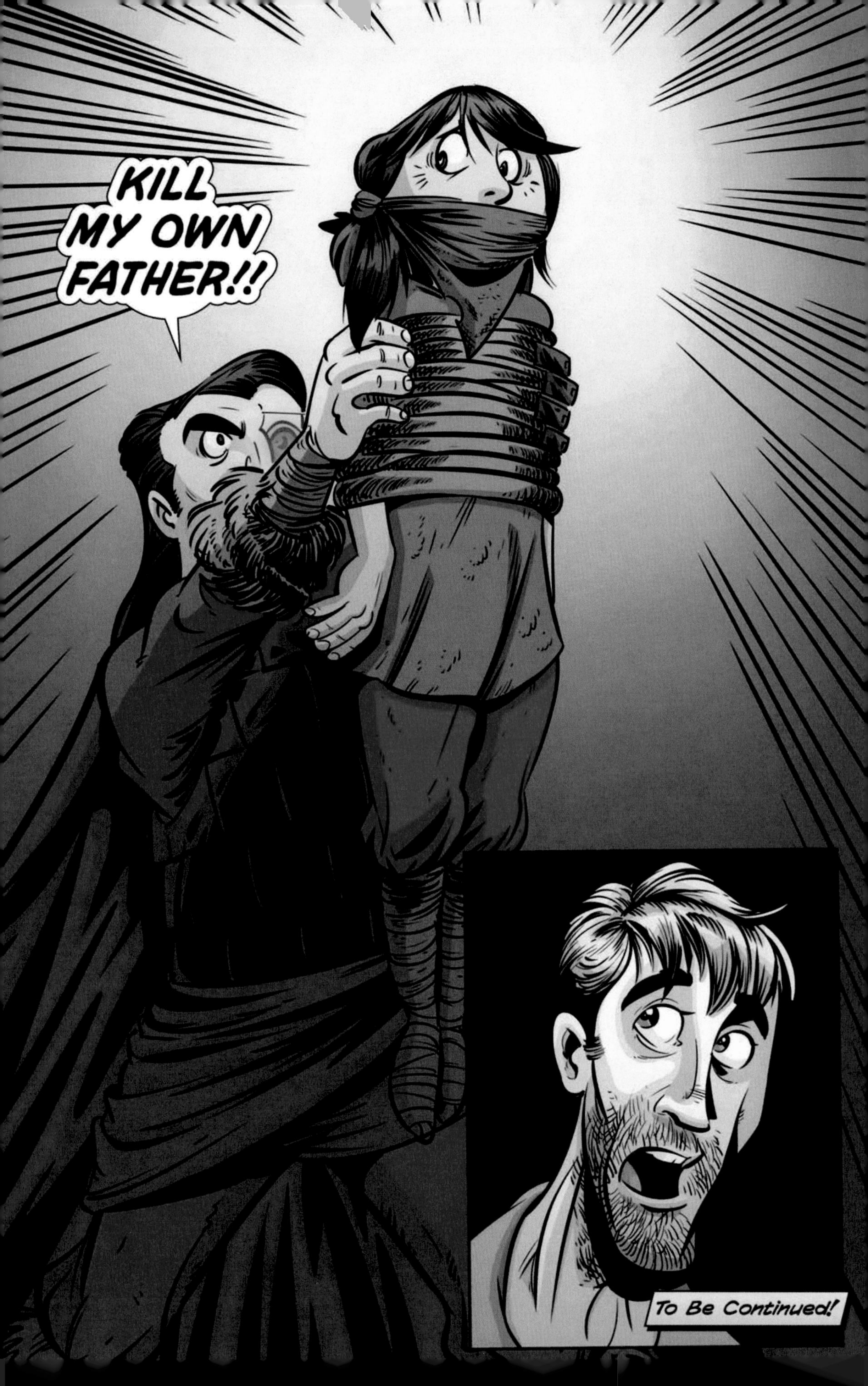
KILL MY OWN FATHER!!
To Be Continued!

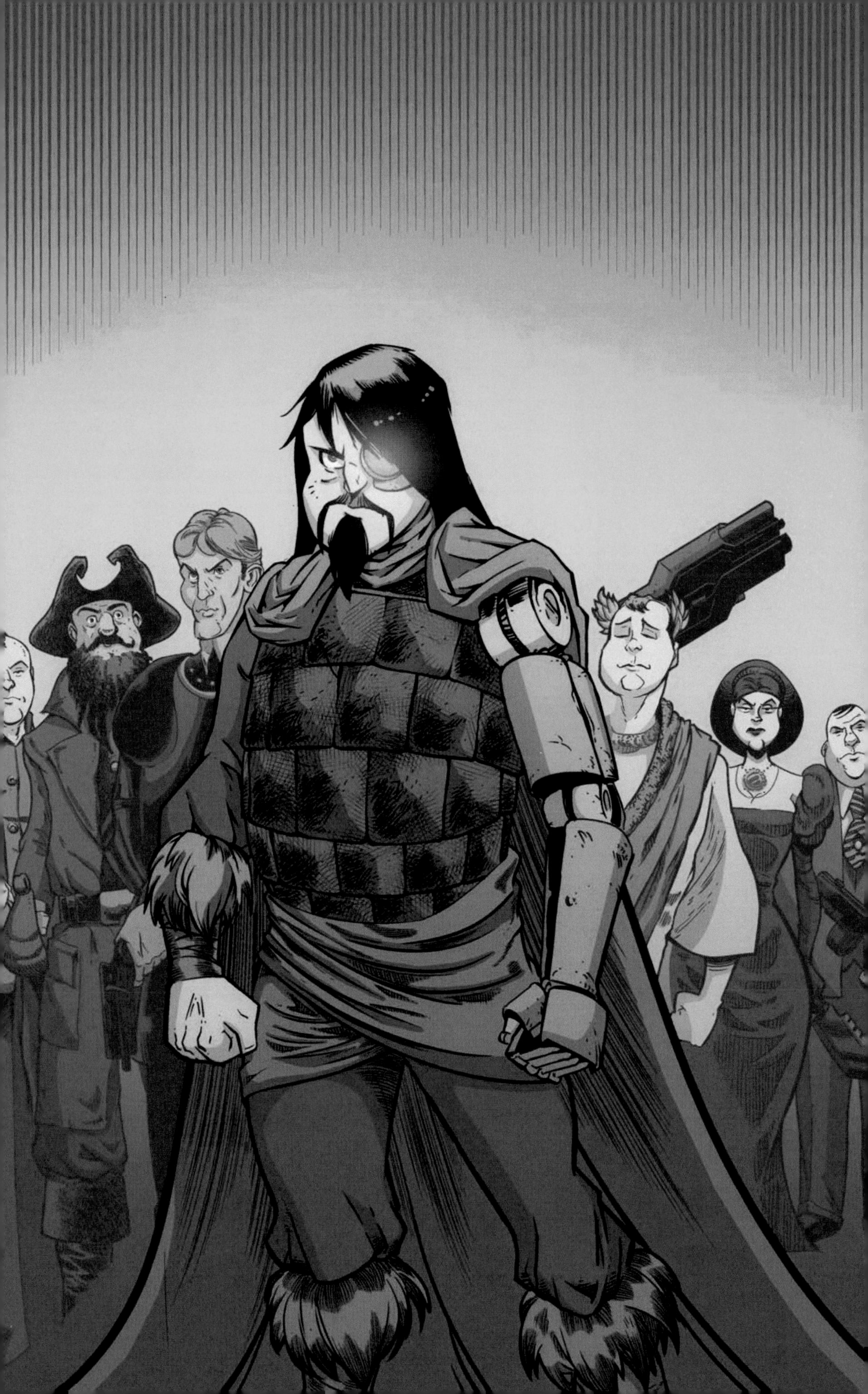

ISSUE FOUR

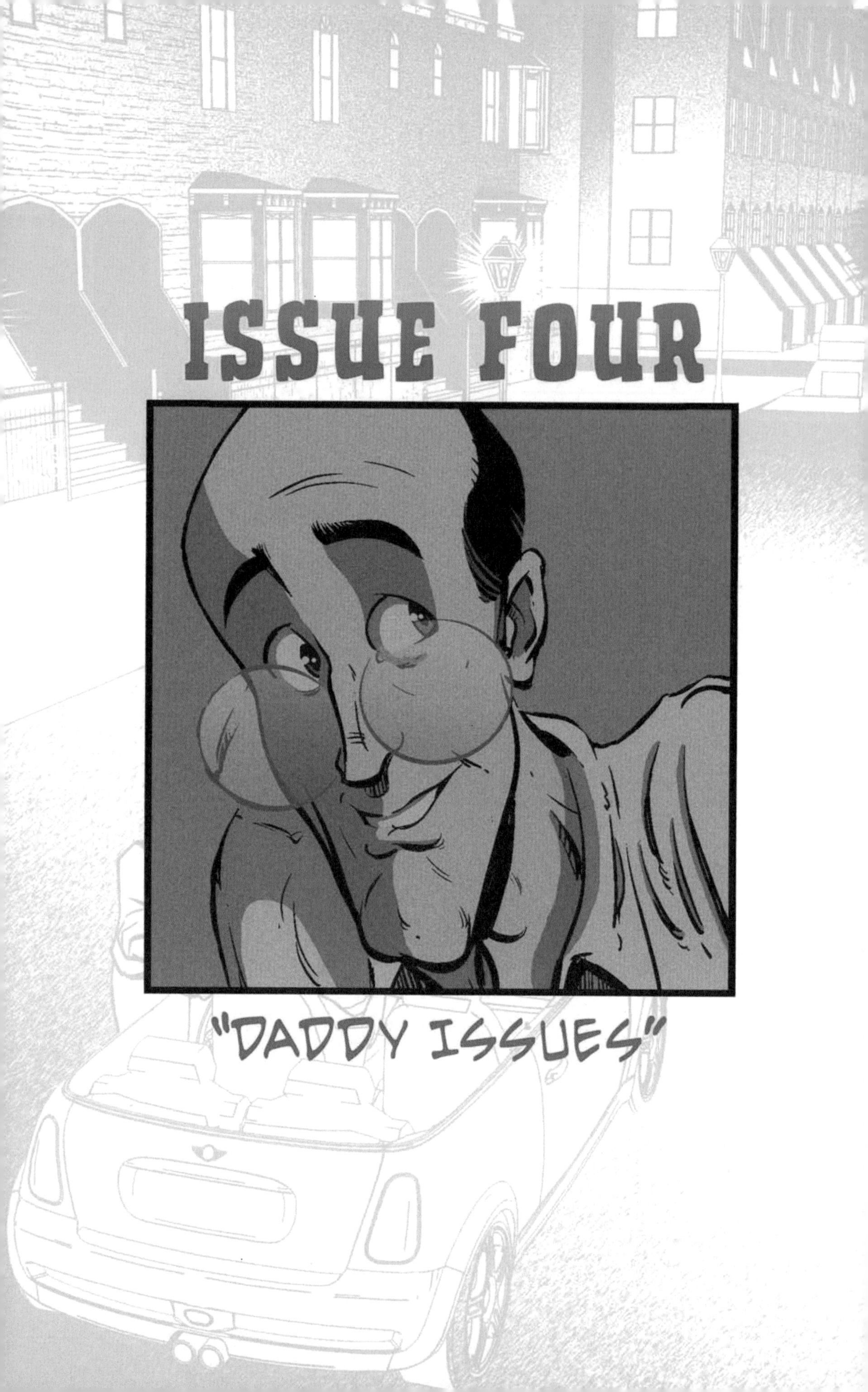

"DADDY ISSUES"

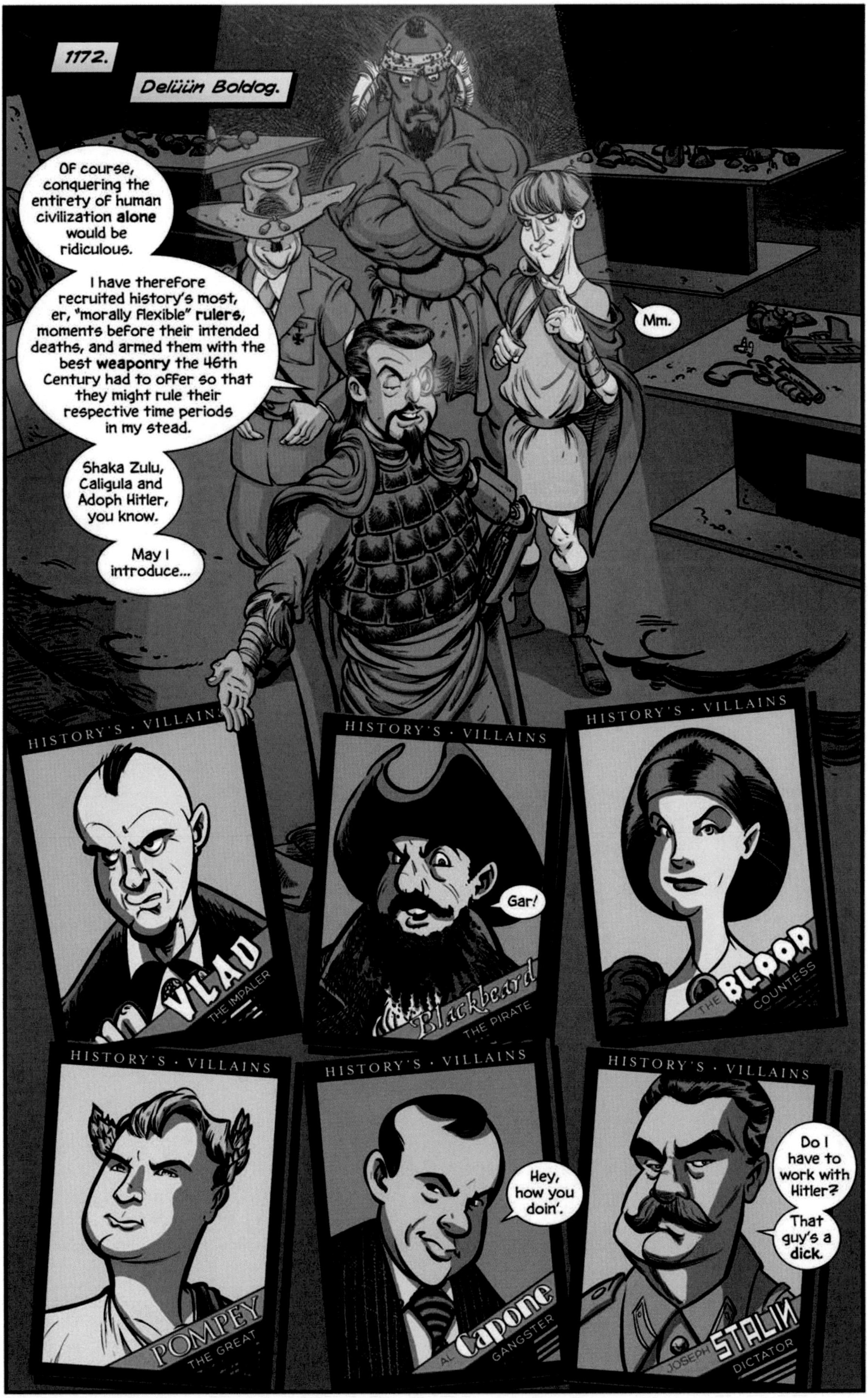
1172.
Delüün Boldog.
Of course, conquering the entirety of human civilization **alone** would be ridiculous.
I have therefore recruited history's most, er, "morally flexible" **rulers**, moments before their intended deaths, and armed them with the best **weaponry** the 46th Century had to offer so that they might rule their respective time periods in my stead.
Shaka Zulu, Caligula and Adoph Hitler, you know.
Mm.
May I introduce...
HISTORY'S · VILLAINS
VLAD THE IMPALER
HISTORY'S · VILLAINS
Gar!
Blackbeard THE PIRATE
HISTORY'S · VILLAINS
THE BLOOD COUNTESS
HISTORY'S · VILLAINS
POMPEY THE GREAT
HISTORY'S · VILLAINS
Hey, how you doin'.
AL Capone GANGSTER
HISTORY'S · VILLAINS
Do I have to work with Hitler?
That guy's a **dick**.
JOSEPH STALIN DICTATOR

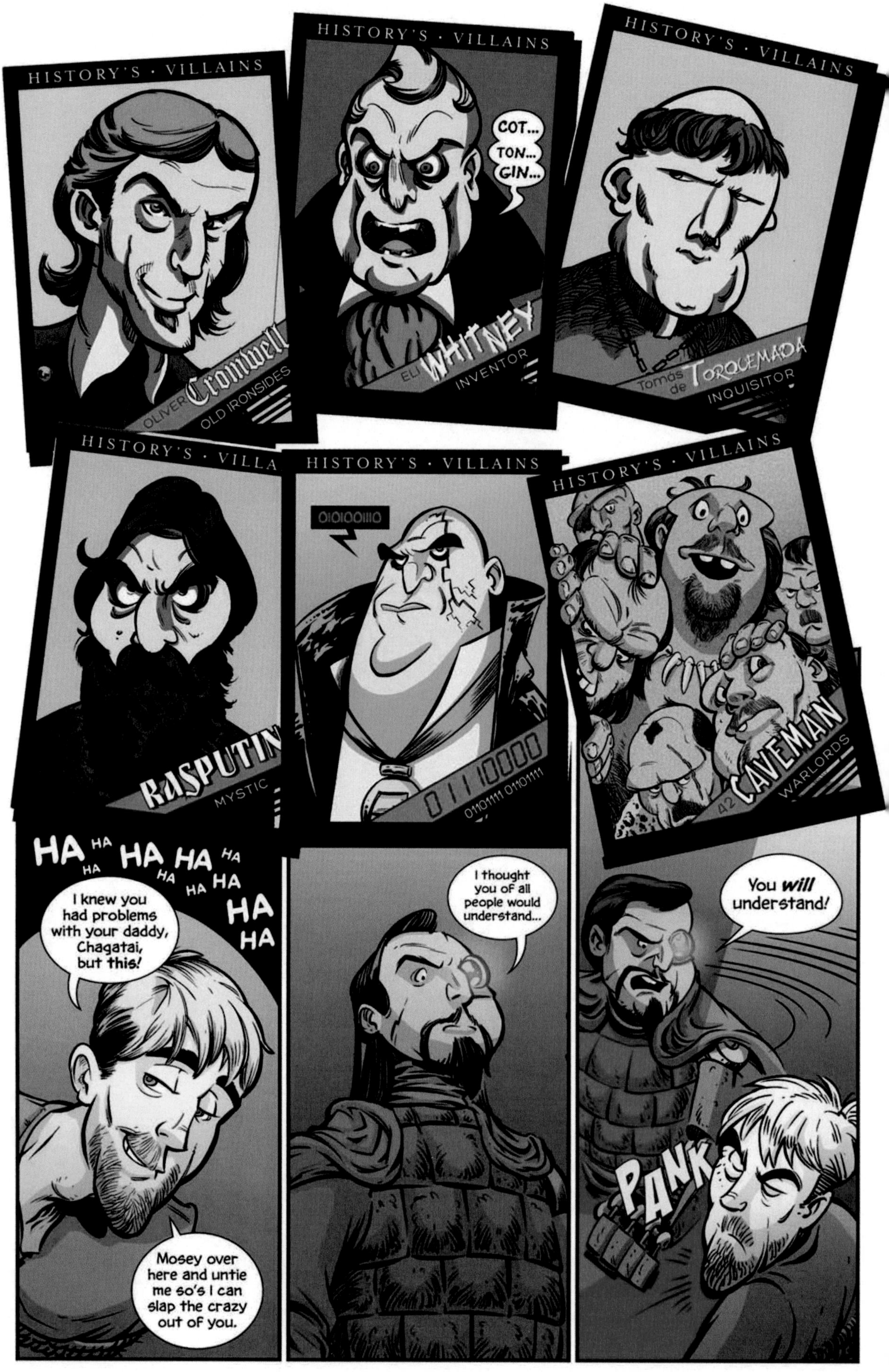
HISTORY'S · VILLAINS
OLIVER Cromwell
OLD IRONSIDES
HISTORY'S · VILLAINS
COT... TON... GIN...
ELI WHITNEY
INVENTOR
HISTORY'S · VILLAINS
Tomás de TORQUEMADA
INQUISITOR
HISTORY'S · VILLA
RASPUTIN
MYSTIC
HISTORY'S · VILLAINS
01010001110
01110000
0110111 0110111
HISTORY'S · VILLAINS
42 CAVEMAN
WARLORDS
HA HA HA HA HA HA HA HA HA HA HA HA
I knew you had problems with your daddy, Chagatai, but this!
Mosey over here and untie me so's I can slap the crazy out of you.
I thought you of all people would understand...
You will understand!
PANK

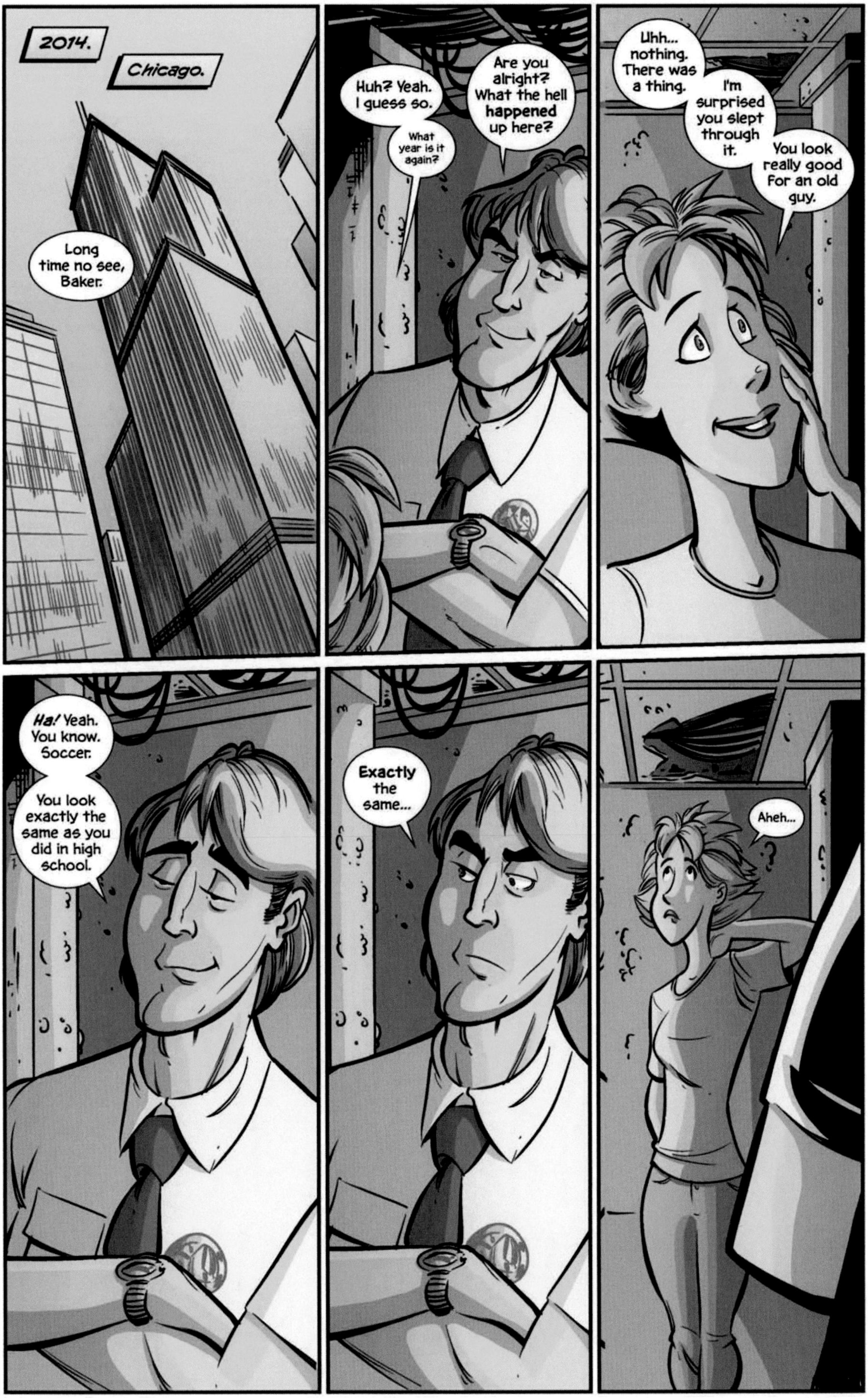
2014.
Chicago.
Long time no see, Baker.
Are you alright? What the hell happened up here?
Huh? Yeah. I guess so.
What year is it again?
Uhh... nothing. There was a thing.
I'm surprised you slept through it.
You look really good for an old guy.
Ha! Yeah. You know. Soccer.
You look exactly the same as you did in high school.
Exactly the same...
Aheh...

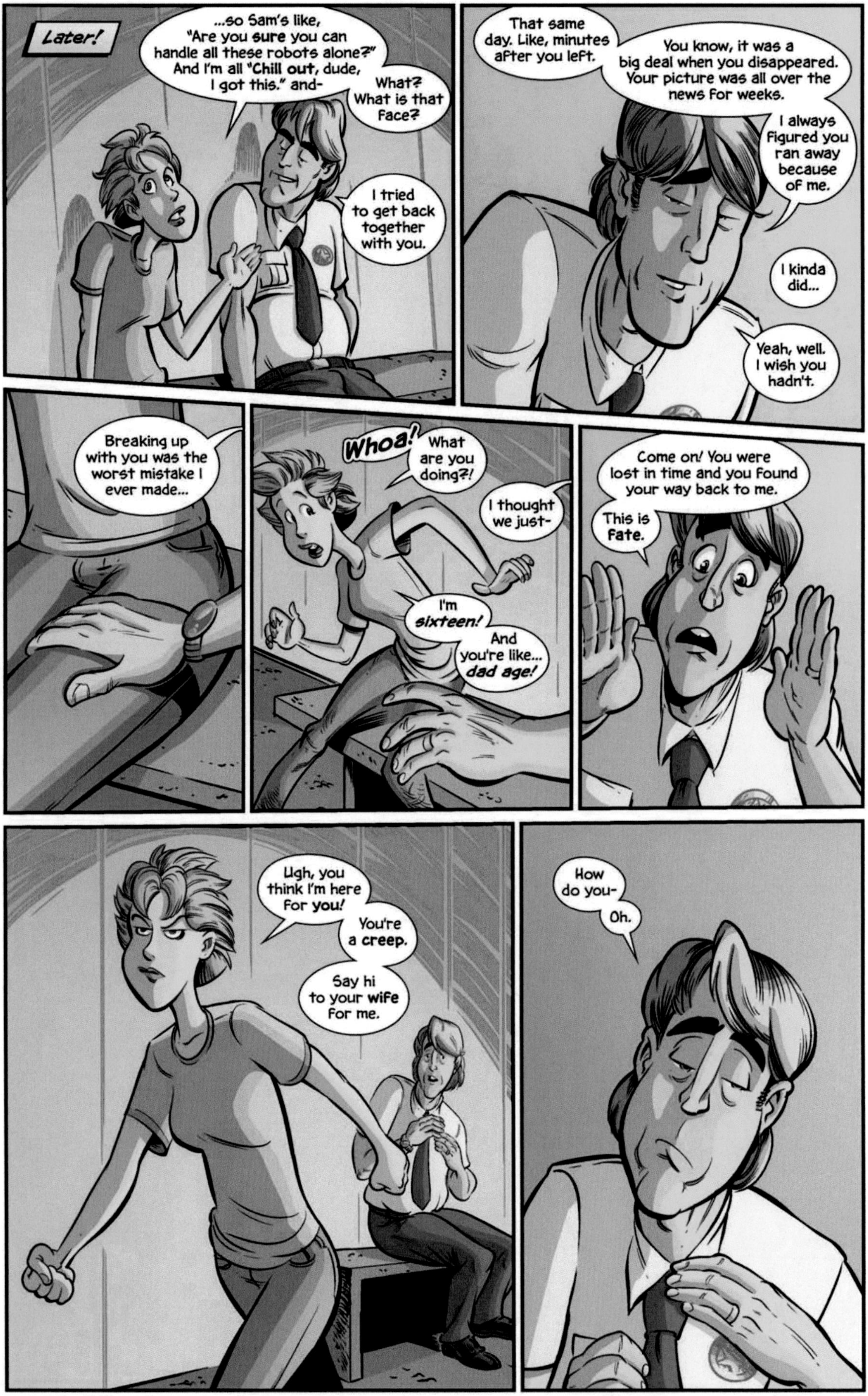
Later!
...so Sam's like, "Are you sure you can handle all these robots alone?" And I'm all "Chill out, dude, I got this." and-
What? What is that Face?
I tried to get back together with you.
That same day. Like, minutes after you left.
You know, it was a big deal when you disappeared. Your picture was all over the news for weeks.
I always Figured you ran away because of me.
I kinda did...
Yeah, well. I wish you hadn't.
Breaking up with you was the worst mistake I ever made...
Whoa!
What are you doing?!
I thought we just-
I'm sixteen!
And you're like... dad age!
Come on! You were lost in time and you found your way back to me.
This is Fate.
Ugh, you think I'm here for you!
You're a creep.
Say hi to your wife for me.
How do you-
Oh.

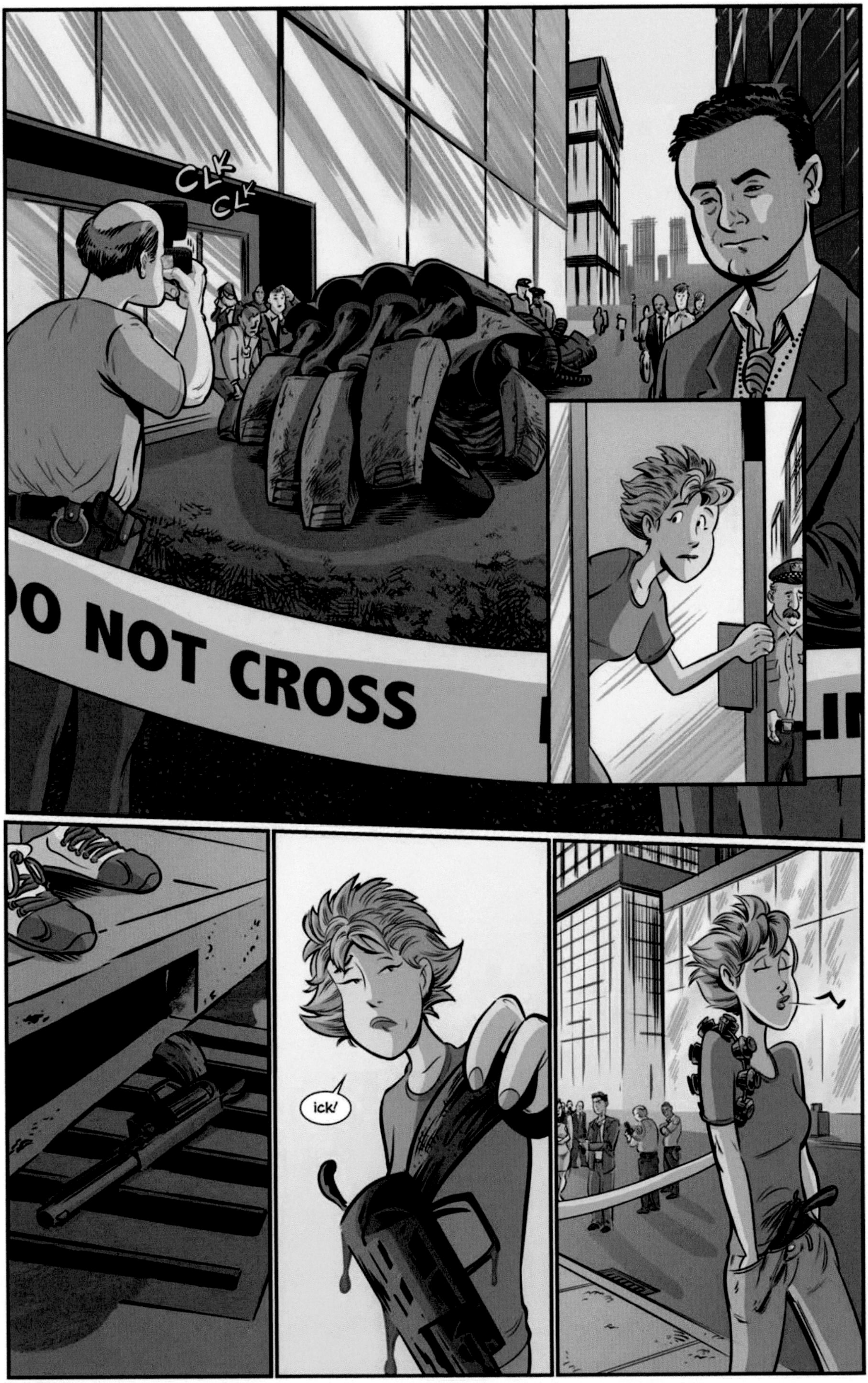
CLK
CLK
DO NOT CROSS
ick!

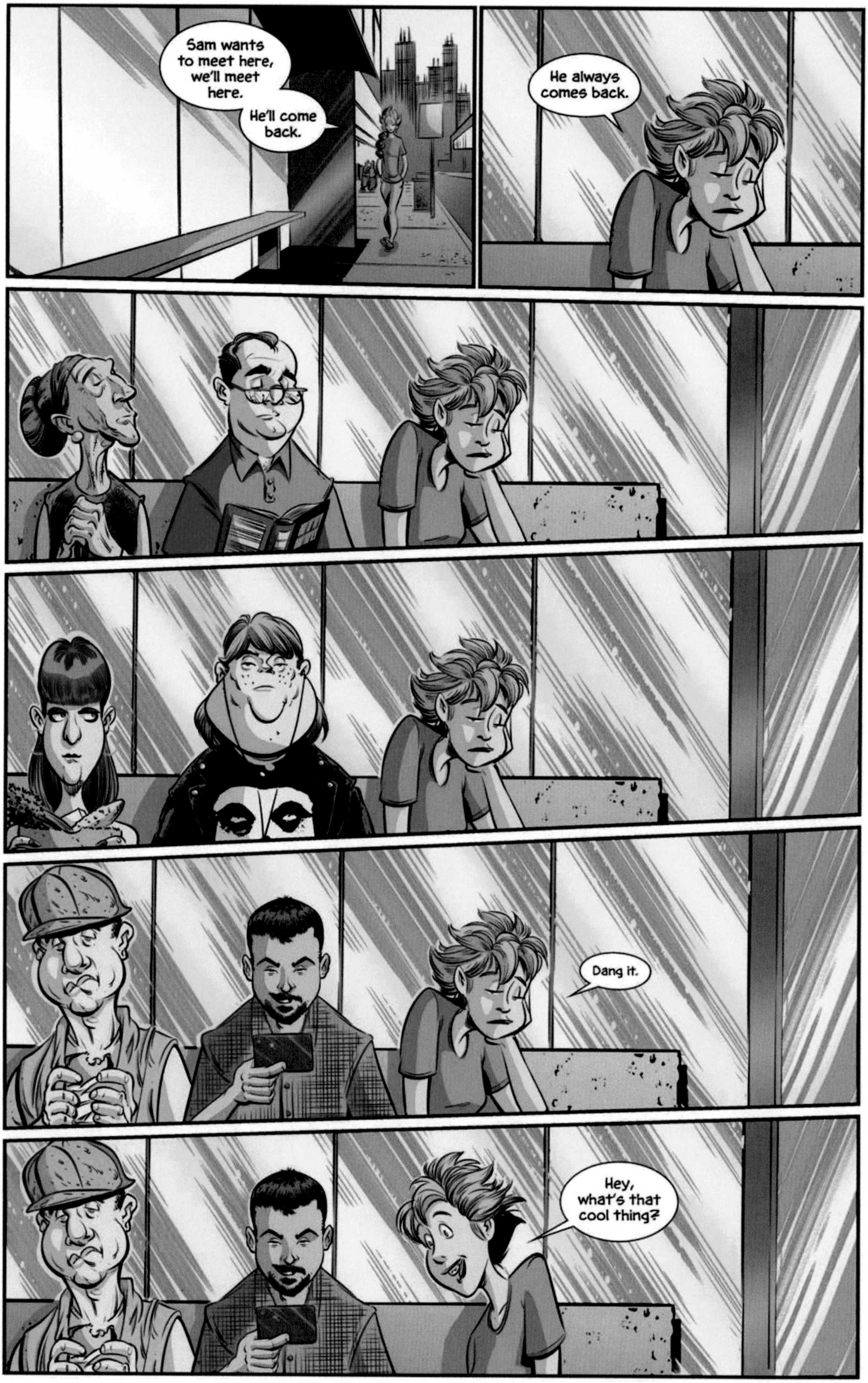
Sam wants to meet here, we'll meet here.
He'll come back.
He always comes back.
Dang it.
Hey, what's that cool thing?

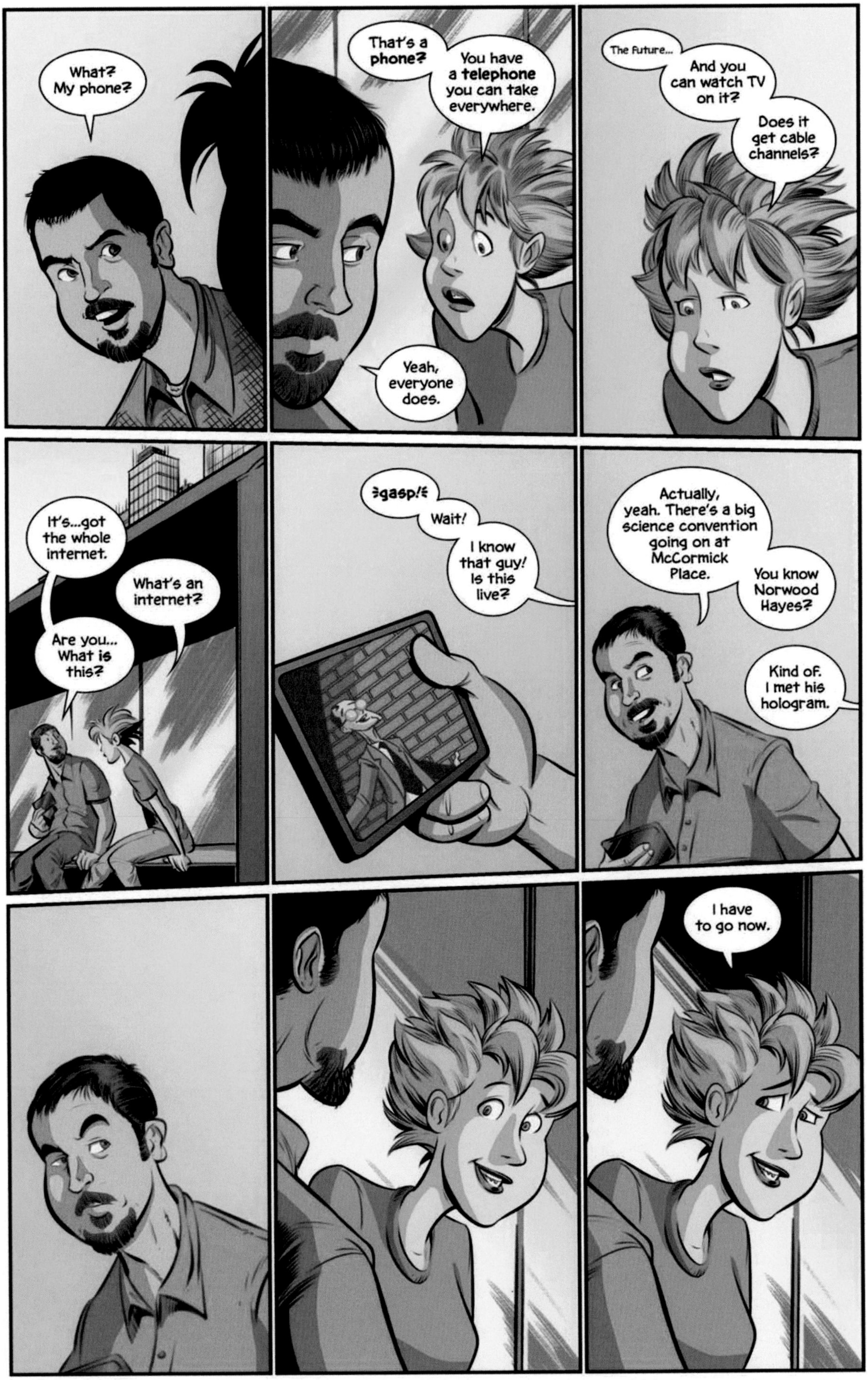
What? My phone?
That's a phone?
You have a telephone you can take everywhere.
Yeah, everyone does.
The future...
And you can watch TV on it?
Does it get cable channels?
It's...got the whole internet.
What's an internet?
Are you... What is this?
gasp!
Wait!
I know that guy! Is this live?
Actually, yeah. There's a big science convention going on at McCormick Place.
You know Norwood Hayes?
Kind of. I met his hologram.
I have to go now.

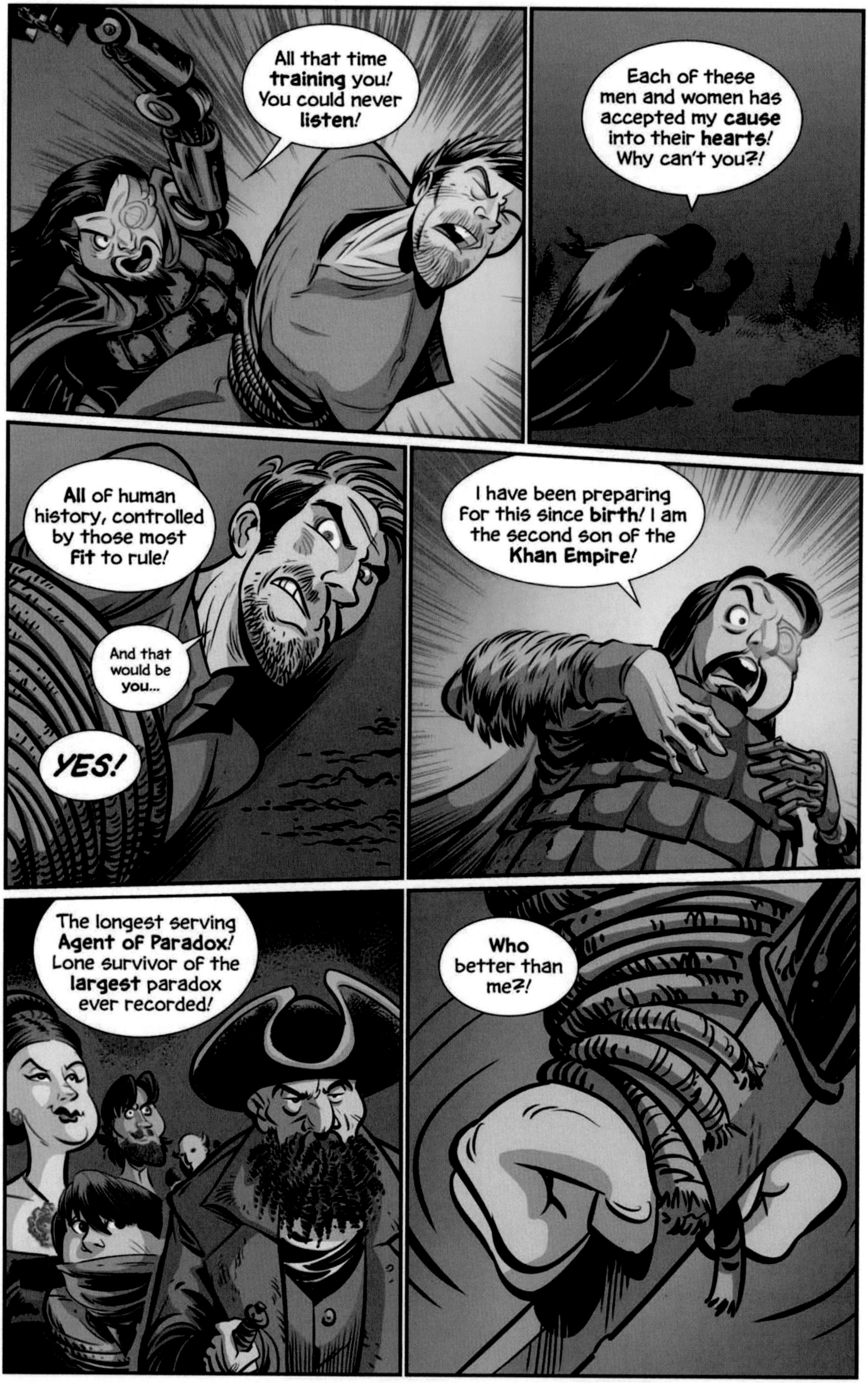
All that time training you! You could never listen!
Each of these men and women has accepted my cause into their hearts! Why can't you?!
All of human history, controlled by those most fit to rule!
And that would be you...
YES!
I have been preparing for this since birth! I am the second son of the Khan Empire!
The longest serving Agent of Paradox! Lone survivor of the largest paradox ever recorded!
Who better than me?!

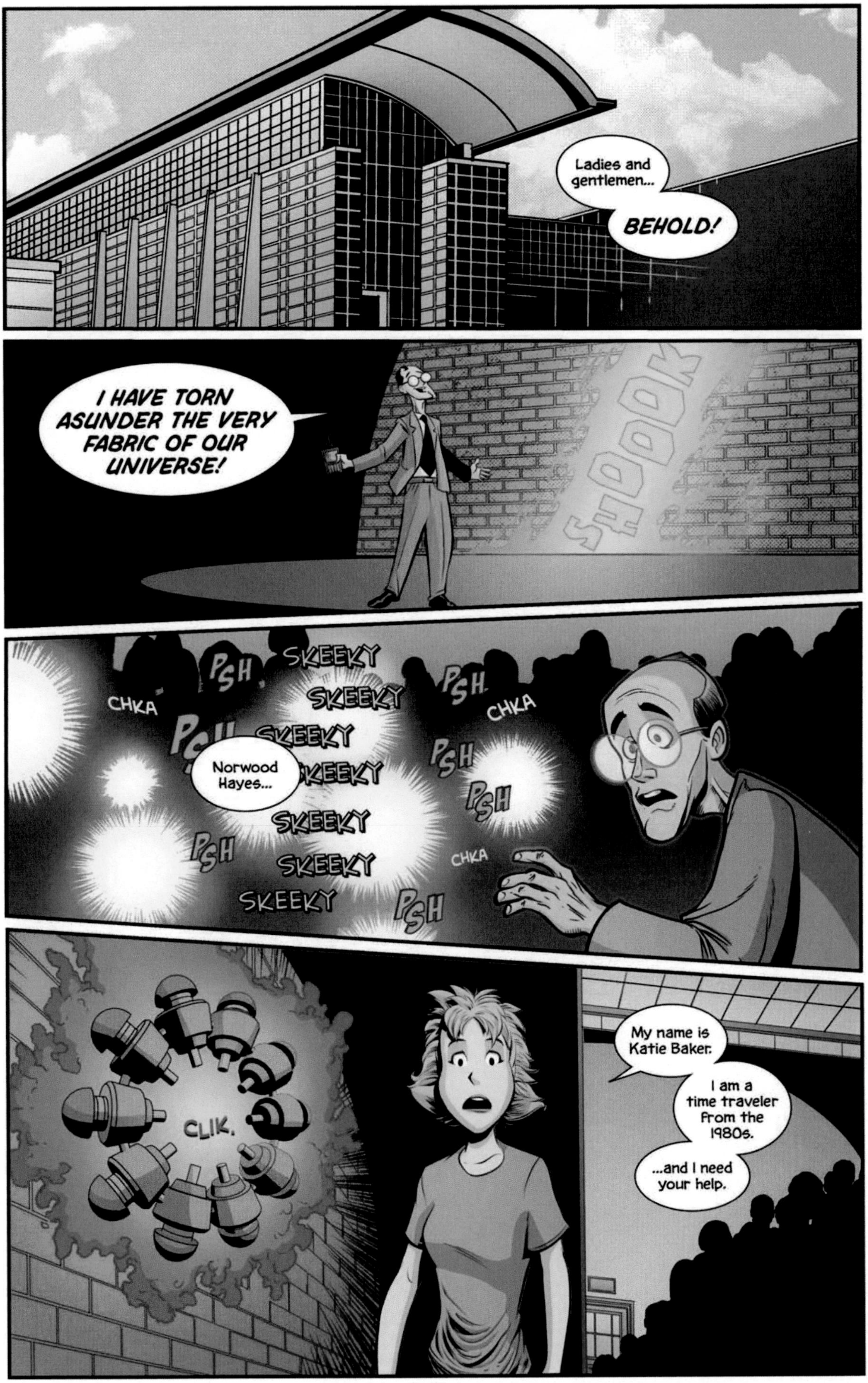
Ladies and gentlemen...
BEHOLD!
I HAVE TORN ASUNDER THE VERY FABRIC OF OUR UNIVERSE!
SHOOOK
PSH
SKEEKY
CHKA
Norwood Hayes...
CLIK.
My name is Katie Baker.
I am a time traveler from the 1980s.
...and I need your help.

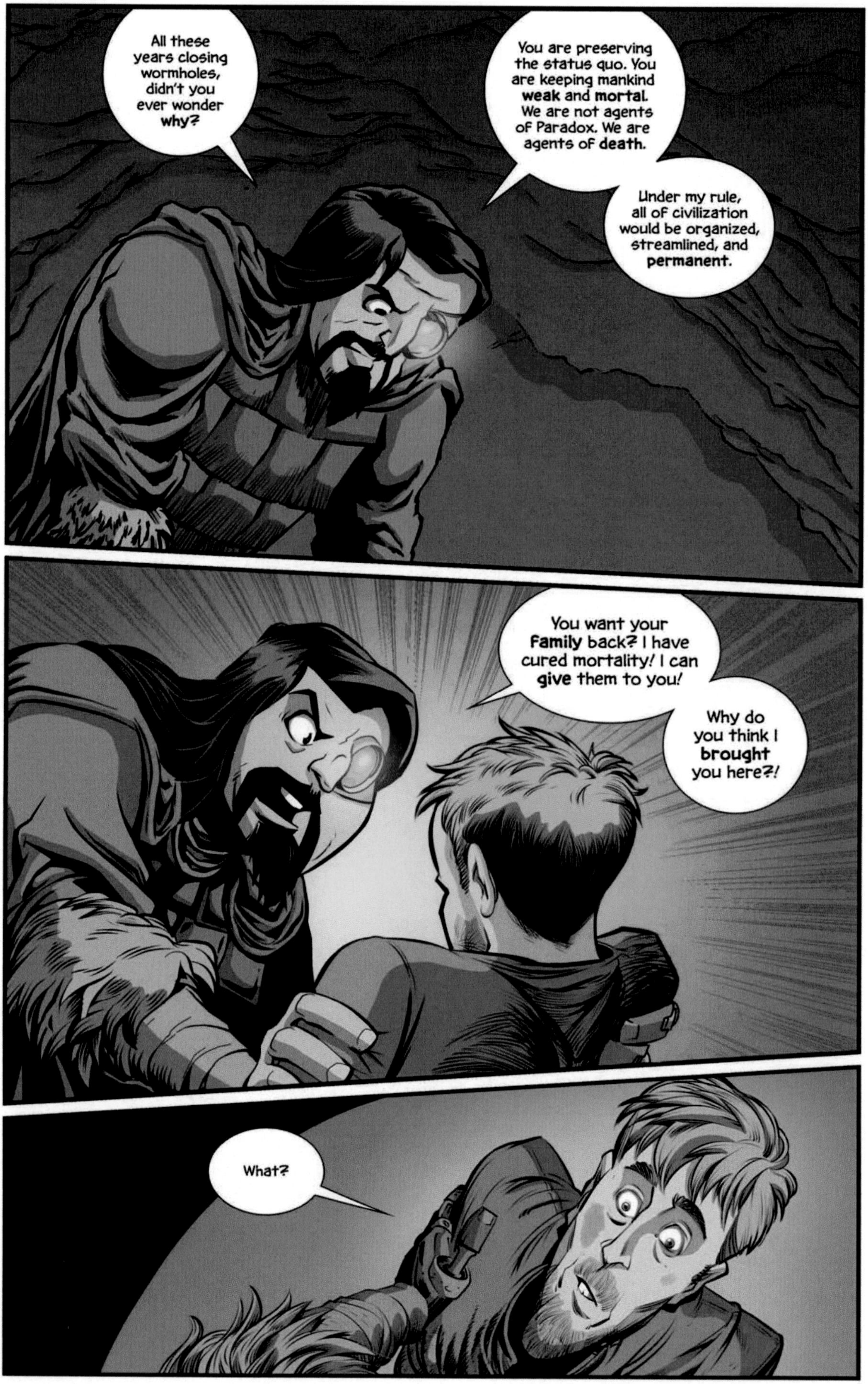
All these years closing wormholes, didn't you ever wonder **why?**
You are preserving the status quo. You are keeping mankind **weak** and **mortal**. We are not agents of Paradox. We are agents of **death**.
Under my rule, all of civilization would be organized, streamlined, and **permanent**.
You want your **family** back? I have cured mortality! I can **give** them to you!
Why do you think I **brought** you here?!
What?

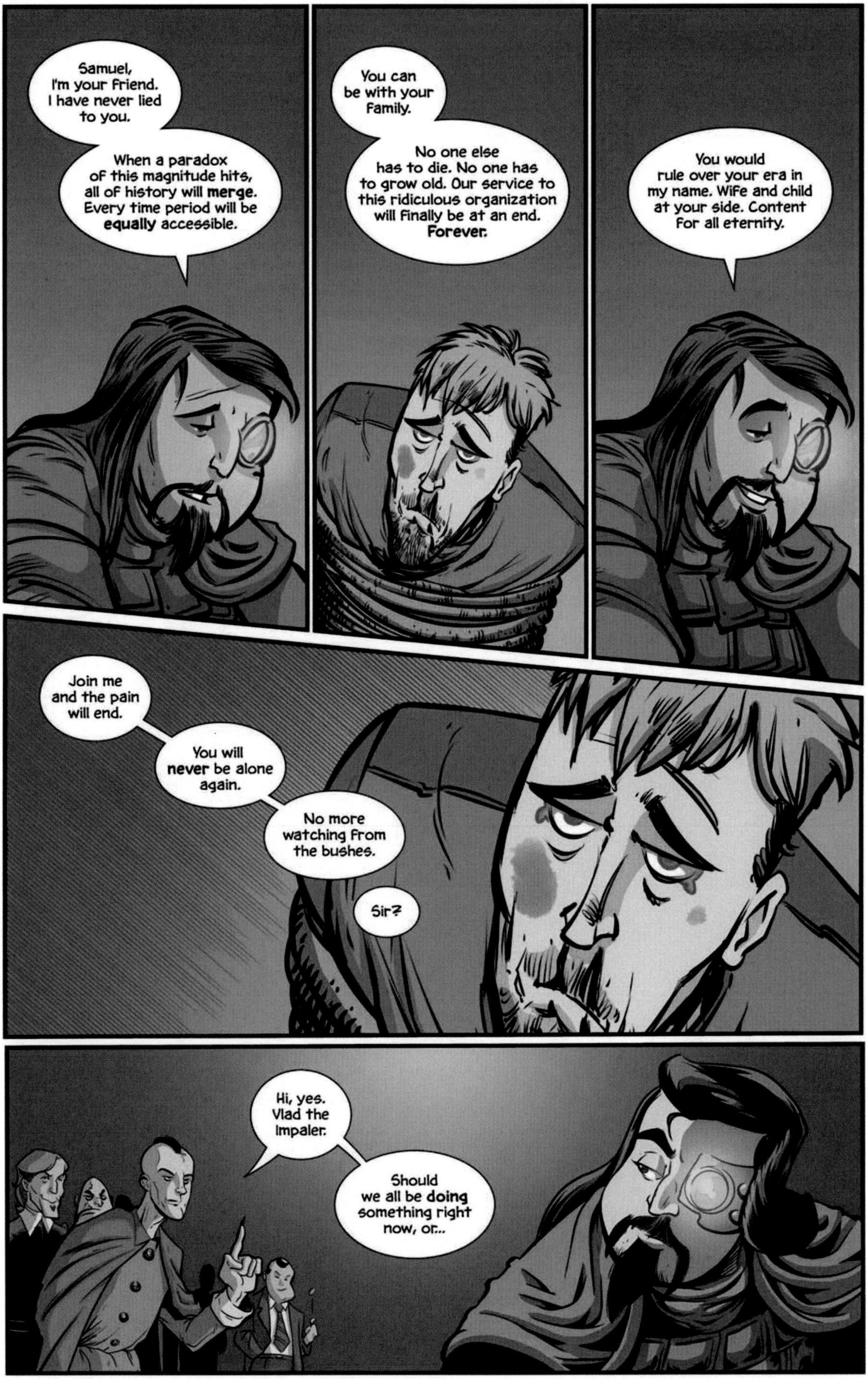
Samuel, I'm your friend. I have never lied to you.
When a paradox of this magnitude hits, all of history will **merge**. Every time period will be **equally** accessible.
You can be with your family.
No one else has to die. No one has to grow old. Our service to this ridiculous organization will finally be at an end. **Forever.**
You would rule over your era in my name. Wife and child at your side. Content for all eternity.
Join me and the pain will end.
You will **never** be alone again.
No more watching from the bushes.
Sir?
Hi, yes. Vlad the Impaler.
Should we all be **doing** something right now, or...

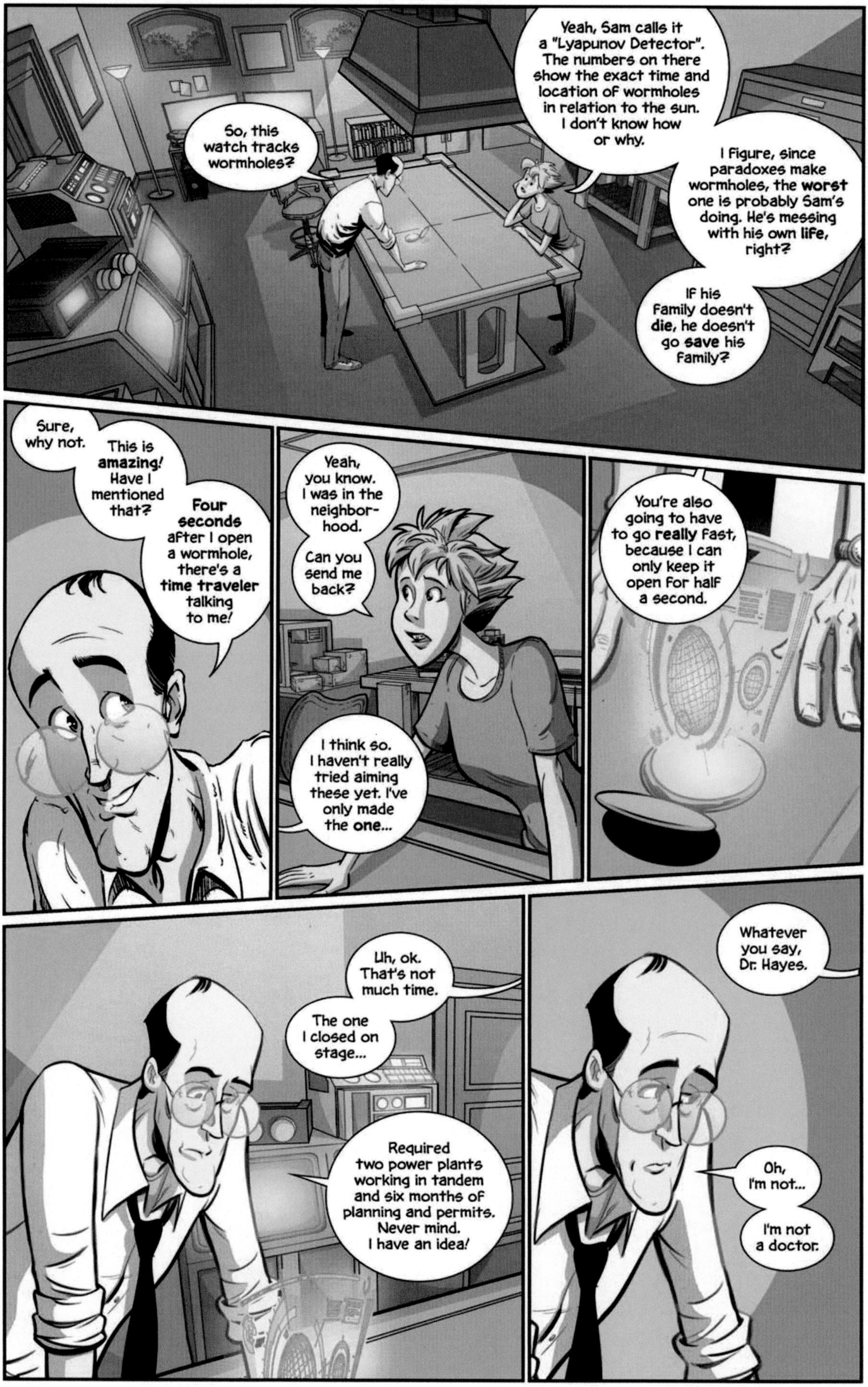
So, this watch tracks wormholes?
Yeah, Sam calls it a "Lyapunov Detector". The numbers on there show the exact time and location of wormholes in relation to the sun. I don't know how or why.
I figure, since paradoxes make wormholes, the **worst** one is probably Sam's doing. He's messing with his own **life**, right?
If his family doesn't **die**, he doesn't go **save** his family?
Sure, why not.
This is **amazing**! Have I mentioned that?
Four seconds after I open a wormhole, there's a **time traveler** talking to me!
Yeah, you know. I was in the neighbor-hood.
Can you send me back?
I think so. I haven't really tried aiming these yet. I've only made the **one**...
You're also going to have to go **really** fast, because I can only keep it open for half a second.
Uh, ok. That's not much time.
The one I closed on stage...
Required two power plants working in tandem and six months of planning and permits. Never mind. I have an idea!
Whatever you say, Dr. Hayes.
Oh, I'm not...
I'm not a doctor.

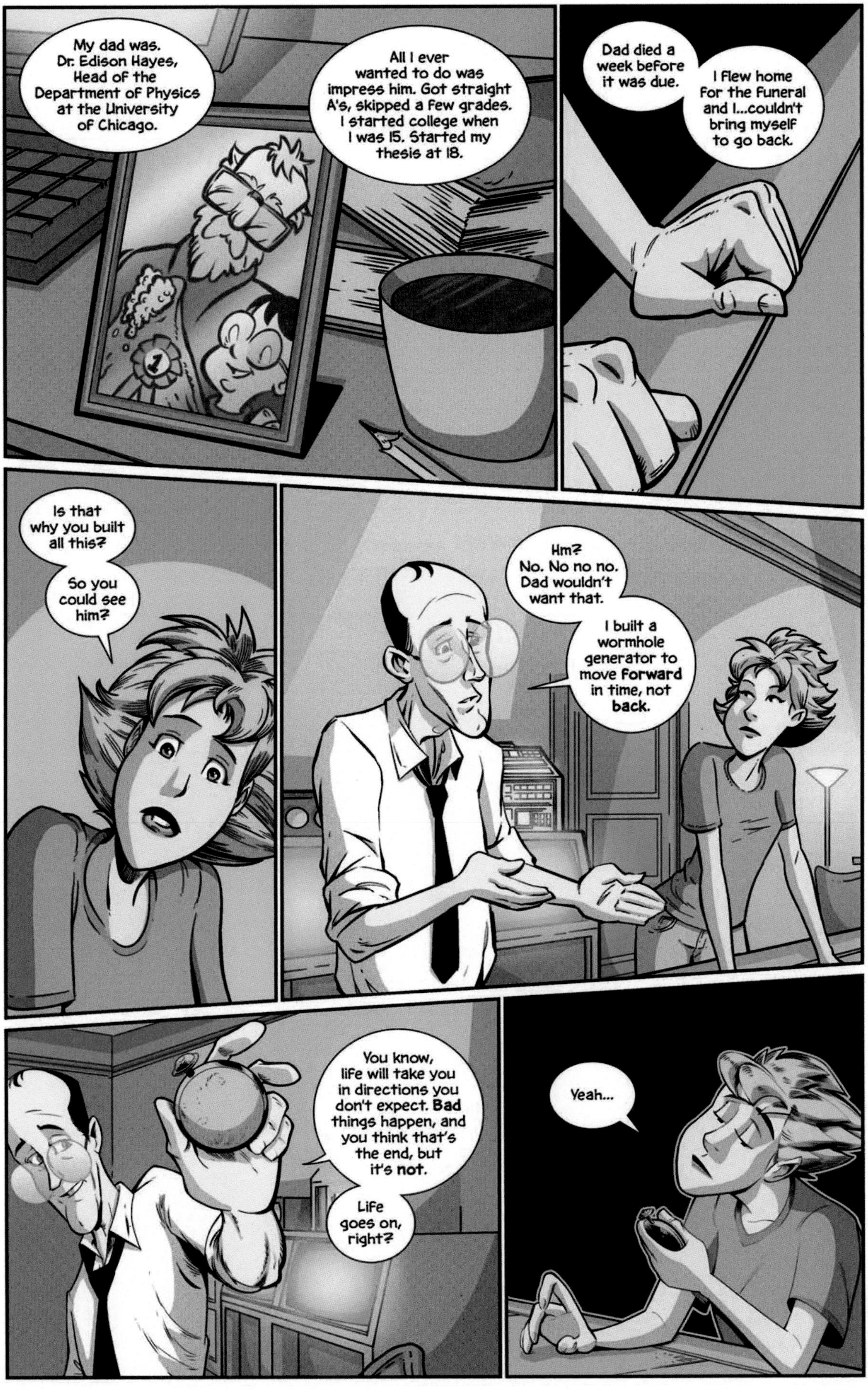

My dad was. Dr. Edison Hayes, Head of the Department of Physics at the University of Chicago.
All I ever wanted to do was impress him. Got straight A's, skipped a few grades. I started college when I was 15. Started my thesis at 18.
Dad died a week before it was due.
I flew home for the funeral and I...couldn't bring myself to go back.
Is that why you built all this?
So you could see him?
Hm? No. No no no. Dad wouldn't want that.
I built a wormhole generator to move **forward** in time, not **back**.
You know, life will take you in directions you don't expect. **Bad** things happen, and you think that's the end, but it's **not**.
Life goes on, right?
Yeah...

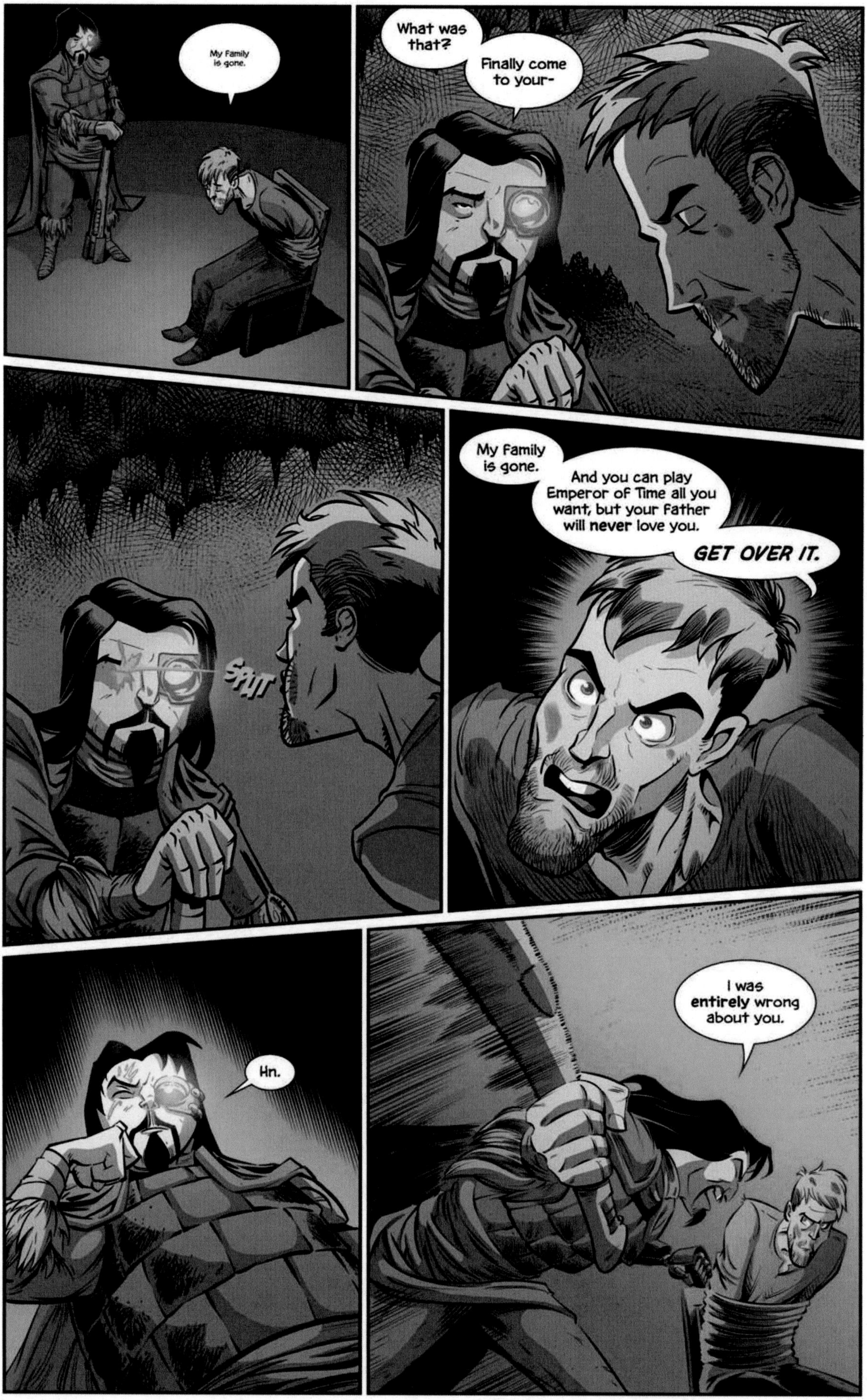

My Family is gone.
What was that?
Finally come to your-
SPIT
My Family is gone.
And you can play Emperor of Time all you want, but your Father will never love you.
GET OVER IT.
Hn.
I was entirely wrong about you.

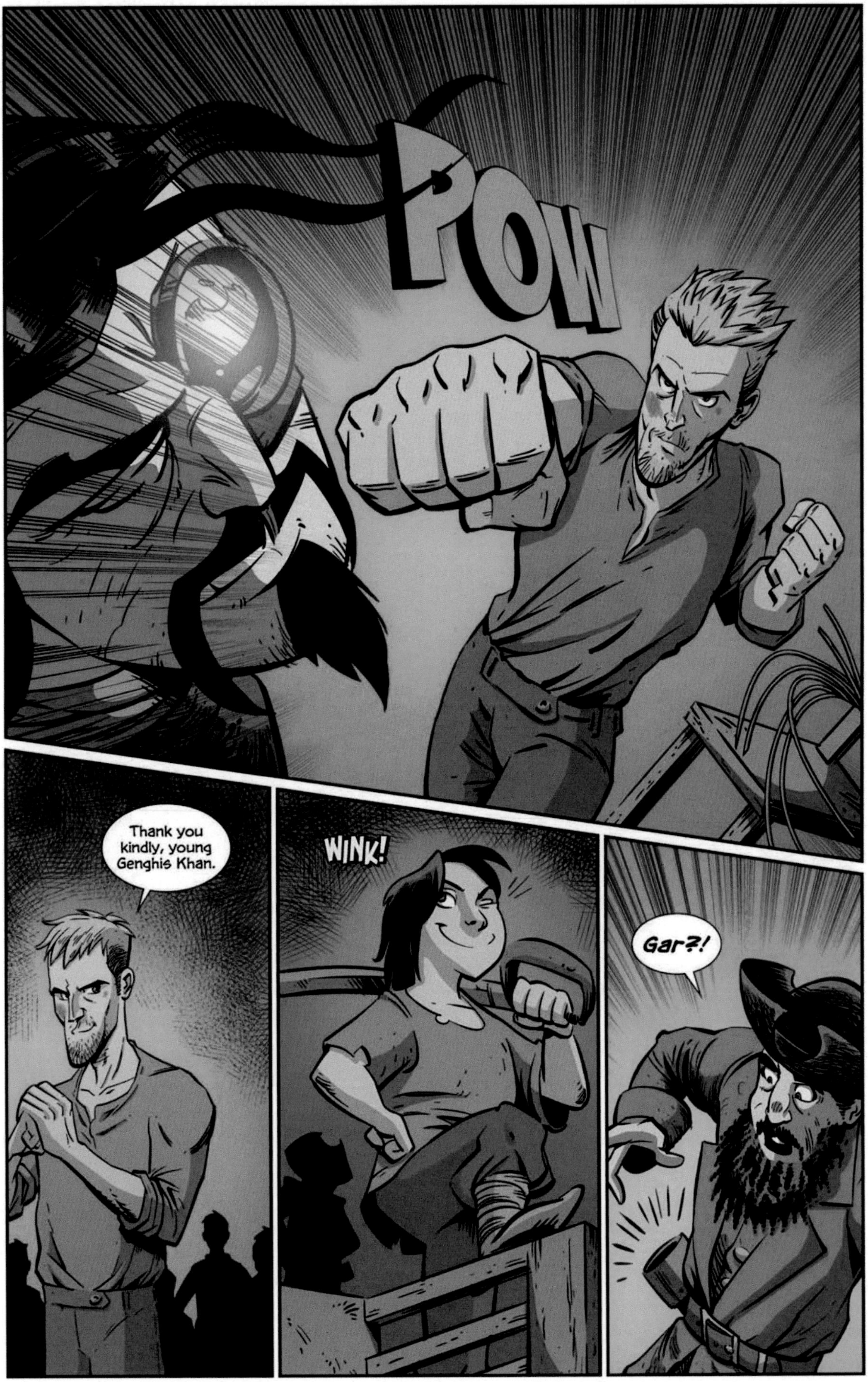
POW
Thank you kindly, young Genghis Khan.
WINK!
Gar?!

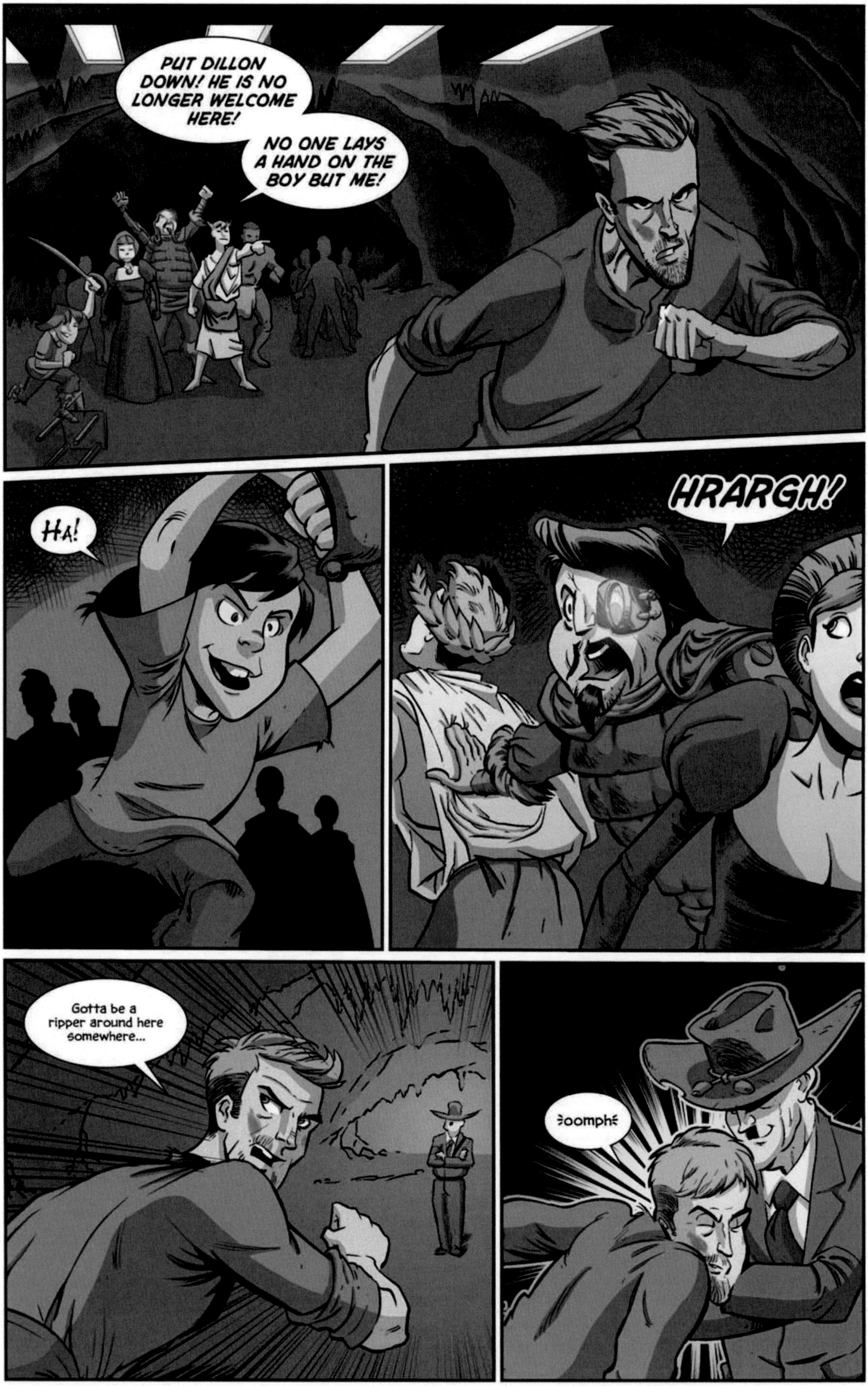
PUT DILLON DOWN! HE IS NO LONGER WELCOME HERE!
NO ONE LAYS A HAND ON THE BOY BUT ME!
HA!
HRARGH!
Gotta be a ripper around here somewhere...
oomph

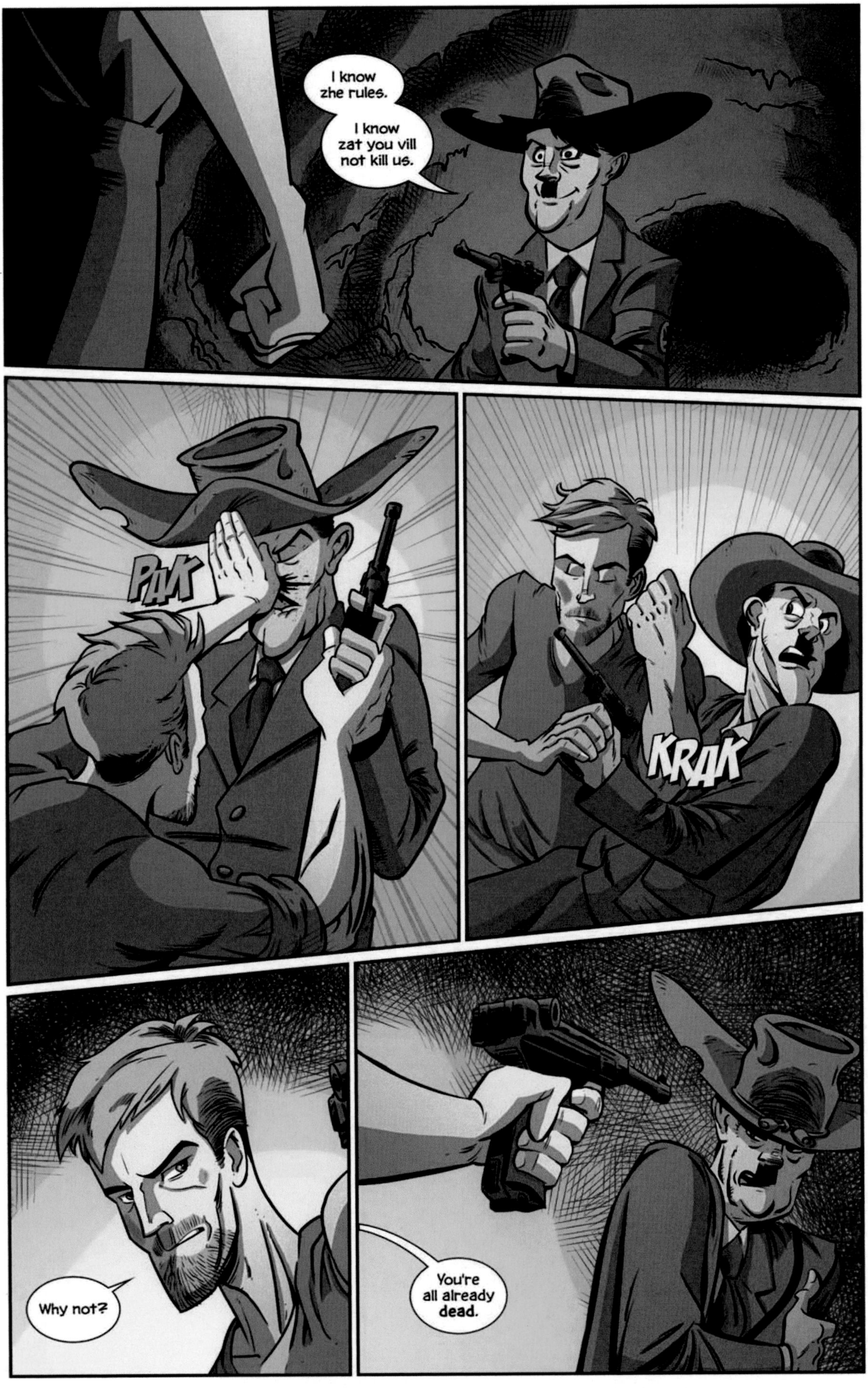
I know
zhe rules.
I know
zat you vill
not kill us.
PAK
KRAK
Why not?
You're
all already
dead.

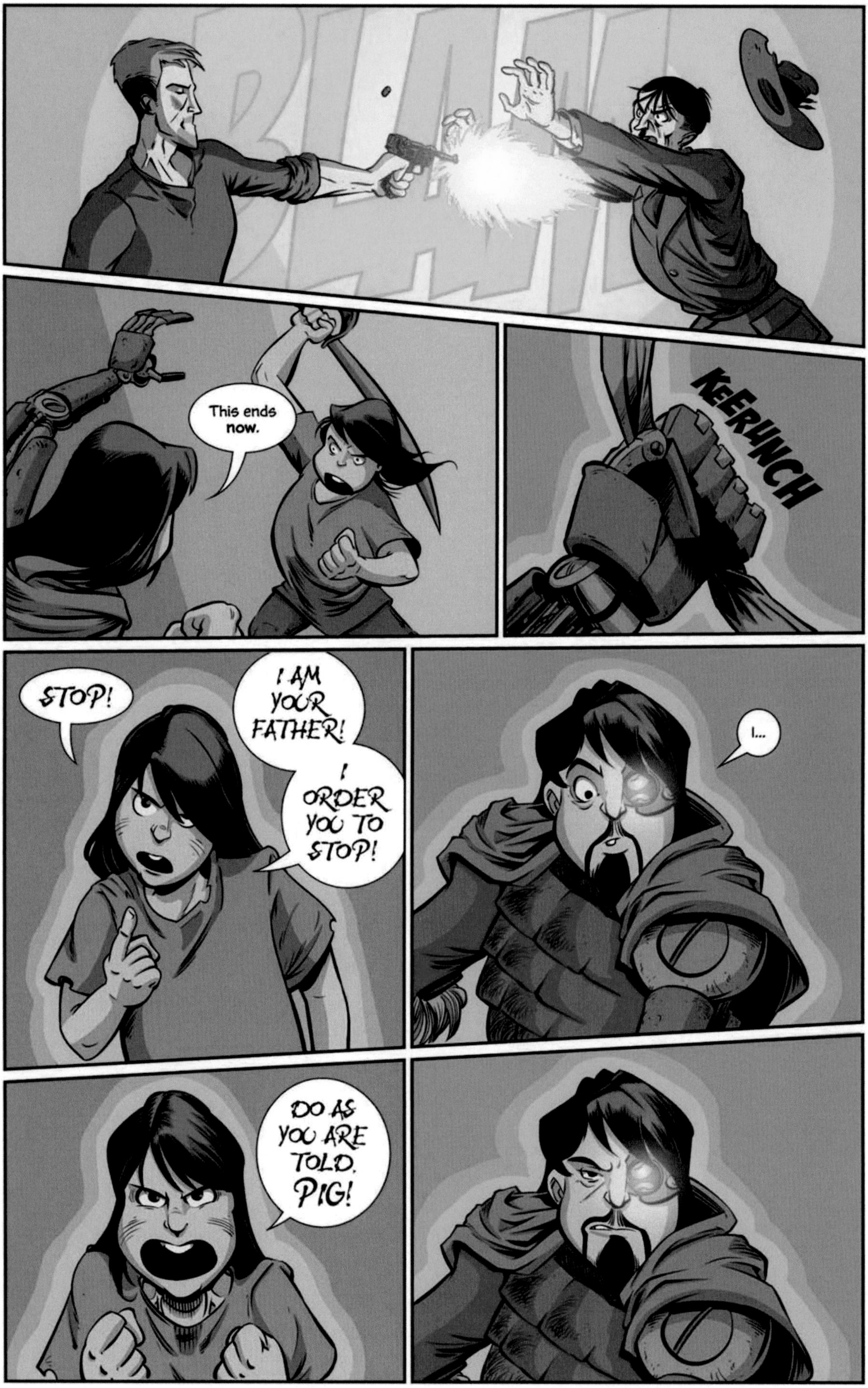
This ends now.
KEERUNCH
STOP!
I AM YOUR FATHER!
I ORDER YOU TO STOP!
I...
DO AS YOU ARE TOLD, PIG!

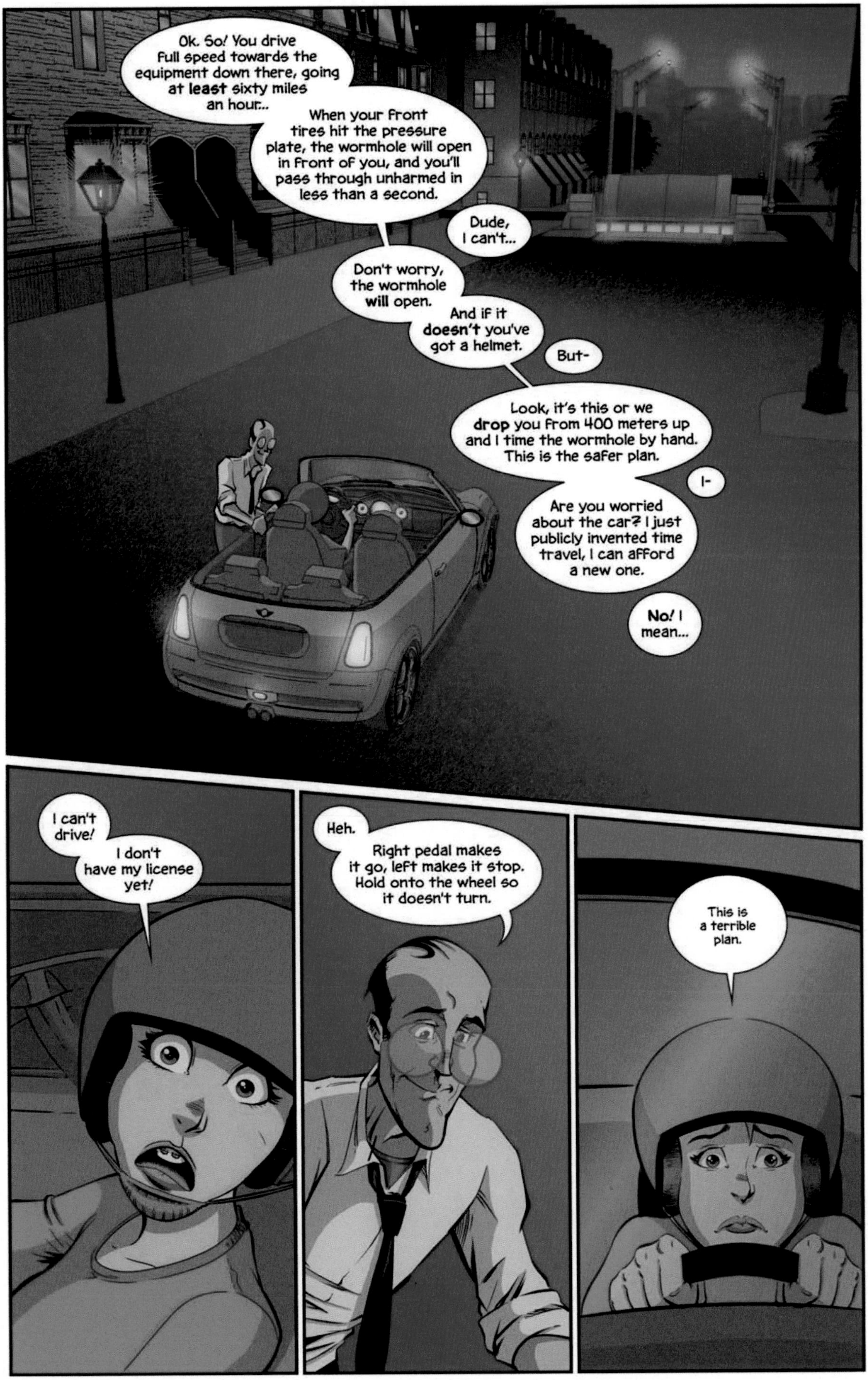
Ok. So! You drive full speed towards the equipment down there, going at least sixty miles an hour...
When your front tires hit the pressure plate, the wormhole will open in front of you, and you'll pass through unharmed in less than a second.
Dude, I can't...
Don't worry, the wormhole will open.
And if it doesn't you've got a helmet.
But-
Look, it's this or we drop you from 400 meters up and I time the wormhole by hand. This is the safer plan.
I-
Are you worried about the car? I just publicly invented time travel, I can afford a new one.
No! I mean...
I can't drive!
I don't have my license yet!
Heh.
Right pedal makes it go, left makes it stop. Hold onto the wheel so it doesn't turn.
This is a terrible plan.

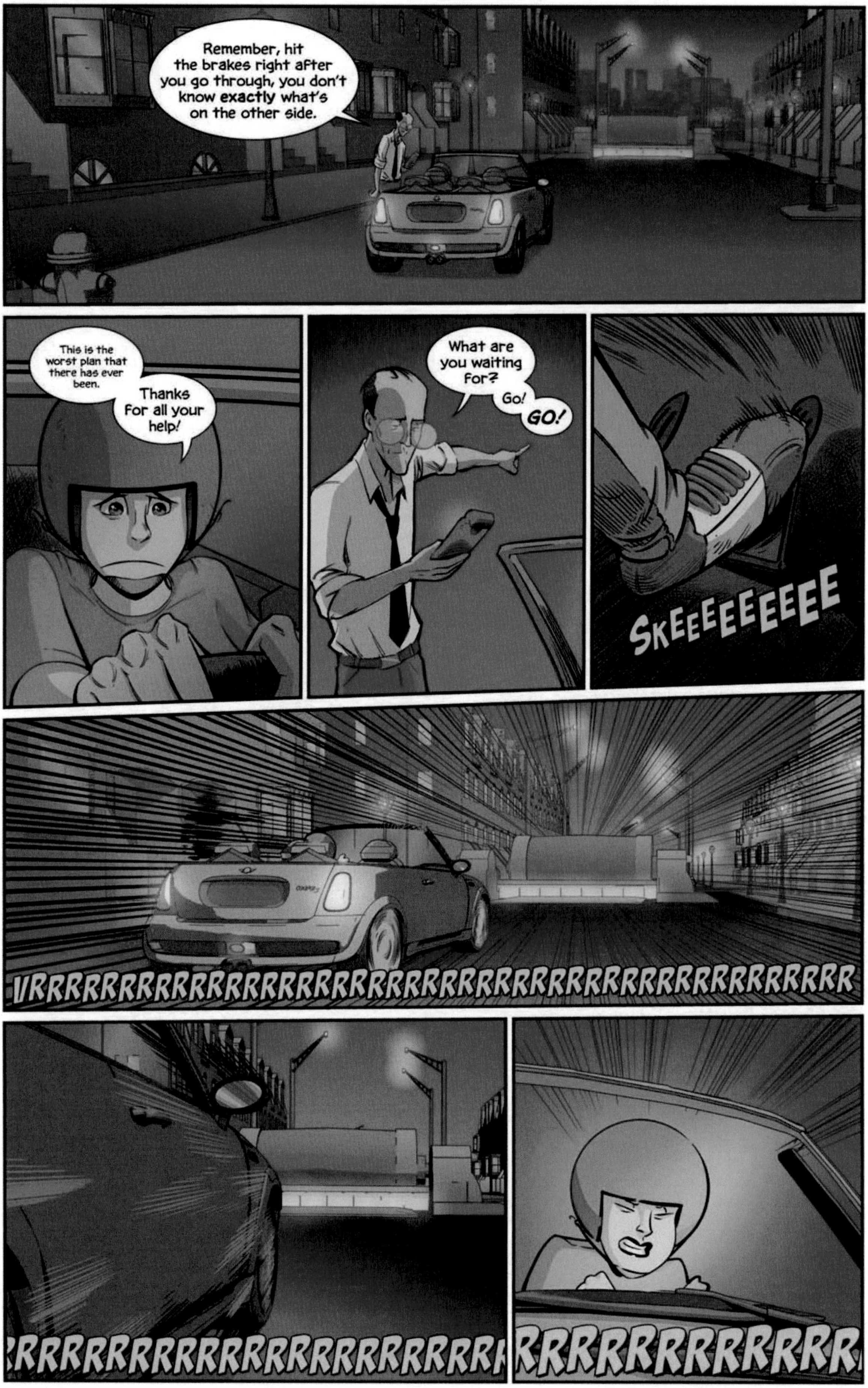

Remember, hit the brakes right after you go through, you don't know exactly what's on the other side.
This is the worst plan that there has ever been.
Thanks for all your help!
What are you waiting for?
Go!
GO!
SKEEEEEEEE
VRRRRRRRRRRRRRRRRRRRRRRRRRRRRRRRRRRRRRRRRRRR
RRRRRRRRRRRRRRRRRRRRRR
RRRRRRRRRRRR

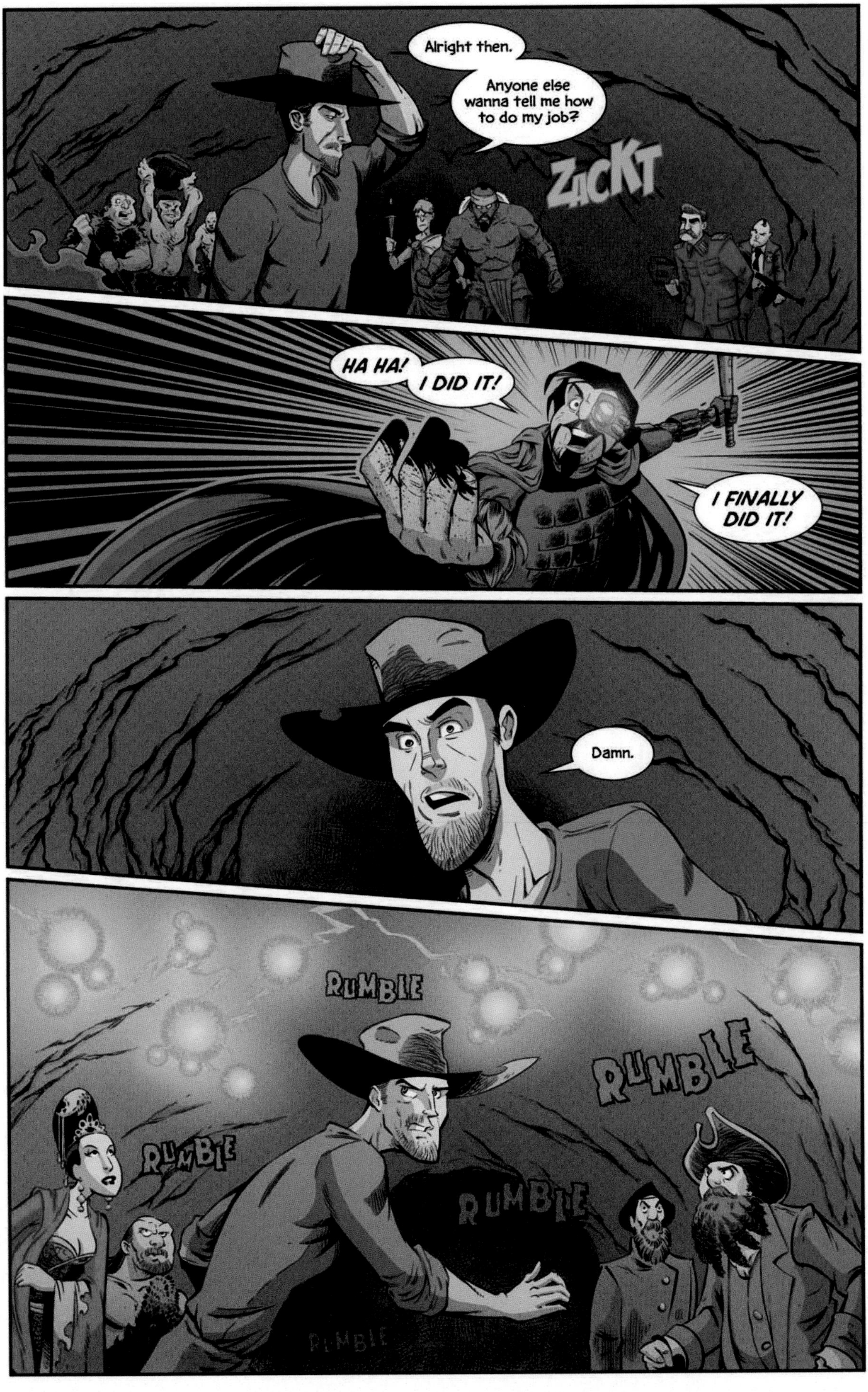
Alright then.
Anyone else wanna tell me how to do my job?
ZACKT
HA HA!
I DID IT!
I FINALLY DID IT!
Damn.
RUMBLE
RUMBLE
RUMBLE
RUMBLE
RUMBLE

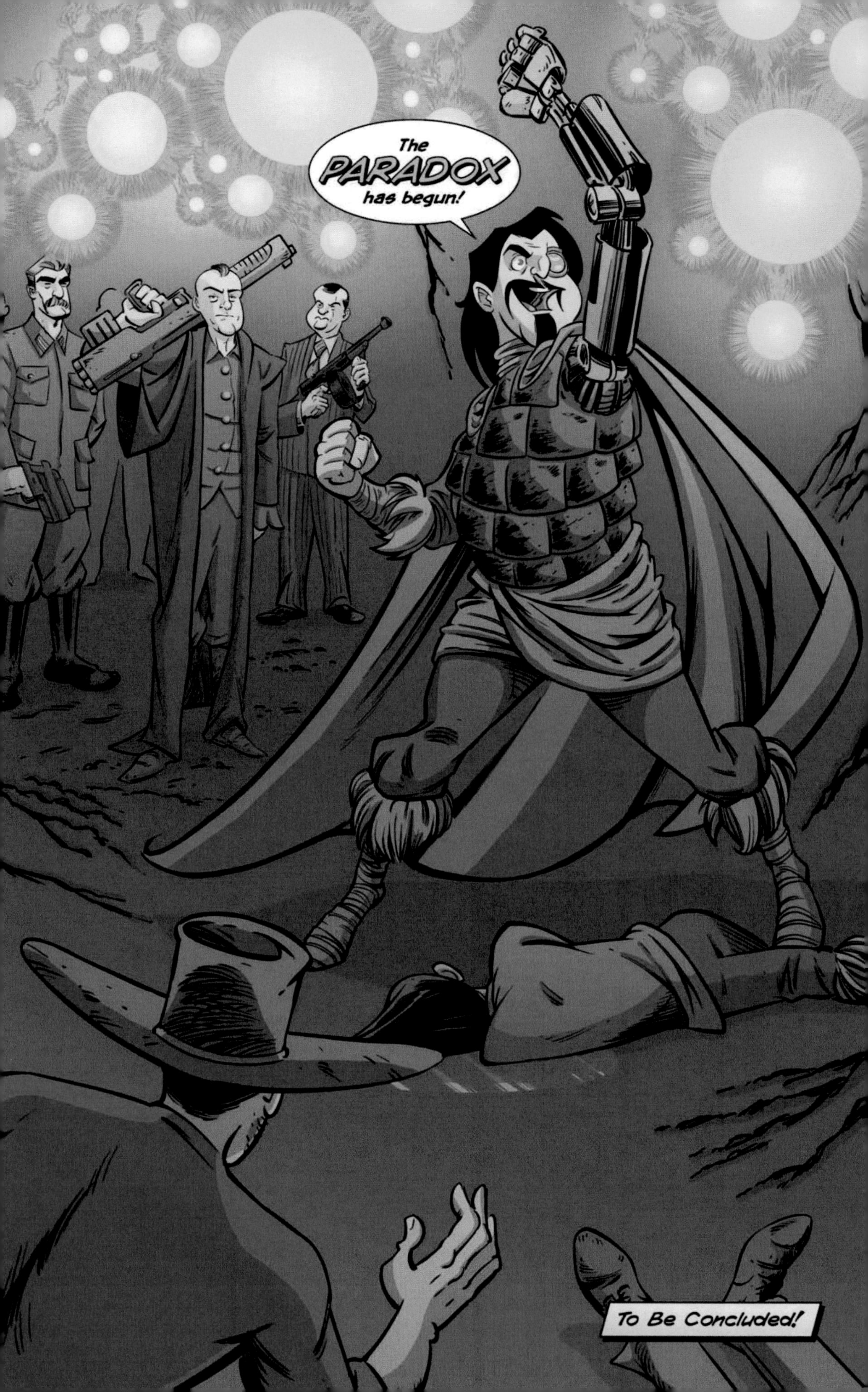
The PARADOX has begun!
To Be Concluded!

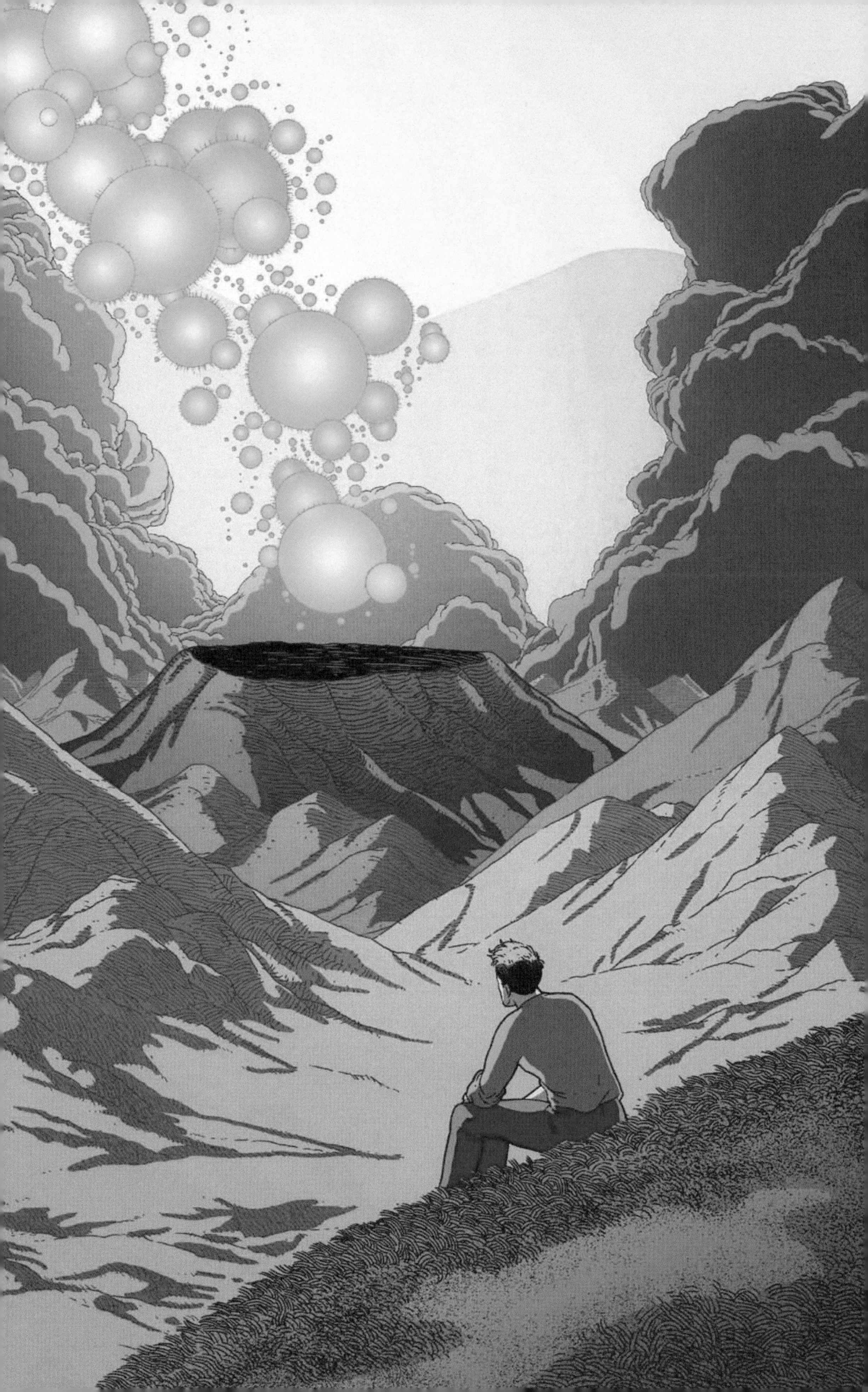

ISSUE FIVE

"MOVING ON"

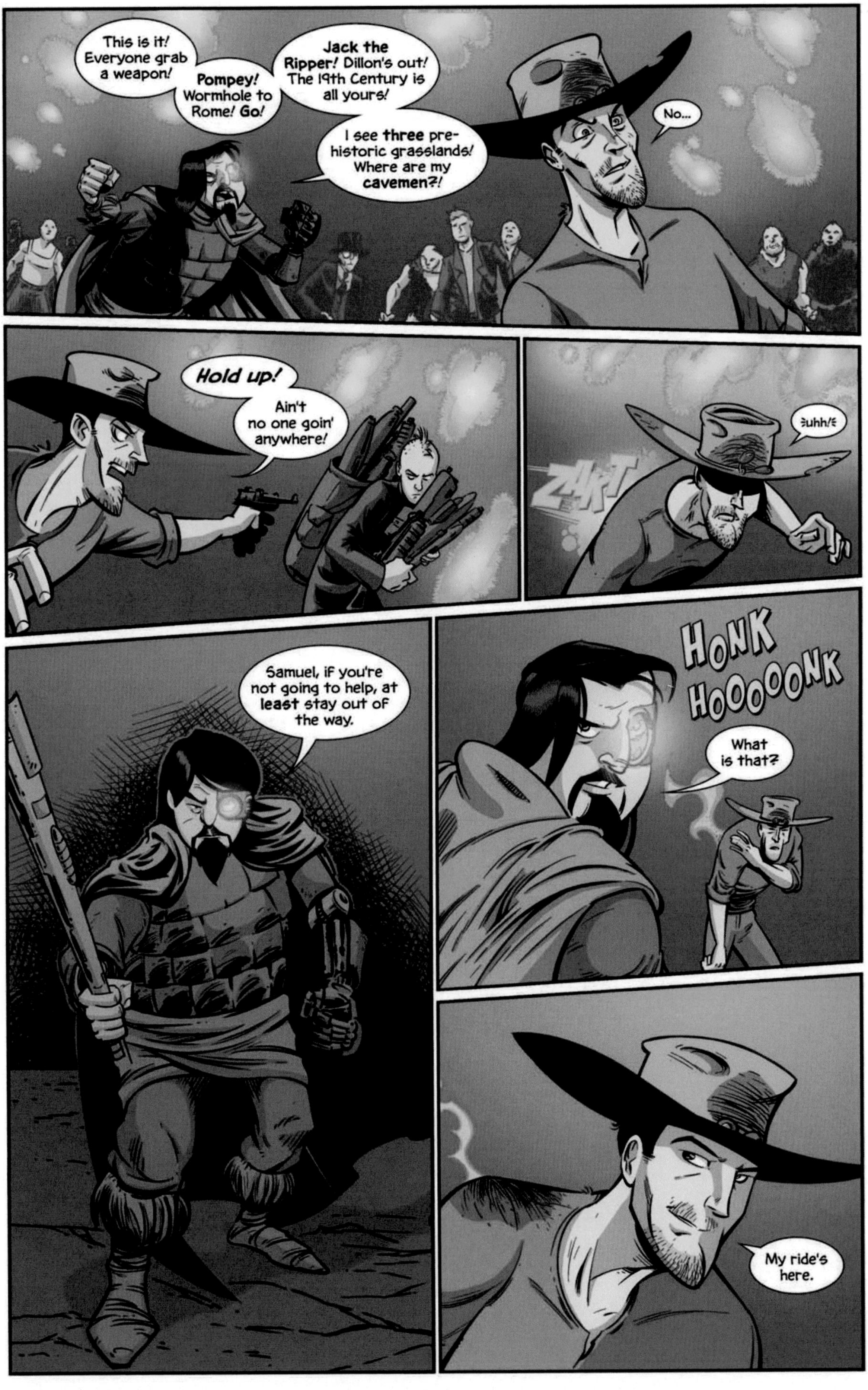
This is it! Everyone grab a weapon!
Pompey! Wormhole to Rome! Go!
Jack the Ripper! Dillon's out! The 19th Century is all yours!
I see three pre-historic grasslands! Where are my cavemen?!
No...
Hold up!
Ain't no one goin' anywhere!
ZAKT
Euhh!
Samuel, if you're not going to help, at least stay out of the way.
HONK HOOOOONK
What is that?
My ride's here.

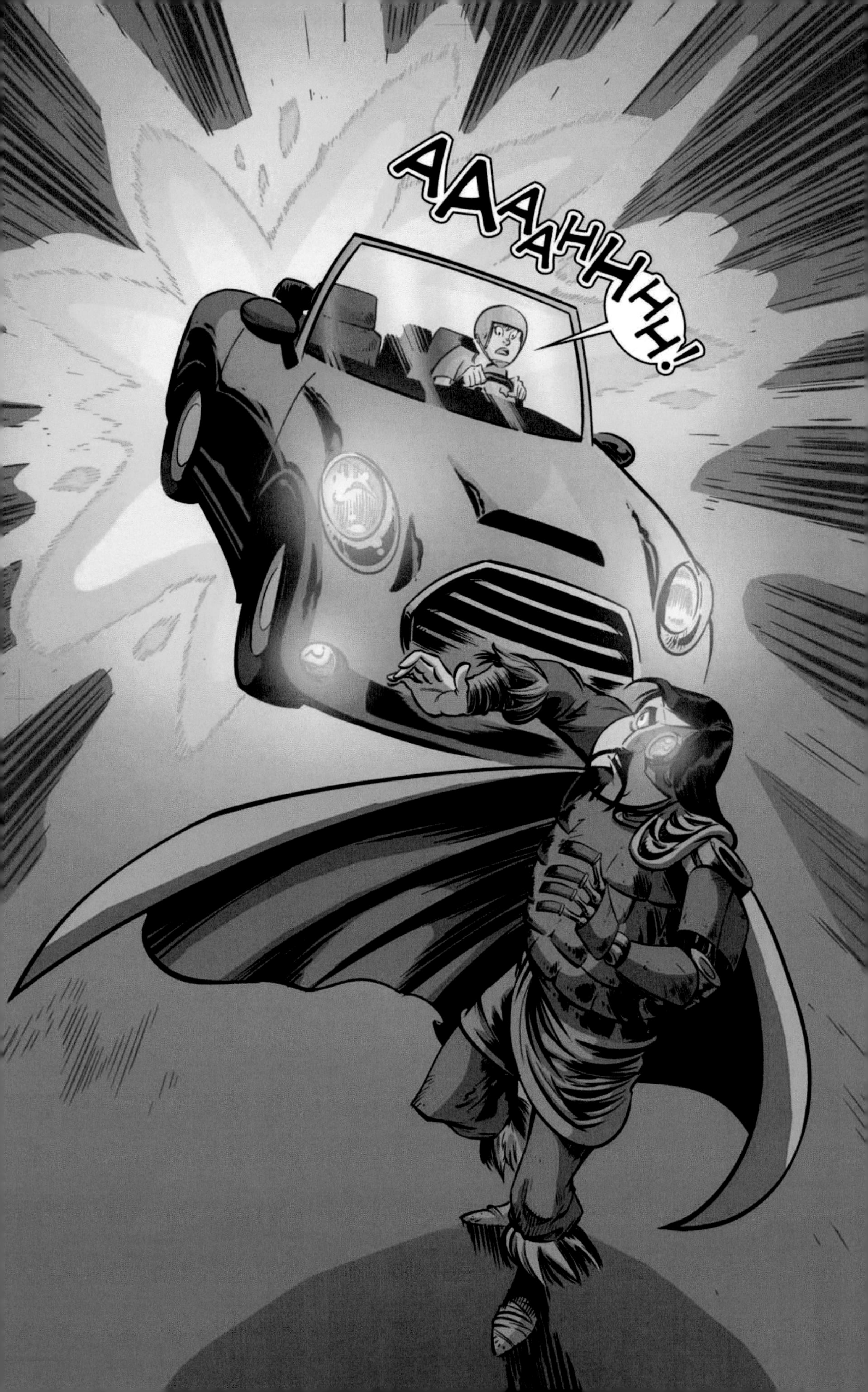
AAAAHHHH!

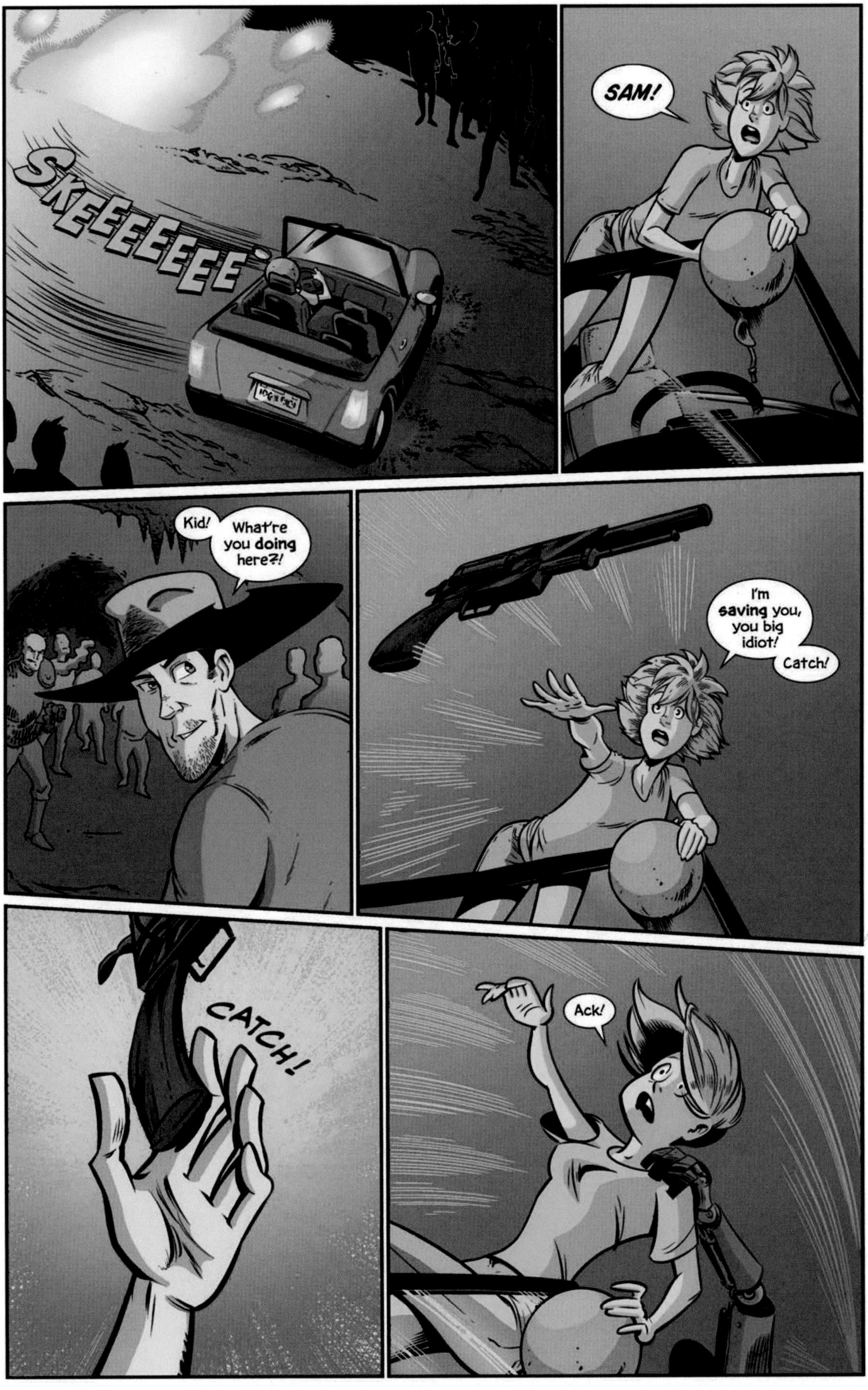
SKEEEEEEEE
SAM!
Kid!
What're you doing here?!
I'm saving you, you big idiot!
Catch!
CATCH!
Ack!

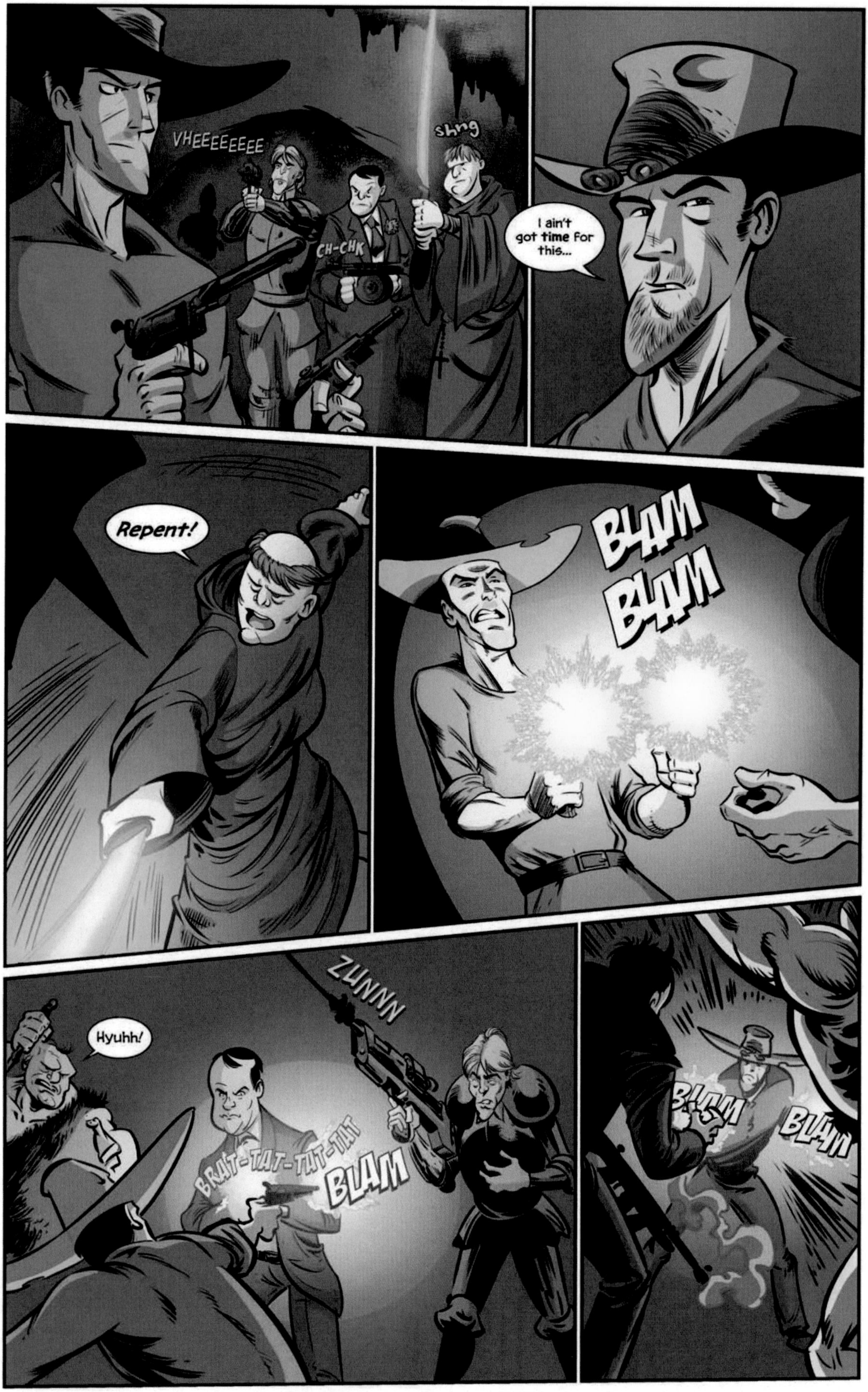
VHEEEEEEEE
CH-CHK
shng
I ain't got time for this...
Repent!
BLAM
BLAM
Hyuhh!
ZUNNN
BRAT-TAT-TAT-TAT
BLAM
BLAM
BLAM

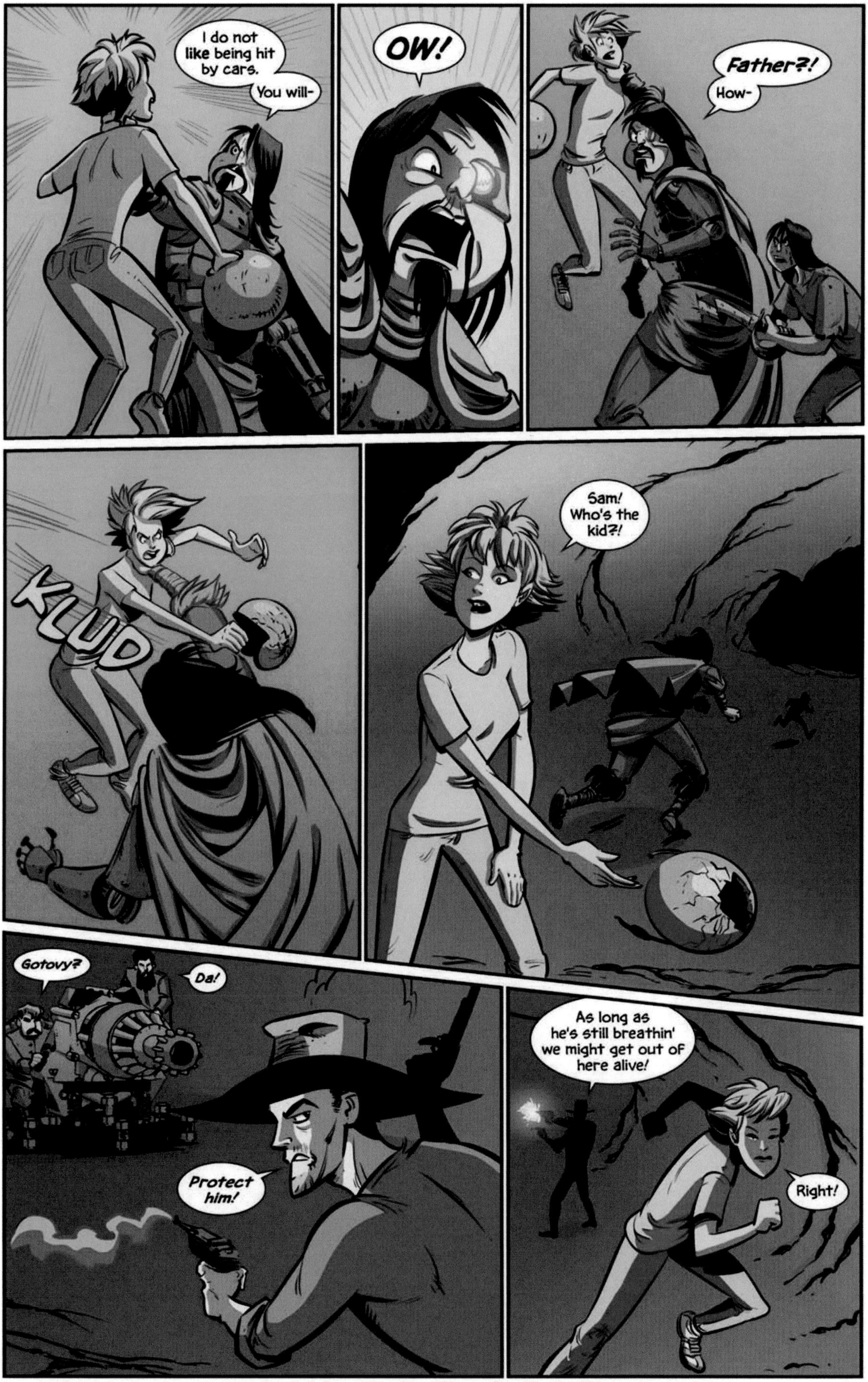
I do not like being hit by cars.
You will-
OW!
Father?!
How-
KLUD
Sam! Who's the kid?!
Gotovy?
Da!
Protect him!
As long as he's still breathin' we might get out of here alive!
Right!

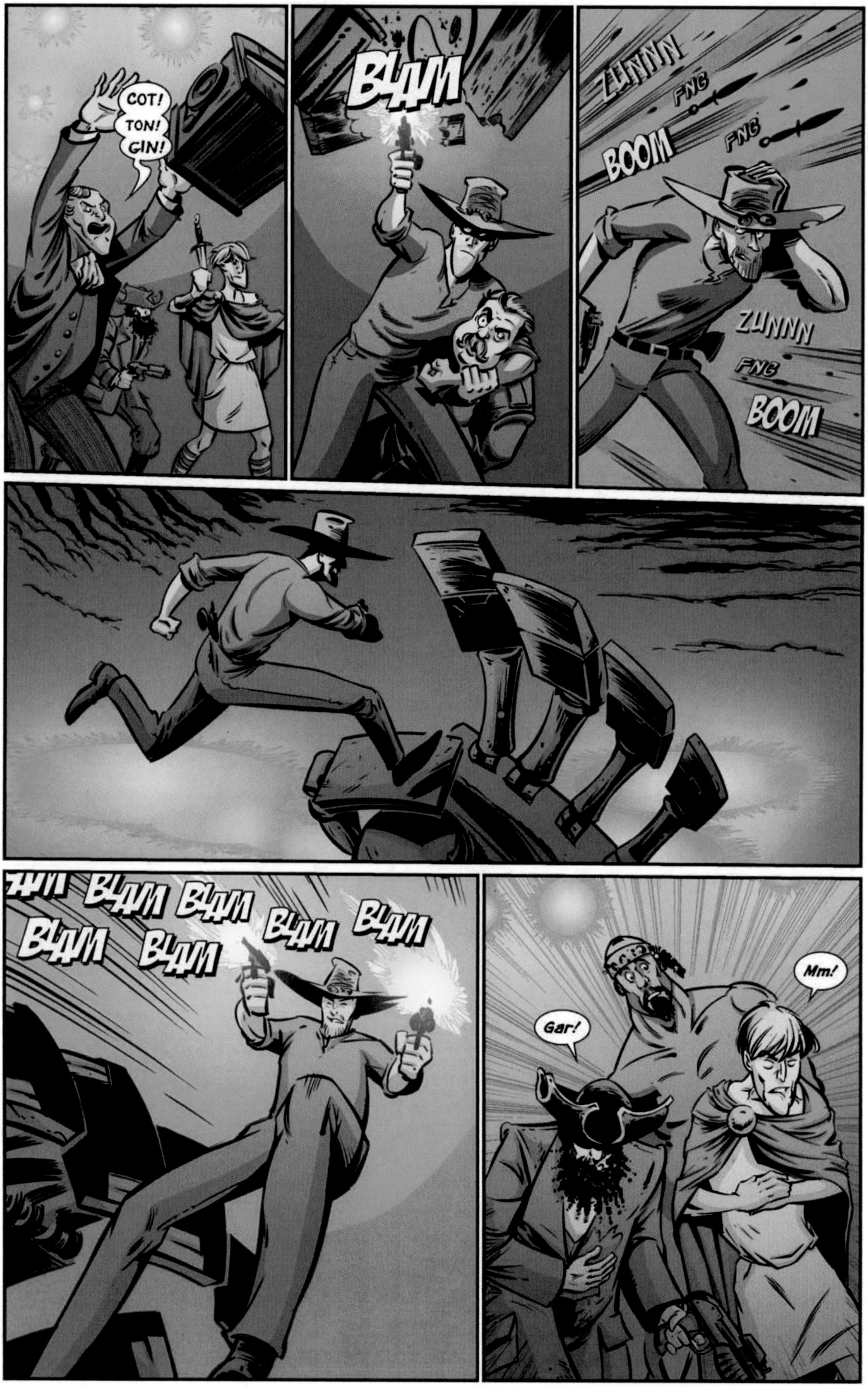
COT!
TON!
GIN!
BLAM
ZUNNN
FNG
BOOM
FNG
ZUNNN
FNG
BOOM
BLAM BLAM BLAM
BLAM BLAM BLAM BLAM
Mm!
Gar!

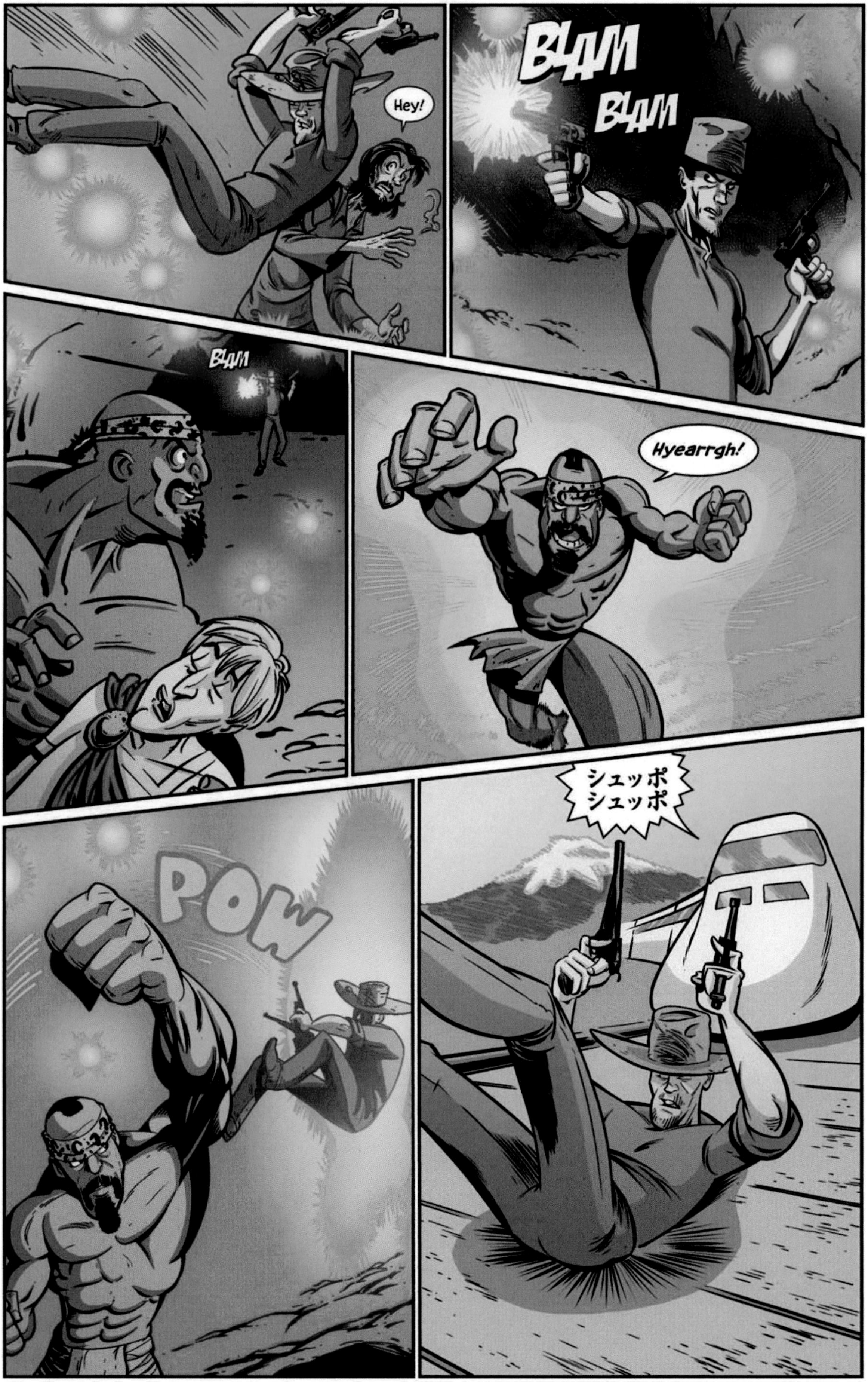
Hey!
BLAM
BLAM
BLAM
Hyearrgh!
POW
シュッポ
シュッポ

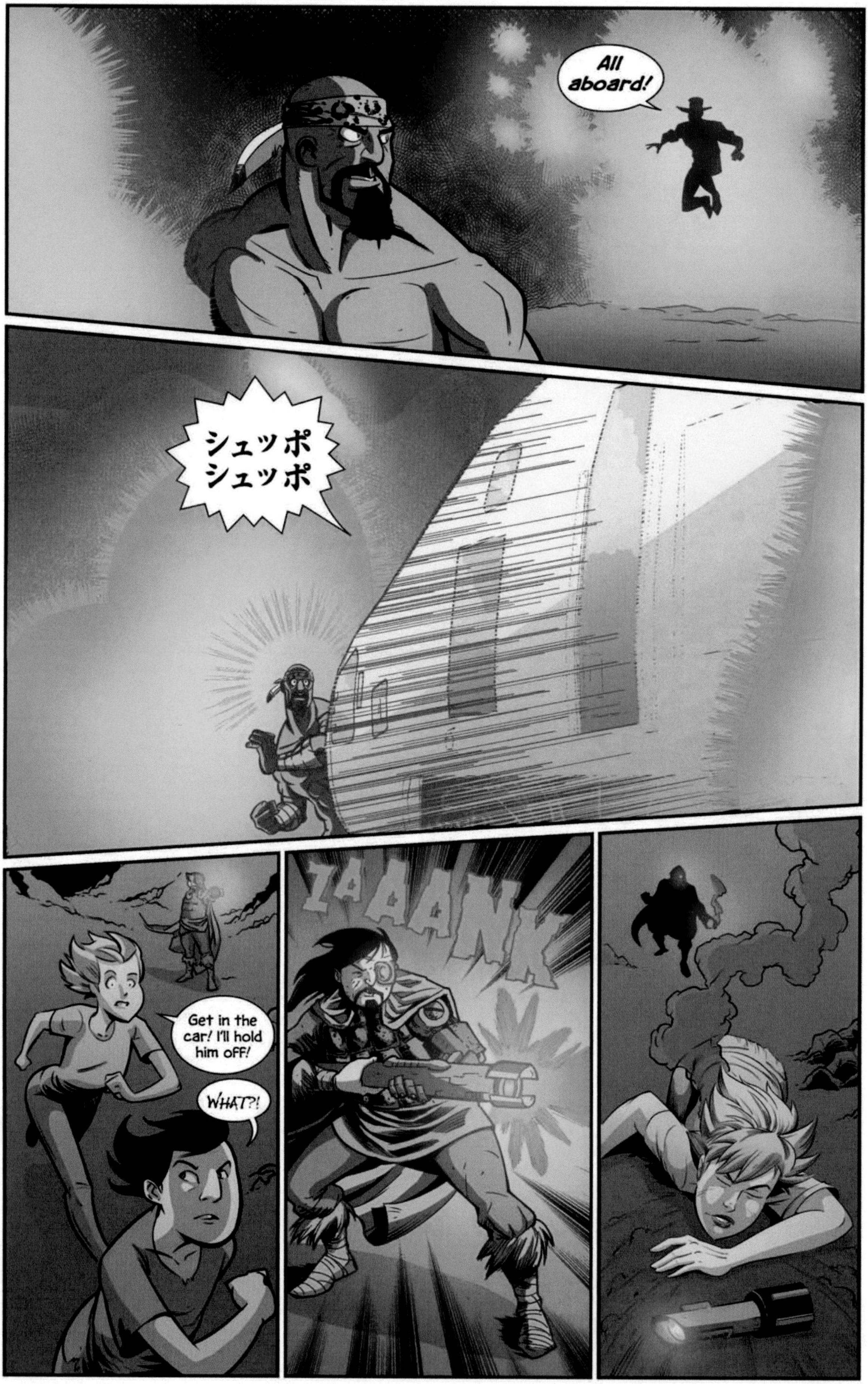
All aboard!
シュッポ
シュッポ
Get in the car! I'll hold him off!
WHAT?!
ZAAANK

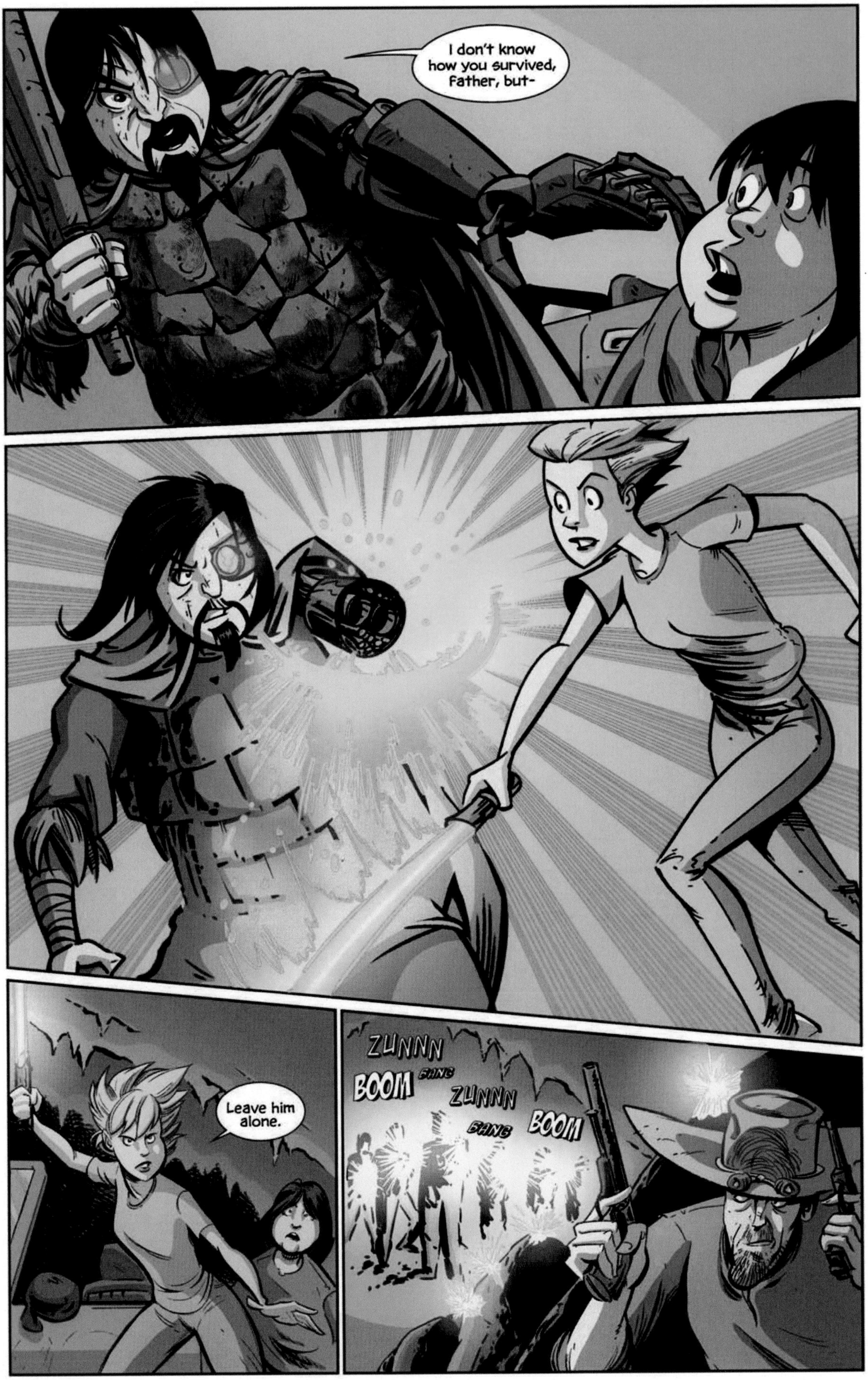
I don't know how you survived, father, but-
Leave him alone.
ZUNNN
BOOM
BANG
ZUNNN
BANG
BOOM

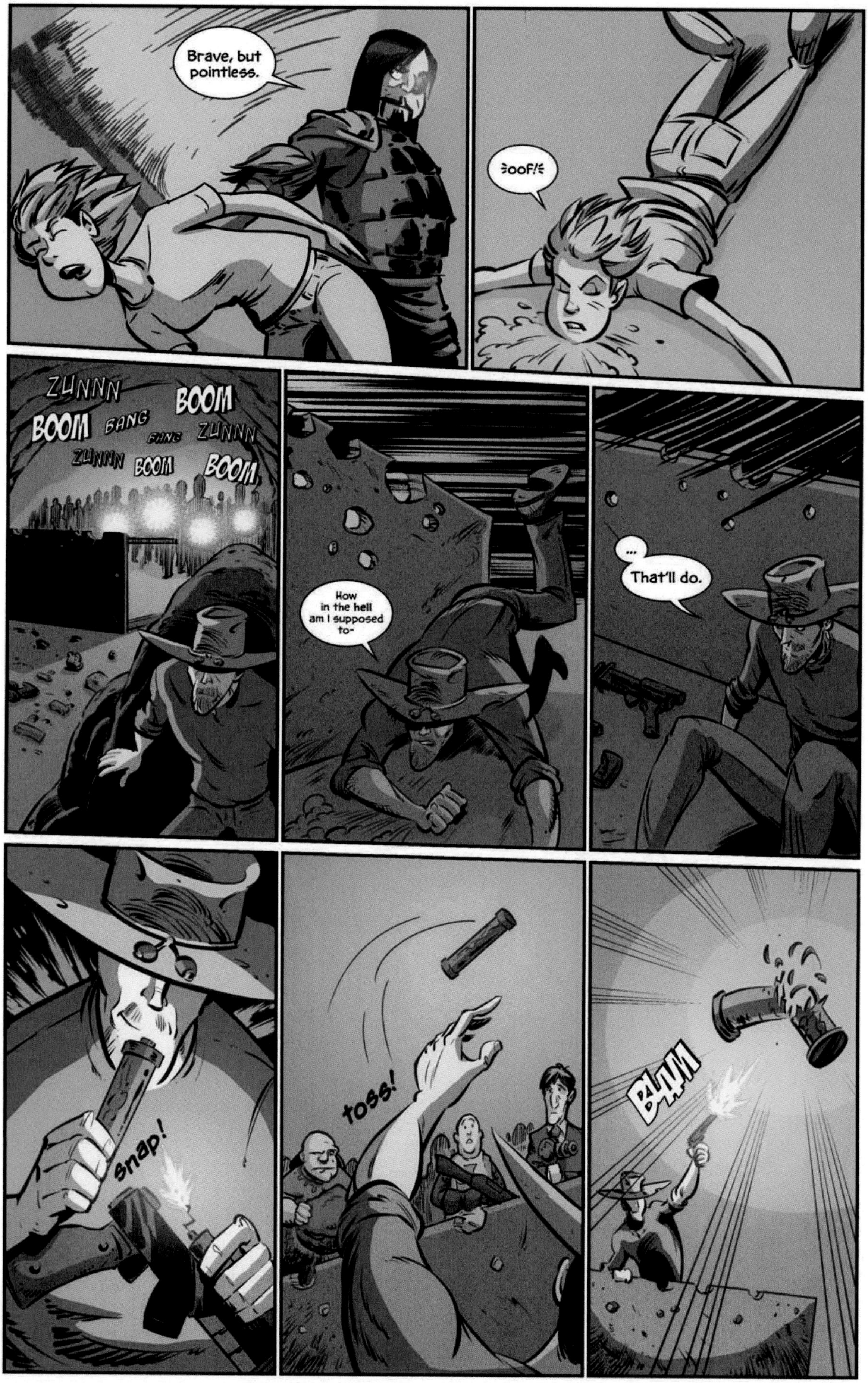
Brave, but pointless.
oof!
ZUNNN
BOOM
BOOM
BANG
BANG
ZUNNN
ZUNNN
BOOM
BOOM
How in the hell am I supposed to-
...
That'll do.
snap!
toss!
BLAM

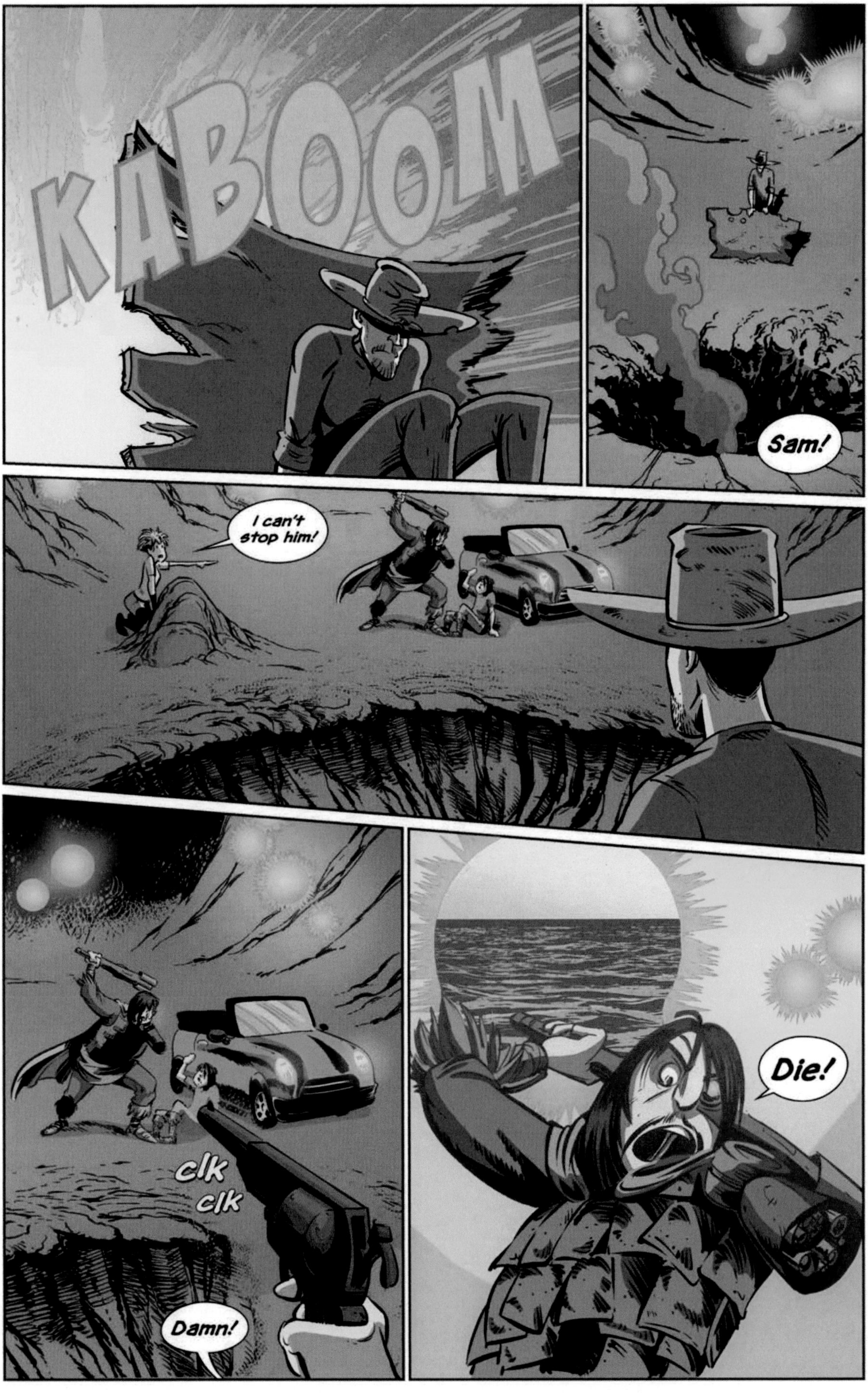
KABOOM
Sam!
I can't stop him!
clk
clk
Damn!
Die!

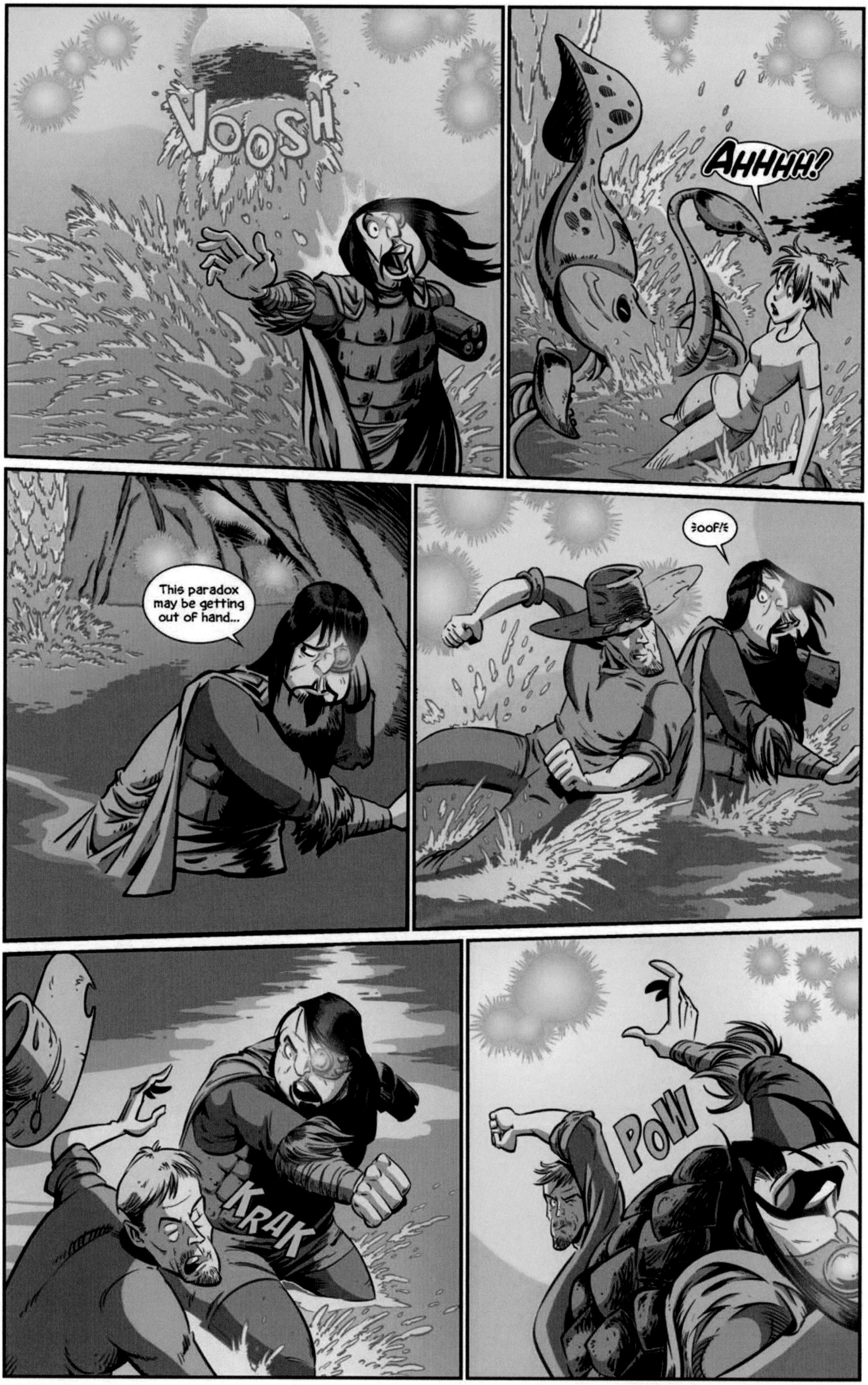
VOOSH
AHHHH!
This paradox may be getting out of hand...
OOF!
KRAK
POW

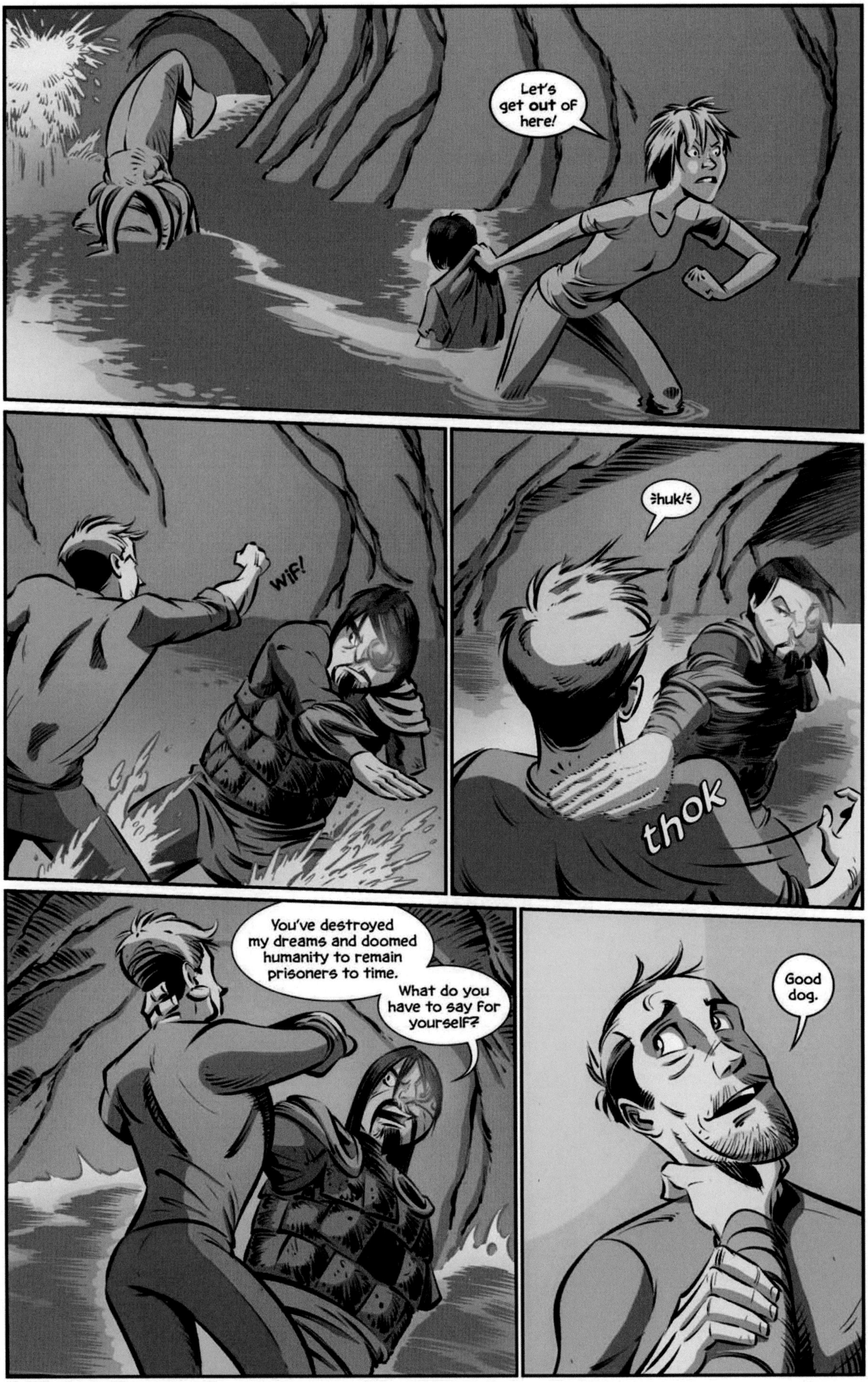
Let's get out of here!
wif!
huk!
thok
You've destroyed my dreams and doomed humanity to remain prisoners to time.
What do you have to say for yourself?
Good dog.

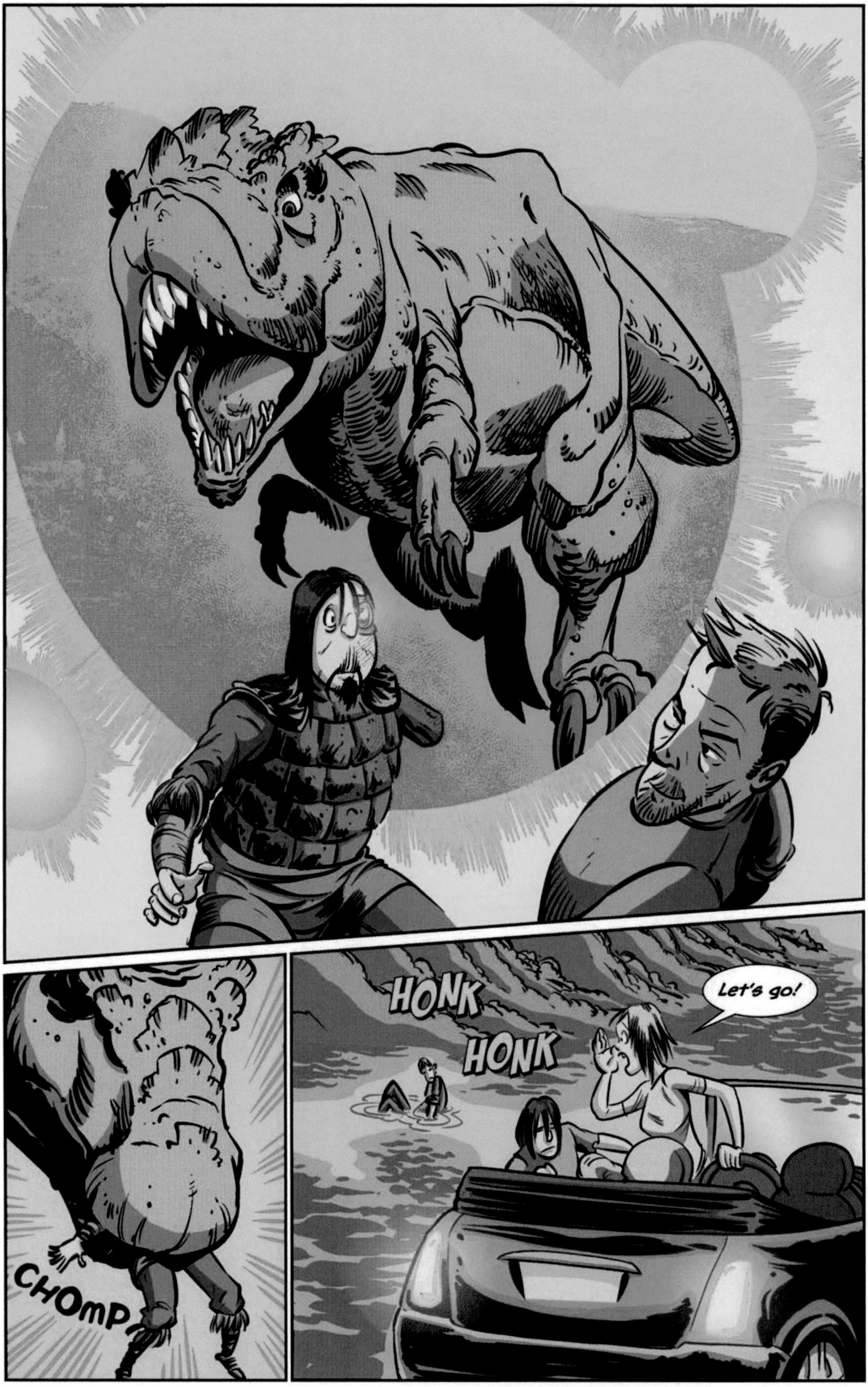
CHOMP
HONK
HONK
Let's go!

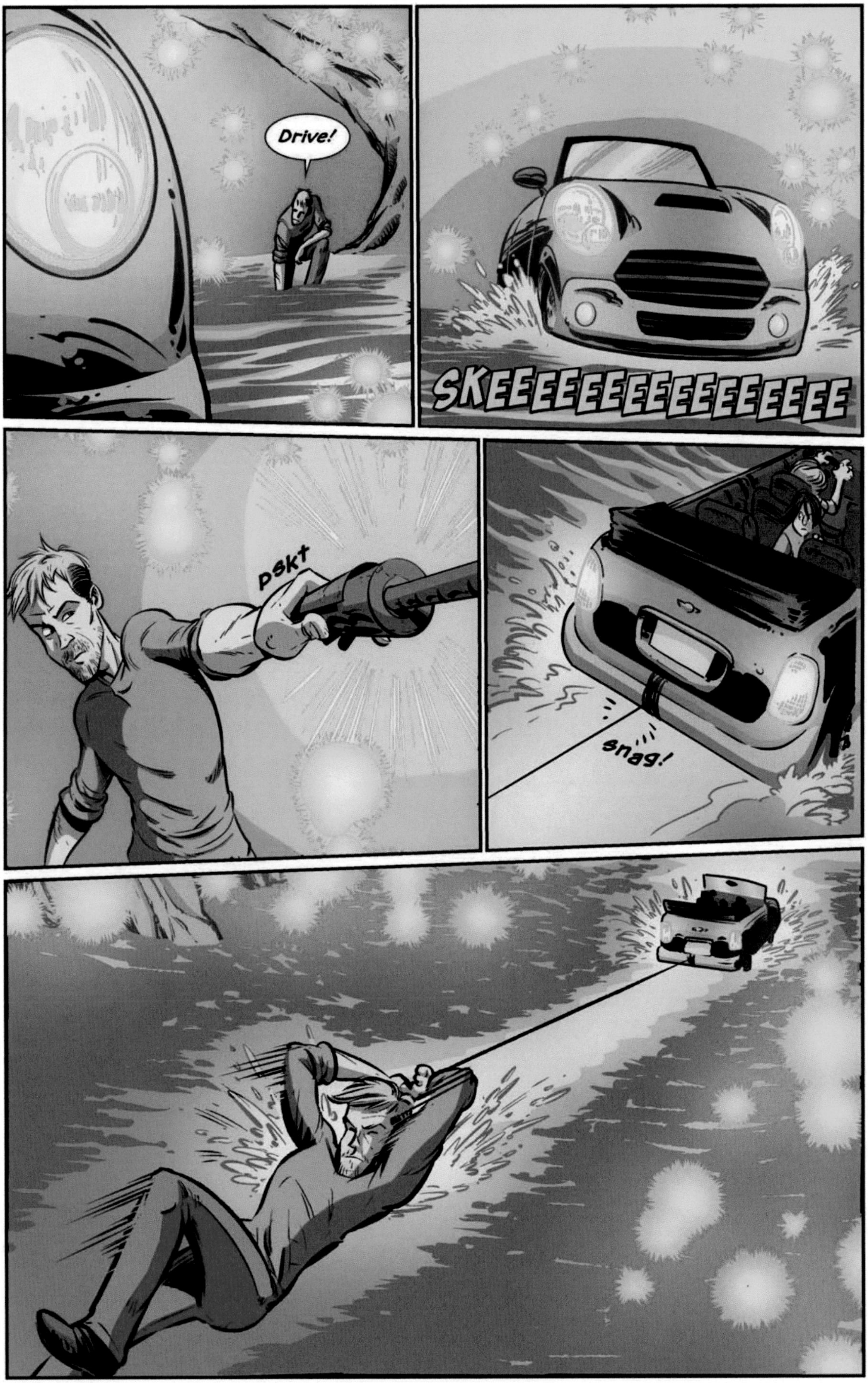
Drive!
SKEEEEEEEEEEEEEEE
pskt
snag!

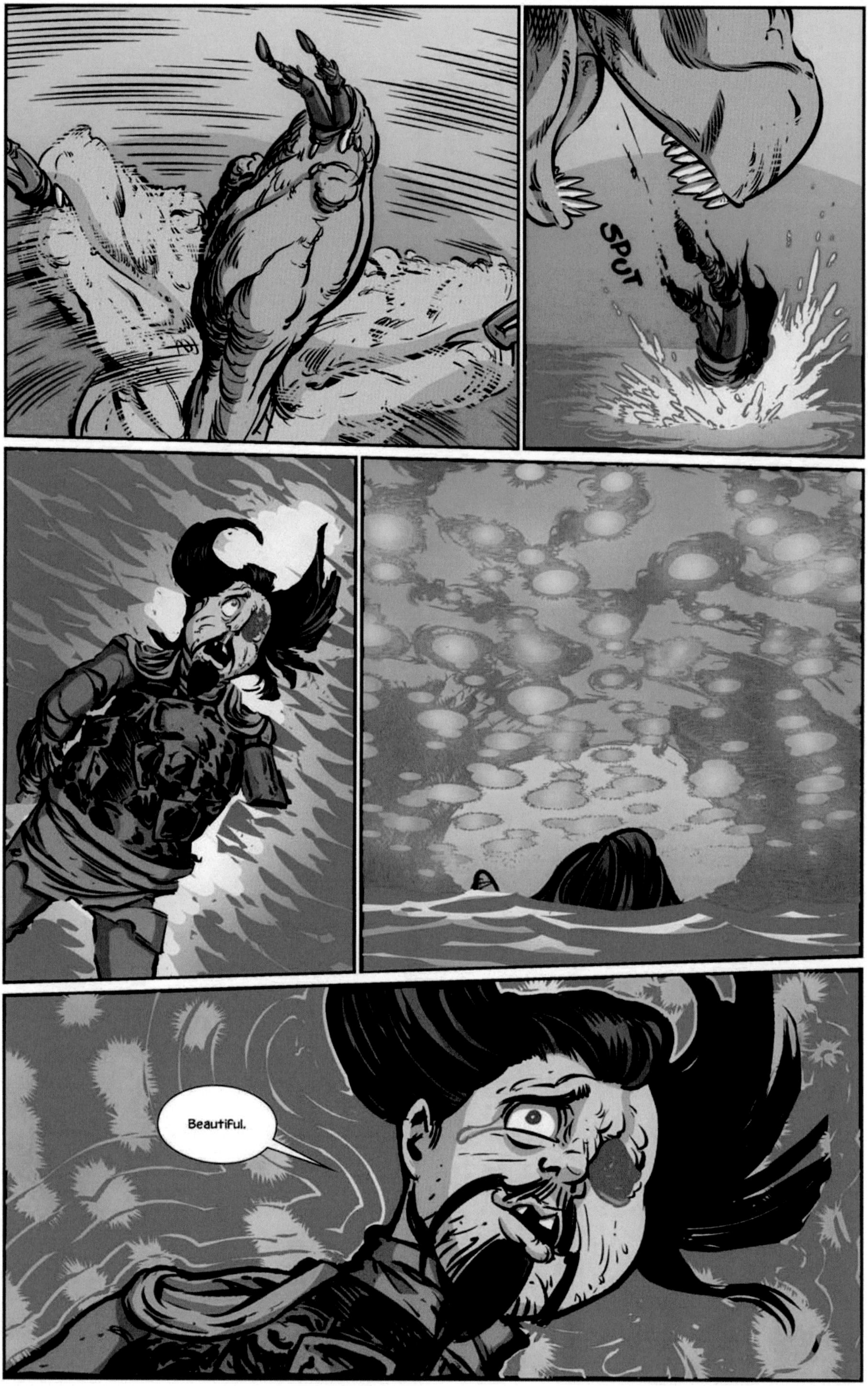
SPUT
Beautiful.

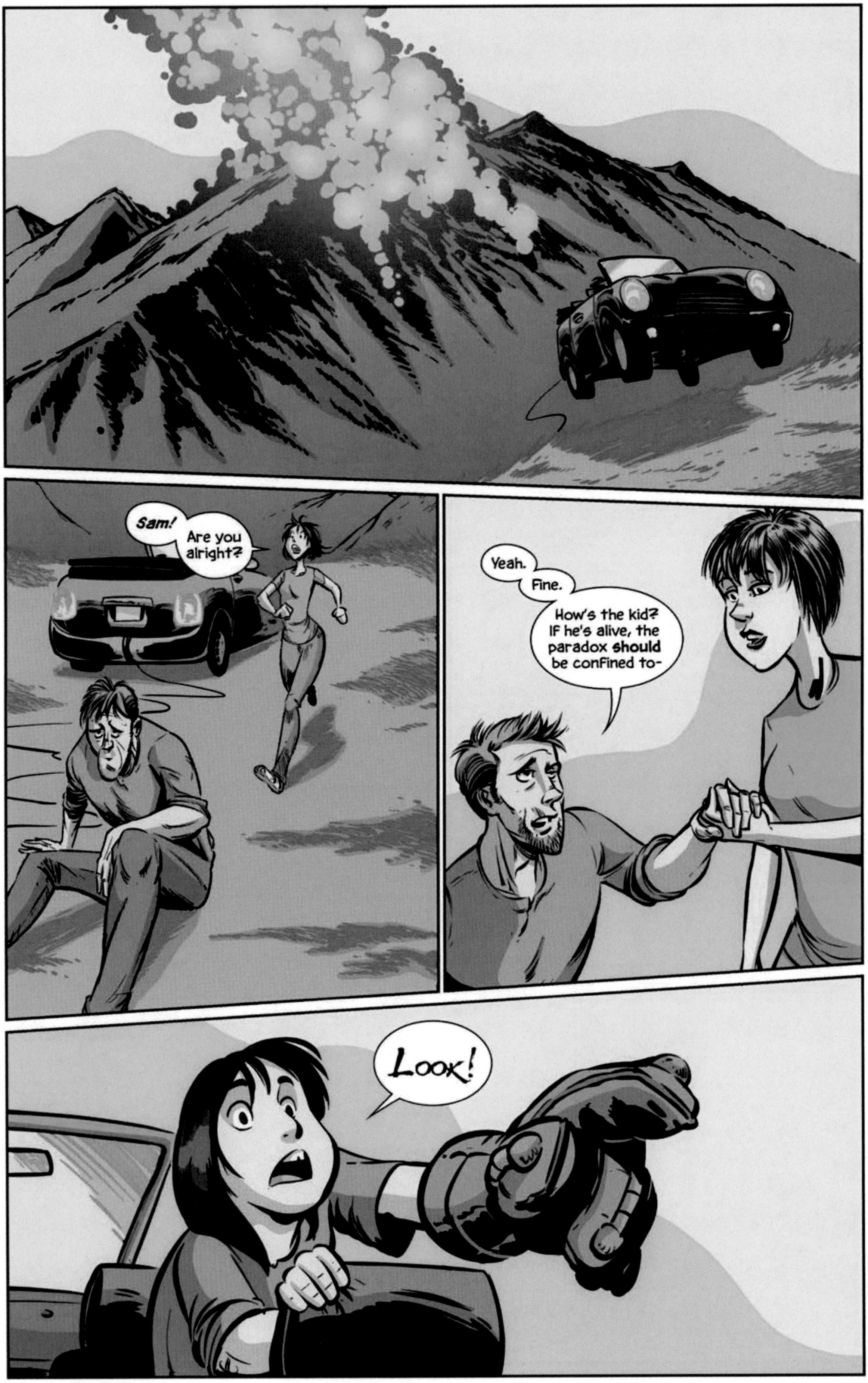
Sam!
Are you alright?
Yeah.
Fine.
How's the kid? If he's alive, the paradox should be confined to-
Look!

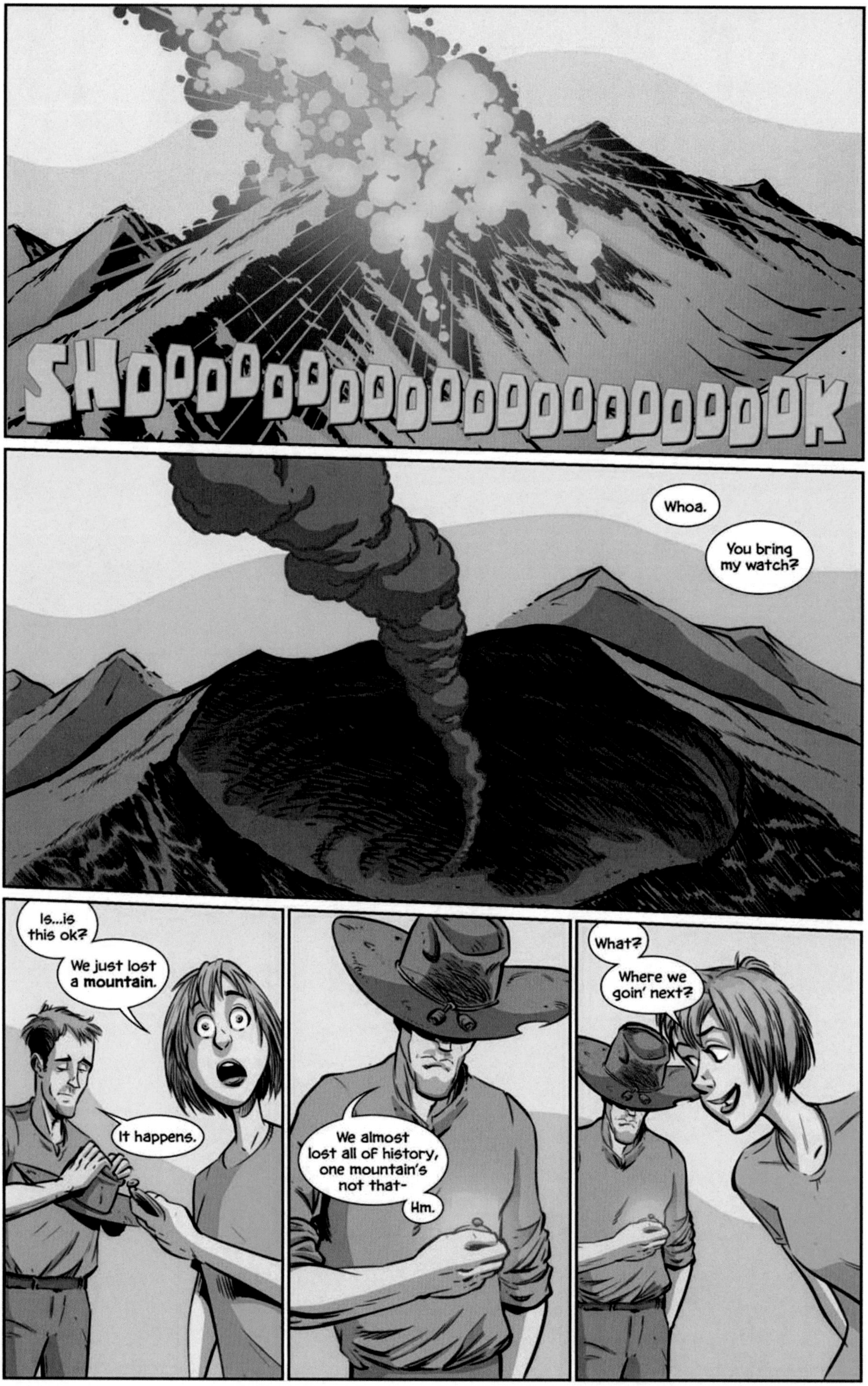
SHOOOOOOOOOOOOOOOOOOOOK
Whoa.
You bring my watch?
Is...is this ok?
We just lost a mountain.
It happens.
We almost lost all of history, one mountain's not that-
Hm.
What?
Where we goin' next?

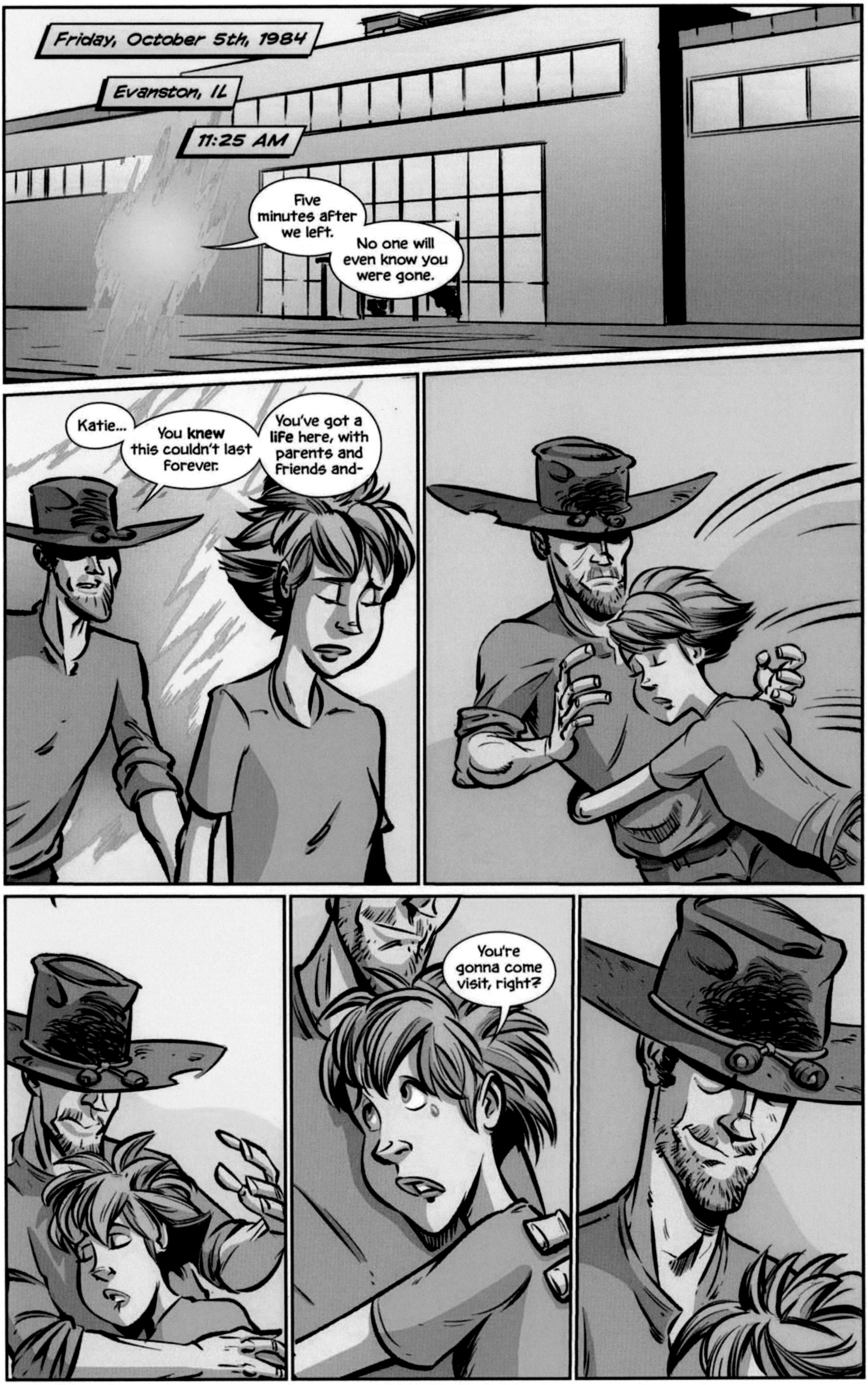
Friday, October 5th, 1984
Evanston, IL
11:25 AM
Five minutes after we left.
No one will even know you were gone.
Katie...
You knew this couldn't last forever.
You've got a life here, with parents and friends and-
You're gonna come visit, right?

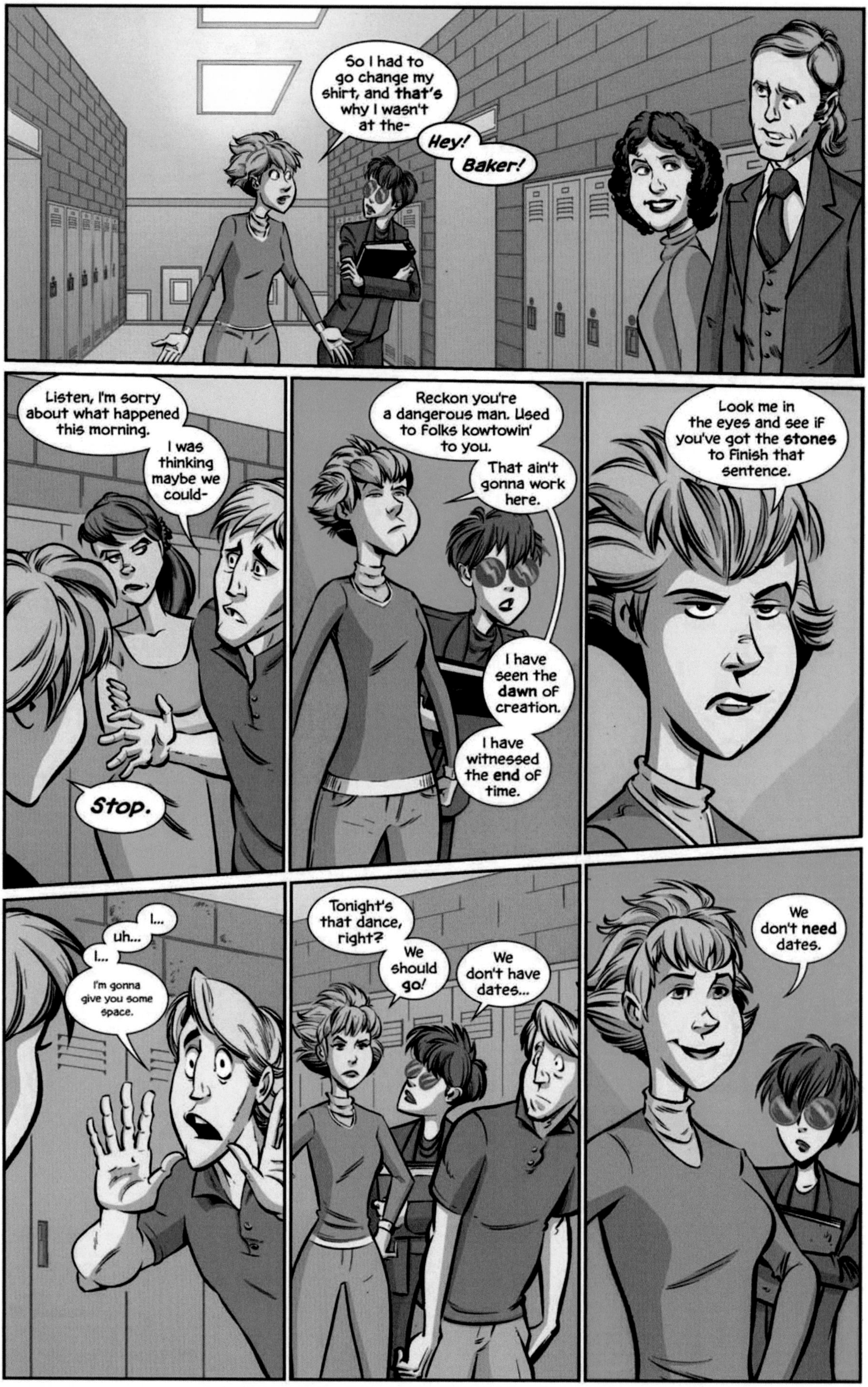

So I had to go change my shirt, and **that's** why I wasn't at the-
Hey!
Baker!
Listen, I'm sorry about what happened this morning.
I was thinking maybe we could-
Stop.
Reckon you're a dangerous man. Used to folks kowtowin' to you.
That ain't gonna work here.
I have seen the **dawn** of creation.
I have witnessed the **end** of time.
Look me in the eyes and see if you've got the **stones** to finish that sentence.
I...
uh...
I...
I'm gonna give you some space.
Tonight's that dance, right?
We should **go**!
We don't have dates...
We don't **need** dates.

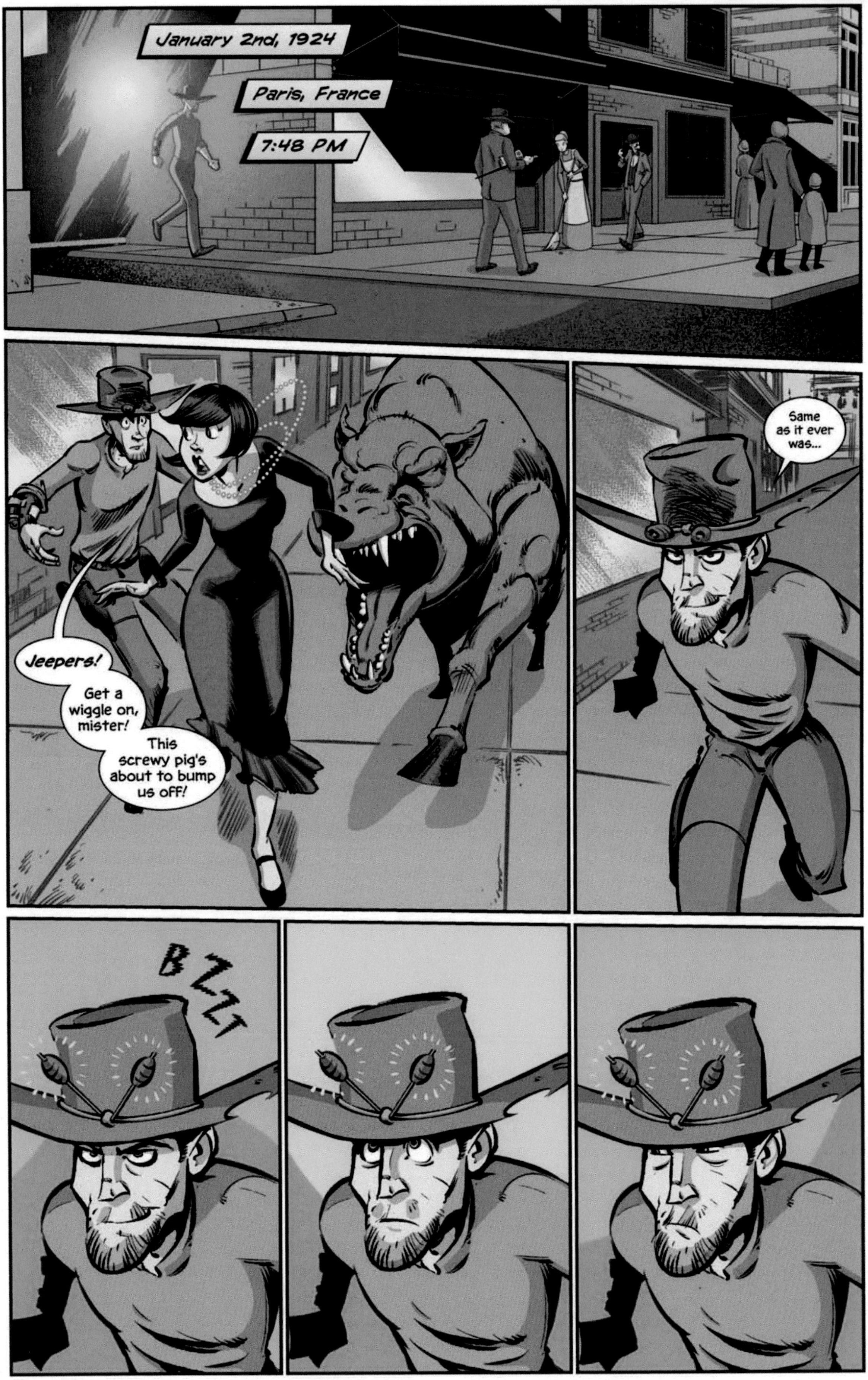
January 2nd, 1924
Paris, France
7:48 PM
Jeepers!
Get a wiggle on, mister!
This screwy pig's about to bump us off!
Same as it ever was...
BZZT

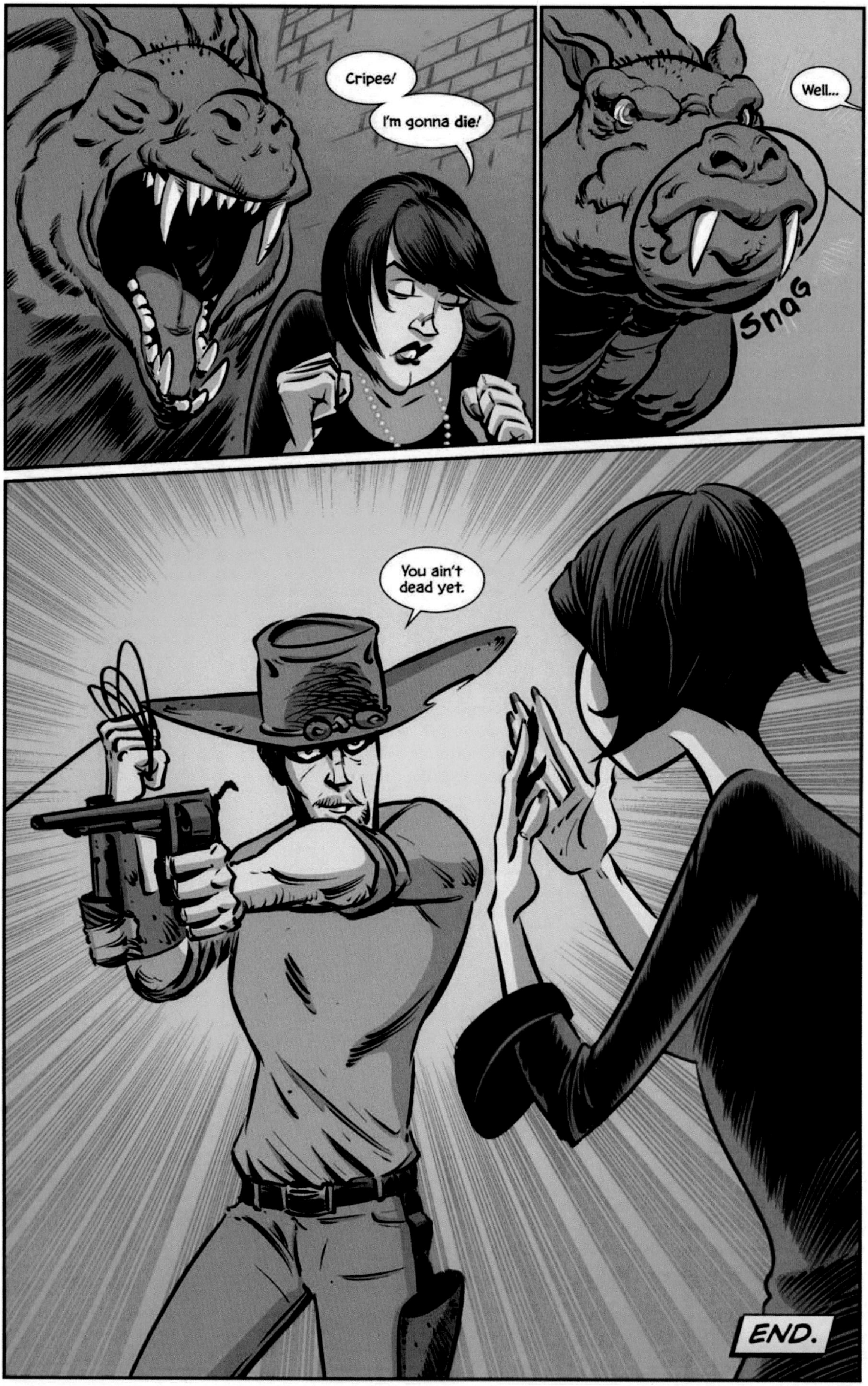
Cripes!
I'm gonna die!
Well...
SnaG
You ain't dead yet.
END.

JACK McGUIGAN is also the author of *Dog Walker*, a horror/comedy novel. In his youth, he made movies under the pseudonym "John McGuigan" which can be found pretty easily on the Internet. He lives in Chicago with his wife, kid and dog. He's never traveled through time, except in the boring way.

web: *jackmcguigan.com*

JOHN FORTUNE is an illustrator and designer in St. Louis, MO. His heroes are Jack Davis, Mort Drucker, Moebius and Franklin Booth. When he's not working he can be found spending time with his wife Michelle and sons, Nate, Joe and Jacob. If you meet him in a bar and say "Agents of Paradox!" he'll probably buy you a beer. Or demand you buy him one. It could go either way.

web: *behance.net/jkf724*

VANESSA KIRBY has been colouring comics since 2007. She lives in Edmonton, Alberta with her husband and cat. She loves cute things, spooky things and of course, colour! While colouring, she tends to binge watch horror movies on Netflix.

web: *vanessabeckmannportfolio. carbonmade.com*

Visit us online at

AGENTSOFPARADOX.COM

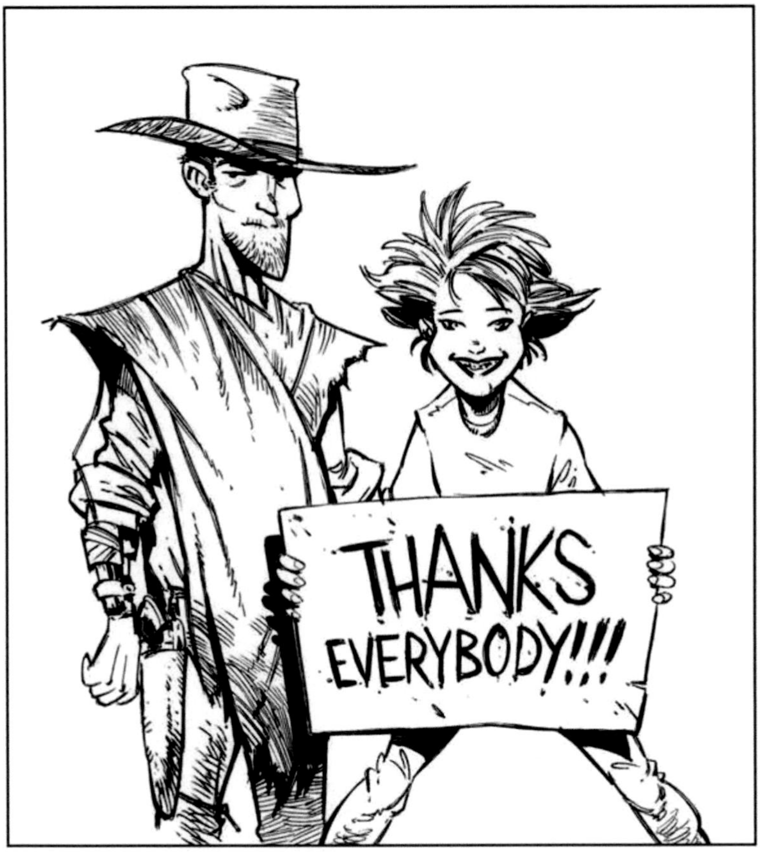
THANKS
EVERYBODY!!!

Made in the USA
Middletown, DE
26 September 2016